The Race for the Rhine Bridges

1940, 1944, 1945

ALEXANDER McKEE

ABRIDGED EDITION

PAN BOOKS LTD
LONDON AND SYDNEY

First published 1971 by Souvenir Press Ltd

This abridged edition published 1974 by Pan Books Ltd,
Cavaye Place, London SW10 9PG

ISBN 0 330 24022 6

Made and printed in Great Britain by
Cox & Wyman Ltd, London, Reading and Fakenham

THE RACE FOR THE RHINE BRIDGES

Alexander McKee was born in Ipswich in 1918. During World War II he served with the British and Canadian Armies and was present at the battles of Emmerich and Arnhem in 1945; in the immediate post-war period he toured extensively along the Dutch and German Rhine. In 1948 he joined the British Forces Network in Hamburg as a writer/producer and four years later, he became a freelance scriptwriter and author. He now has many books to his credit, including *Caen, Anvil of Victory* and *Vimy Ridge*.

By the same author in Pan Books

CAEN — ANVIL OF VICTORY

CONTENTS

Part III THE RHINE: 1945

LIST OF ILLUSTRATIONS
(*between pages 144 and 145*)

Part I

Fortress Holland

1940

CHAPTER ONE

Operation Yellow

Hitler had wanted war, but not war against the Western Powers, unless it was absolutely forced on him. On 3 September 1939 it was forced on him, as a result of his attack on Poland, when Britain and France declared war; all other nations remained neutral, with the single exception of the Soviet Union, which aided the Nazi State in the swift dismemberment of Poland.

On 9 October 1939, a little over a month later, Hitler issued his Directive No 6 for the Conduct of the War. This was his blueprint for 1940.

Two estimates and a number of political facts are basic to its background. The first estimate concerned German war production, which, it was calculated, would not reach its peak until 1943.

Nevertheless, it was not advisable to wait, because of the second estimate, which concerned British war production. The resources of the British Empire, although they would gather more slowly, would in time exceed those of Germany. Therefore, Germany could not afford a long war with Britain. She had to strike immediately, if possible, in 1939.

The political facts must be somewhat brutally summarized. Hitler's ambitions lay in the East. The Franco-British declaration of war was a nuisance. He had hoped to avoid it. But now that it had come he judged his Western adversaries, actual and potential, to be weaker in will than in power. He might secure a negotiated peace after very little fighting, or perhaps none at all, as he had done for so many years on so many occasions. With this in mind, Hitler wrote

Directive No 6 for operation *Fall Gelb* ('Case Yellow'):

1. Should it become evident in the near future that England, and, under her influence, France also, are not disposed to bring the war to an end, I have decided, without further loss of time, to go over to the offensive.

2. Any further delay will not only entail the end of Belgian and perhaps of Dutch neutrality, to the advantage of the Allies; it will also increasingly strengthen the military power of the enemy, reduce the confidence of neutral nations in Germany's final victory, and make it more difficult to bring Italy into the war on our side as a full ally.

3. I therefore issue the following orders for the further conduct of military operations:

(a) An offensive will be planned on the northern flank of the Western front, through Luxembourg, Belgium, and Holland ...

(b) The purpose of this offensive will be to defeat as much as possible of the French Army and of the forces of the Allies fighting on their side, and at the same time to win as much territory as possible in Holland, Belgium and Northern France, to serve as a base for the successful prosecution of the air and sea war against England and as a wide protective area for the economically vital Ruhr.

(c) The time of the attack will depend upon the readiness for action of the armoured and motorized units involved ... it will depend also upon the weather conditions ...

There were five more paragraphs, but these were the vital ones. Later directives show this plan evolving. It was to be an on-off, on-off affair, capable of cancellation at any time up to five hours before the attack was due, and as it was cancelled on a number of occasions this greatly favoured the success of the actual operation when it finally was launched. For although many Germans blindly believed in their leader, and most considered that he had done well up to that time to achieve so much with so little trouble and bloodshed, senior officers in the German Army knew better. They regarded him as a common little guttersnipe, possessing in an extraordinary degree the ability to hypnotize the common people, who were now started on a reckless adventure that could lead in the long run only to catastrophe. Some of them were in a position to keep the Allies informed of the impending attack and so, each time the German Army was alerted for Operation Yellow, so too were the Allied armies and the neutral victims.

Regarding the neutral Dutch, Hitler's Directive No 8 stated:

> The attitude of the Dutch forces cannot be foreseen. Where no resistance is offered the invasion will assume the character of a peaceful occupation . . . Operations against the Dutch Navy will be undertaken only if the latter displays a hostile attitude . . . Neither in Holland nor in Belgium–Luxembourg are centres of population, and in particular large open cities and industrial installations, to be attacked without compelling military necessity.

Directive No 9, of 29 November 1939, dealt exclusively with the final objective of Operation Yellow – Great Britain.

> In our fight against the Western Powers, England has shown herself to be the animator of the fighting spirit of the enemy and the leading enemy power. The defeat of England is essential to final victory. The most effective means of ensuring this is to cripple the English economy by attacking it at decisive points. Early preparations must therefore be made . . . to deal an annihilating blow to the English economy . . . Should the Army succeed in defeating the Anglo-French Armies in the field and seizing and holding a sector of the coast of the Continent opposite England, the task of the Navy and Air Force to carry the war to English industry becomes paramount.

On 10 January 1940 a German aircraft carrying detailed

plans of Operation Yellow force-landed in Belgium, the pilot apparently having lost his way in fog. The major carrying the documents managed to burn most of them, but not all, before capture by Belgian soldiers. It was almost too good to be true. In any event, it was yet another cry of 'Wolf! Wolf!' and served also to focus attention on Holland and Belgium, when later variants of the plan shifted the emphasis of the attack southward to the Ardennes, while the armies advancing into Belgium were to 'divert to themselves the strongest possible Anglo-French forces'. In short, the Allies' mobile force was to be drawn northward, away from the Maginot Line, while the main attack cut in behind them. Nevertheless, both Belgium and Holland were to be taken, but it would have to be done quickly, before the French and the British could come effectively to their aid.

All very well to direct this and that to be done, but how was it all to be actually achieved? The events of the First World War, still no less bitterly remembered in Germany than in France and Britain, had shown the superiority of the defence over the attack, even when the defenders had only trenches to protect them. Now, most of the French border was covered by the elaborate concrete forts of the Maginot Line, from which a small number of troops should be able to hold off much greater numbers of attackers, thus freeing many Allied formations for an unopposed advance into Belgium and Holland, where they would be welcomed in the event of invasion.

And in Holland itself the traditional water defences, plus the large areas of marsh, would impose a serious obstacle even to tanks and at the very least delay an attacker sufficiently for the Netherlands forces to retire from one waterline to another until they were safe behind the inner and very formidable lake and river obstacles surrounding the heart of the country, which they called 'Fortress Holland'.

The demolition of some half-dozen key bridges would be the modern equivalent of pulling up the drawbridge of a medieval castle. The castle might fall, but only after prolonged investment and assault, and long before that the Allied forces would have come to their relief, by both land and sea. This was indeed the Dutch plan, and in ordinary circumstances it would have been a good one.

Two facts were to destroy it. The first was that the Dutch defences were designed to cope in the manner of 1918 with an attack on the lines of 1918. That is to say, a ponderous, slow-moving assault of masses of men covered by the fire of masses of guns, giving ample time for counter-measures. Even to small details, the Dutch defences were precisely 1918 – the forts were small pillboxes armed mostly with heavy machine-guns, deadly to unprotected infantry, extended by primitive wooden-revetted trenches with fire-steps.

The second ominous fact was Hitler himself. General-leutnant Kurt Student, commander of the German airborne forces, told the British military critic Captain B. H. Liddell Hart that all the basic ideas were Hitler's and that he, Student, merely worked them out in detail and then led the key assault. Even discounting something for modesty, this must have been true, for the plan bears an unmistakable political imprint at many points. Hitler was a man accustomed to calculating and working on both the thought processes and the emotional reactions of people; the people of his own nation, and the people of other nations also.

Operation Yellow was not a traditional military stroke, and is best understood by studying Hitler's technique during that series of bloodless successes, from the reoccupation of the Rhineland to the invasion of Czechoslovakia, where everything turned on bluffing and bewildering an irresolute or unready opponent and calculating the extent of his reactions precisely.

The Dutch were expecting a heavy attack, whereas what was coming was an exceedingly light attack, which itself lent surprise, carried out with lightning speed and on unexpected lines, including that 'Trojan Horse' element that Hitler had already used in both Poland and Norway. This was to be popularly called the 'Fifth Column', implying a mass of local sympathizers and traitors, a panic belief that was to help Hitler considerably.

In fact, the greater part of the 'Trojan Horse' element consisted of German soldiers, in or out of uniform, infiltrated into the enemy's fortress in an unusual way. In both Poland and Norway it had been largely a 'Trojan Seahorse', consisting of ordinary soldiers concealed in merchant ships lying in harbours. A variant of this plan was intended for the Dutch waterways. Local helpers were not scorned, but there were fewer of them and they played a smaller active part than is generally believed.

The effect of surprise on individuals in bewilderment and indecision, purely temporary, lasting possibly for a few minutes only; and this can always be achieved, even if the troops to be attacked have been notified in advance of the attack, provided that it is the first attack they have ever sustained, the enemy the first enemy they have ever seen. Up to that moment, they do not really believe. This was what was to happen to the Dutch, all the more effectively because Holland had not been at war for over a century.

On 2 May 1940, Hitler ordered the commanders of his airborne forces to Berlin. They were Generalleutnant Kurt Student, commanding the 4,500 highly trained parachutists of 7 Flieger Division, and Generalleutnant Graf Sponeck, responsible for the 12,000 air-transportable infantry of 22 Airlanding Division.

Both divisions were not merely small in numbers, but lightly armed and equipped. Machine-guns and light mortars were the heaviest weapons that could be dropped with the parachutists, and although the infantry division had some air-transportable artillery, its ground transport (which had to be loaded into the aircraft) consisted of bicycles and small trailers. Theoretically, an ordinary division could wipe them out in a short time, because of its much greater mobility and fire power.

On 6 May that is, in four days' time, they were to be launched into the heart of Holland to play a major role in the swift defeat of that country, and this conference was to finalize the details of what seemed to some German Generals an insane gamble.

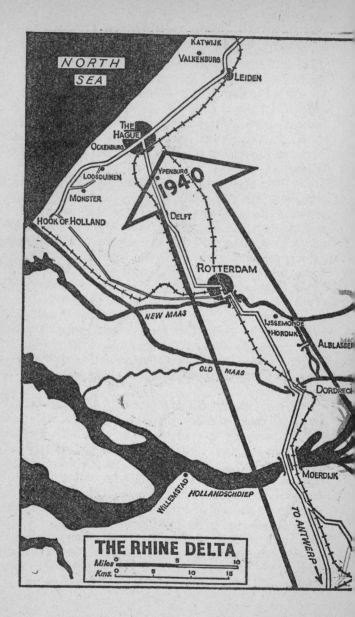

THE RHINE DELTA

Miles 0 — 5 — 10
Kms. 0 — 5 — 10 — 15

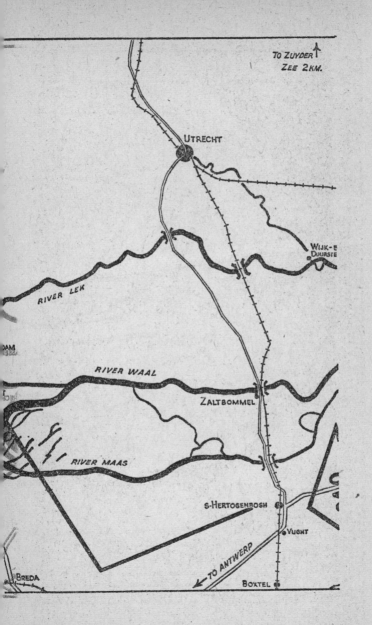

TO ZUYDER ↑
ZEE 2 KM.

THE RHINE DELTA
CONTINUATION

WIJK·BIJ·
DUURSTEDE

RENKUM   OOSTERB

WAGENINGEN

RHENEN

NEDER RHINE

RIVER WAAL

NEERBOSH

ᴏMMEL

RIVER MAAS

HATERT
MALDEN
HEUMEN
GRAVE

MOC

1940

OGENBOSH

ᴛWERP   VUGHT

SUDEN

VEGHEL ←TO EINDHOVEN

BOXTEL

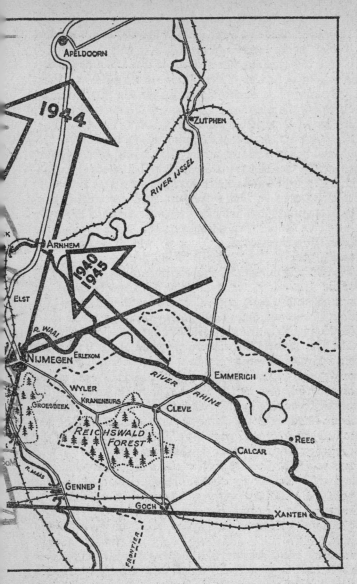

The theme of the plan was speed, surprise, and disruption. Key points in the enemy's defences were to be occupied, in the first hour of hostilities, not by his own troops but by German troops. And to add to the confusion such a swift and unexpected series of moves would cause, the Dutch government itself was to be the target of a secondary attack by soldiers dropping out of the sky, again in the first hour of the war.

The political task, that of capturing the queen of the Netherlands and her government at The Hague, was given to Count Sponeck. He was to have two parachute battalions from Fallschirm Regiment 3 and with them capture the three airfields of Ypenburg, Ockenburg, and Valkenburg. After capture, two brigades of air-transported infantry – Regiments 47 and 65 – were to be flown in and then advance on the Dutch capital, The Hague. Hitler stressed that Queen Wilhelmina was not to be harmed.

But the main military blow, the seizure of key bridges spanning the great waterways of the Rhine delta, was given to General Student, the paratroop expert. These bridges carried the main road and rail routes leading from Antwerp into the heart of Holland – the 'fortress' that the German Army had to attack.

The first obstacle was the wide expanse of the Hollandsch Diep, a great waterway formed by the main stream of the Rhine (here known as the Waal) joining the main stream of the Meuse (here known as the Maas). The motor road and the railway crossed side by side at a little village called Moerdijk. After dive-bomber attack on the Dutch defences, one parachute battalion was to drop right on top of them, at both ends of the bridges simultaneously, and overwhelm the defenders.

This was what General Student called the 'short method' – delivery of assault troops right on the objective, ready to fight at once, instead of a drop some distance away, a forming up, and then an approach to – by now – alerted defenders. Shock and surprise were to make up for the lack of weight in the assault.

The same principles were to be used against the bridges over the Old Maas at Dordrecht, which were a more formidable proposition because they were in a built-up area, with room only for a single company of parachutists to drop.

The third great waterway, the New Maas at Rotterdam, which also takes water from the Rhine via the Lek and Neder Rijn, was spanned over an artificial island by a complex of huge bridges in an almost entirely built-up area. Therefore Student proposed the bold stroke of using the waterway itself as a landing place – a dozen old seaplanes would fly in an infantry company and land on the Maas by the bridges – another example of the 'short method'. But because this force would be too weak to hold the bridges for long – in effect, they were in the centre of Rotterdam – Waalhaven airfield south of the river was to be captured simultaneously by parachutists who would be immediately reinforced by three battalions of air-transported troops – Regiment 16 from Sponeck's division. This regiment would reinforce not merely to the north, towards the Rotterdam bridges, but also to the south, towards the Dordrecht bridges.

With bridges across all three waterways in their hands, the Germans would in effect have laid an airborne 'carpet' right across the Rhine delta, over which their tanks could roll forward into the heart of the country, to the seat of government itself.

The weak point of the German plan was that light airborne forces were to be dropped ahead of the armour for road distances varying from 60 to 100 miles, and would be required to hold their positions for many days against heavy odds. The swift relieving force was to consist of Generalleutnant Hubicki's 9 Panzer Division only. But before it could even get started, it had to cross a major river – the Maas – and possibly also the Maas–Waal Canal.

Bridges on both waterways were to be taken; not by mass or weight, but by small groups of between ten and thirty men dressed as Dutch soldiers or civilians and already positioned inside the Dutch border beforehand. If any of these parties succeeded, they in turn would have to wait until relieved by regular units of the German Army advancing out of Germany; and these units also, although extremely fast-moving, had little fire power. In fact, the Germans had no overwhelming mass of troops anywhere; they were indeed somewhat inferior in numbers, overall, to their Dutch opponents, secure behind the water defences of the Rhine delta.

To orthodox tacticians, the plan seemed reckless to the point of madness. And maddest of all was the decision to divert 500 of the mere 4,500 paratroops available to an attack on the Albert Canal in Belgium. These 500 were to capture three bridges and the mighty modern fortress of Eben Emael, garrisoned by 1,200 men. To capture that concrete battleship, the Germans allotted 11 gliders made of wood and canvas, carrying 85 specially equipped assault engineers.

For the operation overall, there was no precedent. Although valuable lessons in air and tank warfare had been learned in Spain, and small bodies of paratroops had been used in the Norwegian campaign a month earlier, the bold sweep of this conception by far exceeded even the imagination of tank enthusiasts. It was much more daring than the two previous plans, involving Belgian objectives, which had been worked out and then scrapped when a breach of security had revealed them to the potential enemy. Had Hitler known that some of the details of the third plan, and also the projected date of attack, 6 May, had been communicated to the Dutch almost as soon as they had been finalized, the operation would have been cancelled also, as being probably too perilous.

Such was indeed the case, but Hitler did not know it. What the Germans were doing, consciously, was to reintroduce to the battlefields of Europe the Napoleonic concept of war, 'that he who remains behind his entrenchments is beaten,' but in the context of twentieth-century technology. The Russians, who first formed parachute forces, never did anything notable with them; the British, who invented and first used the tank, were strangely slow to grasp its potentialities. It was the Germans who were going to demonstrate, not only how to use air power, airborne forces, and armoured forces, but how to use them to their utmost effect – simultaneously, together, and where possible, concentrated.

CHAPTER TWO

Battles for the Bridges and Build-up of the Waalhaven 'Airhead': 10 May

On the night of 9–10 May 1940, the German side of the German border was still open. It was to be kept open until the last minute, in order to help achieve surprise. Only now was 9 Panzer Division crossing the Rhine at Wesel and coming into its forming-up area under cover of the Reichswald Forest, where the German border lances forward to Wyler among the hills south-east of Nijmegen.

On the Dutch side of the border there had been periodic alerts since 7 May, the day after the German attack had been timed to start, originally. But nothing had happened, because bad flying weather had caused a temporary postponement. On 8 May, the Dutch Army was ordered to be at immediate readiness for war. By 2200 hours on 9 May – two hours before midnight – the Dutch had closed their frontiers, stopped telephone communications, closed the barriers on railway bridges, prepared road-blocks, and were ready to blow all bridges at a moment's notice. Units manning forward defences were ordered to 'stand to' at 0300 hours on 10 May. That is, one hour before the Germans were due to attack.

Dawn was at about 0400 hours, Dutch time, but this was not the only reason for the 'stand to'. Hitler had held his final conference with the airborne planners on 2 May. On 3 May the Dutch military attaché in Berlin, Colonel Sas, learned that the invasion of Holland was imminent. His informant was a

German intelligence officer – Oberst Hans Oster, head of Department Z of the Abwehr, controlled by the enigmatic Admiral Wilhelm Canaris. Both were later to pay with their lives for their opposition to Hitler's plans. The information received by the Dutch government from their military attaché in Berlin was reinforced by a similar message passed on to them from the Vatican in Rome. But nothing happened.

These warnings were from the German opposition led by General Ludwig Beck, who had stated: 'If any offensive takes place without the Allies having received previous warning, we can hardly expect them to continue to make a distinction between the Hitler regime and the decent Germany.'

The final, authentic warning came late in the evening of 9 May. What the Anglo-Saxons call 'D-Day', the Germans call 'A-Day' (*Angriffstag*) – merely a method by which planning can take place without the exact date of an operation being known, the days being counted as 'A plus' or 'A minus' the key, unknown date. At 1900 hours on 9 May, Colonel Sas was told by Hans Oster that A-Day was 10 May, that Hitler was reported to have gone to the front, and that the chance of another cancellation was small. In any event, no cancellation could be made after 2300 hours that night – A-Day minus one – and that, even so, the decision would have to be taken earlier, in Berlin, at 2130 hours, to allow time for the message to reach the forward commanders.

The code-word *Danzig* had already been flashed to all units. 9 Panzer Division began to move forward into the Rhineland to take up springboard positions. From the Westphalian airfields of Delmenhorst, Fassberg, and Gutersloh flew the Heinkels of Kampfgesschwader 4, which was to strike at the airfields of Rotterdam and The Hague.

The mass of planes, more than seventy bombers, droned slowly out over the North Sea before turning to port to fly parallel with the coast of Holland until they were opposite their targets. Then the formations slowly wheeled towards The Hague and Rotterdam, approaching now from the direction of England in the vain hope of achieving surprise. 'Air raid alarm red! The sirens howled in city and harbour,' wrote a Dutch officer stationed at Waalhaven, the airport of Rotterdam. 'Through the misty dawn came the deep droning of many aircraft.'

As the bombers attacked Waalhaven, individual Dutch aircraft made gallant but ineffectual sorties in machines as unsuitable as Lockheed Hudsons, which were easily picked off even by the twin-engined Messerschmitt 110s. Against the stream of returning aircraft, and passing them under the protection of the fighters, came the first waves of Junkers 52 transports carrying the parachutists, queuing up to jump at dawn into the bombed airfields.

The whole operation was under the control of the Luftwaffe, to whom the parachutists also belonged, and the air organization involved was considerable because of the many targets and the differing speeds and flight endurance of the various aircraft types involved. The streams of transport aircraft – 430 triple-engined Junkers 52s – were very slow, taking nearly an hour to cross Holland; and these machines had to be marshalled in the correct tactical formations, according to their loads, so that military units would land more or less as units and not as groups of scattered soldiers. Unlike the bomber formations, the transports flew in one great wave direct from Westphalia, just to the north of Arnhem and the Neder Rijn, dividing into two separate streams only when nearing Rotterdam and The Hague.

Great clouds of oily black smoke were rising from the hangars at Waalhaven. Although the leader's machine had been shot down, the 28 Heinkels of II Gruppe of KG4 had bombed well and accurately. Forewarned, the Dutch had hidden an infantry battalion in the hangars in order to surprise the Germans when they landed; but now those reserves had been decimated.

The drop was a good one, most of the parachutists landing, as planned, around the outside perimeter of the airfield, and then pressing inwards with machine-pistols and grenades against the Dutch pillboxes and trenches. That forced the

Dutch defenders — mostly from the Queen's Grenadiers — to take up positions firing outwards from the airfield perimeter. When they were thus pinned down by the parachutists, an unexpected event occurred. The next squadron of transport planes, instead of dropping more parachutists outside the airfield, roared in low over the airfield boundary — and landed. They were not carrying paratroops at all, but two platoons of airlanding infantry from Regiment 16. The great transports, touching down in the middle of the defences, were an easy target for the flak — one of them was streaming smoke and flame from two engines simultaneously — but land they did, all of them; and out of them poured the fieldgrey infantry to take the defending Queen's Grenadiers in the rear. The way was clear for the bulk of Regiment 16 — three battalions of air-landing infantry — to come in to the newly created Waalhaven 'airhead'. A continuous stream of aircraft came in to land, spilled out their men, guns, munitions, trollies, and motor cycles, and then took off again. It was like an airborne conveyor belt in operation.

The capture of the airfield was only a preliminary to the crux of the operation — the capture of the bridges. It was to serve as a springboard, first for III Battalion to drive north for Rotterdam, second for the two other battalions of the regiment to drive south for Dordrecht. III Battalion landed first, because their main task was infinitely harder. Instead of open country, they had to advance for miles through a built-up area to the centre of Rotterdam, through streets where a handful of men with rifles and machine-guns could easily hold up superior numbers of advancing infantry. In the meantime, the bridges might have been blown.

To reduce this risk, the Germans gambled two tiny forces in an extremely bold manner. At the same time as the attack on Waalhaven began, 50 paratroops dropped on a stadium in South Rotterdam, close to the southern end of the bridges, while 12 Heinkel 59 seaplanes carrying 120 infantrymen and engineers landed on the river on both sides of the great

Willems bridge, before taxiing clumsily to the north bank. Then the soldiers had to inflate their rubber dinghies, board them, paddle to the wall, and climb up on to the river bank.

During this time, they were hopelessly vulnerable. But the very boldness of their arrival helped. 'Workmen crossing the big bridge on their way to work had mistakenly decided that the seaplanes were English, and so they helped the soldiers to climb up the river bank,' recorded the regimental historian.

Shortly afterwards, the 50 paratroops joined them, in an equally unorthodox manner – they simply commandeered some of the city's trams and, bells ringing madly, drove through the streets and across the complex of bridges, which were linked in mid-river by an artificial island, to the north bank. And here they were to remain for five days and four nights, completely cut off from the south bank, for although III Battalion fought its way through the streets to the river, by then the bridges were being so swept by Dutch fire as to be impassable. On the other hand, the Dutch could not retake them, though they tried bitterly.

There was nothing slow about the Dutch reaction. Within hours, they had a fleet of patrol boats and small warships up the river, engaging the German parachutists and infantry on both banks, and had brought Waalhaven under fire from long-range guns sited in the suburbs and directed by observers watching from tall buildings or the tops of cranes at the docks. Although the German hold on the north bank of the Maas was extremely precarious, they refused to depart from their orders and continued to hold on stubbornly to what had been gained.

The airhead was at the northern side of what was in effect an elongated island created by the New Maas flowing through Rotterdam in the north and the Old Maas flowing past Dordrecht to the south, and was secure only if main bridges and ferry sites could be held. To the south-east, both road and rail bridges at Dordrecht had been taken by a single company of parachutists, but the Dutch had reacted vigorously, and the railway bridge had been recaptured.

I and II Battalions were directed towards Dordrecht to reinforce the precarious hold of the paratroops. Bruns, a
company commander in I Battalion, piled his company into two
Dutch trucks and led off early, driving down the motor road
through Hordijk and Alblasserdam to one of the crossing sites
at the Old Maas, where they took the 650-metre-long swing-
bridge, but found the Dutch in possession of the ferry, having
driven back the German platoon holding it. In failing light, and
with the aid of two grenade-throwers and two machine-pistols,
the Germans now retook it from about 100 Dutchmen equipped
with heavy machine-guns as well as light machine-guns.

During the night the Dutch made four attacks against the
German positions in Dordrecht, supported by suspiciously
well-aimed artillery fire. It was being directed by a Dutch
officer who was sitting at an undiscovered telephone in the
middle of the German-held area. The most embarrassing dis-
covery, however, was at Alblasserdam, where the Germans
were astonished to find the river spanned by a major bridge
that, although indisputably there, was not marked on their
maps or listed among their objectives! They occupied it, all the
same.

There was no news of the fate of the paratroops dropped
near The Hague, north-west of Rotterdam and the rivers, nor
of the airlanding infantry who were to support them. Nor was
there any physical contact with Group South, consisting of
Hauptmann Fritz Prager's reinforced II Fallschirmjäger Battalion, which had dropped at both ends of both bridges at
Moerdijk, and swiftly captured them. These bridges carried the
main road and rail communications over viaducts respectively
1,300 yards and 1,400 yards long. They were still intact. But
what tanks would be the first to come roaring up the Antwerp
road from Breda – German or French? Armoured divisions
from the German and the French armies were both racing for
the bridges over the Hollandsch Diep at Moerdijk, and with the
same geographical objective – the German airhead at Waalhaven that was nourishing the entire bridge battle inside 'Fortress
Holland'.

CHAPTER THREE

Arnhem, Nijmegen, and the Maas–Waal Canal: 10 May

Although the complicated lock-bridge at Heumen on the Maas–Waal Canal, was only a small bridge over a small canal connecting the great waterways of the Meuse and the Rhine, it was the Dutch second line of defence, to which the units guarding the frontier with Germany five miles to the east would retire in due order in the event of attack. Consequently, there were Dutch sentries on the eastern end of the bridge, although their headquarters were on the western bank. Their unit, I Battalion of the 26th Regiment of Infantry, stationed along the southern half of the canal, had done very little during the winter to improve the defences.

It was about dawn when these sentries saw a small, disorderly crowd of some thirty men in civilian clothes, guarded by four others in the uniforms of Dutch field gendarmes, shambling down the road to the bridge from the east, the direction of the frontier. While three of the men dressed as military police kept the civilians corralled like prisoners, the fourth gendarme approached the sentry and, in native Dutch, explained that the men in civilian clothes were deserters from the German Army who had escaped across the border, and that his job was to hand them over to the nearest Dutch Army headquarters.

The sentry checked the man's documents, which seemed all right, and gave the order for the lock-bridge to be lowered for their crossing. A sergeant and two corporals of the bridge guard came out to assist the field gendarmes in controlling the mob of Germans in civilian clothes.

The sergeant of the guard suggested that it might save time if he went with the field gendarmes and their prisoners to show them the way. The senior gendarme agreed – the other three men in military police uniform never spoke – and they all moved off towards the west bank.

They had taken no more than a few steps when the 'field gendarmes' and their 'prisoners' suddenly acted in concert. The Dutch sentries were seized and overpowered in an instant. Then, spreading out and drawing machine-pistols and grenades from their clothing, the thirty men in civilian clothes stormed the three nearest casemates and the garrison office, making such skilful use of dead ground and covering fire that it was clear they were highly trained soldiers.

The Dutch sector commander, hearing shots in the distance, broke off the tour of inspection he was making and returned to his command post near the bridge. There he learned that the order to destroy the bridge had been received; so he sent off a cyclist, who quickly returned, having failed to deliver the message. The captain then mounted his own bicycle and pedalled down the road towards the bridge; just before he reached it, he was shot down.

In a matter of a few minutes, the bridge and its immediate defences had been captured, the senior Dutch officer killed, and two of the section leaders taken prisoner, thus making immediate counter-attack unlikely. It was a brilliant success, achieved by a German force numbering less than three dozen lightly armed individuals.

At Malden, north of Heumen, there was another bridge, less important. Here, the German force consisted of eight men in civilian clothes and two more wearing some items of Dutch uniform. With machine-pistols and grenades they drove off the Dutch sentries, who were armed only with rifles, and occupied all the buildings before the Dutch had time to blow the structure. This bridge also was in German hands by dawn, but it did not long remain so.

The Dutch sector commander telephoned battalion headquarters for help, was refused it, and by mustering his clerks

and cooks, found he had a further eight men, plus a light machine-gun. Using this to give covering fire, the Dutch rushed
the building held by the Germans, and killed or captured them
all, apart from one man in civilian clothes who sniped at them
for some hours from cover in a field.

North of Malden was yet another bridge over the canal at
Hatert. Just before dawn, a Dutch sentry noticed a number of
men in civilian clothes loitering suspiciously by the bridge.
Before he could check on them, one opened fire on him with a
machine-gun, but missed. He was able to telephone the news to
sector headquarters, who did not believe him; they did, however, shoot one of their own sentries as he tried to get away
from the Germans by running across the bridge, and shortly
afterwards fresh bursts of German machine-gun fire prompted
them to fire the demolition charges. A cloud of black smoke
rose up at the roar of the explosion, and after it had drifted
away, the bridge was still there, damaged, but with the span
unbroken.

With the Germans holding the far bank, it was impossible to
lay fresh charges, and the captain of the Dutch garrison made
for his casemate to organize a defence. The casemate, however,
was well defended – by the Germans, who had got there first –
and he was taken prisoner. Shortly after, the German follow-up
force arrived, having driven hard across the border. This consisted of a small group of Waffen SS and a couple of tanks.

While the rest gave covering fire over the canal, four SS
scrambled across the damaged structure and formed a small
bridgehead on the west bank. The rest of the SS followed,
stormed the two casemates by the bridge, then turned north
along the canal bank, methodically rolling up the others and
taking about 200 prisoners.

At Neerbosch, still further north towards the Waal, there
were two bridges carrying the main road and rail links from
Nijmegen to Antwerp. Here, the garrison commander acted on
his own initiative. At 0417 he blew both bridges, some minutes
before receiving the order to do so. He was only just in time,
for almost immediately a German mobile force appeared on the

far bank – an SS storm troop riding motor cycles and supported
by two tanks. The Germans opened fire at once, and the Dutch
replied, killing most of the motor-cyclists. One of the tanks
blew up and the other began to burn. Into this smoke and
confusion rolled a German armoured train; but this too was hit
by Dutch fire and began to burn, before backing away towards
Nijmegen.

But now it was around 0500 hours Dutch time, an hour after
the bombing of The Hague, Waalhaven, Dordrecht, and Moerdijk had begun; an hour after the Germans had crossed the
border into Holland; an hour after the initial assaults on the
bridges of the Maas–Waal Canal had been carried out. The
tiny 'Trojan Horse' units had been infiltrated across the frontier during the night, so that they were in position to strike at
the bridges by 0355.

The result, reading from north to south, from the Waal to
the Maas, was that the Germans had failed completely to
secure the two important bridges at Neerbosch; that they had
captured the bridge at Malden and lost it again; that they had
captured the bridge at Hatert in a damaged but usable state;
and that they had taken the locks and bridge at Huemen completely intact. But this was not enough.

The main water barrier south-west of Nijmegen was the
great River Maas, where it looped west near the Waal to follow
a parallel course to the sea; and the main highway to the west
was carried over it by a great bridge at Grave, between Maas
and Waal. This was the priority target, in theory, but the
Germans had no paratroops to spare for its capture and the
'Trojan Horse' units were thinly spread already. Everything depended on the speed with which the ground forces could exploit the successes on the Maas–Waal Canal.

The whole front southwards from Nijmegen down to
Afferden, nearly 20 miles, was the responsibility of the German
XXVI Corps, which attacked with only two divisions, the 254th
in the north and the 256th to the south, with 9 Panzer Division
behind them ready to advance over any bridges that were
seized intact. The more bridges the better, because an ar-

moured advance goes faster when a number of routes are used than it does when everything has to go along one road only in one great traffic jam.

For their assault, 254 Division formed two special forces – the Gruppe Nijmegen and the Gruppe Grave. The former was to take the two great Waal bridges at Nijmegen, the latter to take the Maas–Waal Canal bridges as stepping stones to the main highway bridge over the 800-foot-wide Maas at Grave. Speed was essential, so that the Dutch would have no warning and fail to blow the bridge in time, but the Germans never even came near to achieving it. The Dutch blew it up by mistake at 0645, before any threat had actually developed.

If Gruppe Grave failed to get their Maas bridge, they were instead to turn south and assist in a crossing of the Maas at Mook, which was not screened by a forward canal line. But this, too, they failed to do, and 254 Division crossed without their aid; while farther south at Gennep a bridge was taken intact, and two German trains thundered over it, carrying guns and infantry to the rear of the Dutch positions.

Failure in the north and success in the south meant that 9 Panzer Division initially would have to advance along narrow, congested country roads, instead of breaking through on to the main east–west road route that runs from Nijmegen via Grave, 's Hertogenbosch, Tilburg, and Breda to the Antwerp–Rotterdam motorway. Ominously, none of the great bridges on that motorway – Moerdijk, Dordrecht, Rotterdam – were prepared for demolition. They were to be preserved for the use of the French Seventh Army, and if General Hubicki's 9 Panzer Division was too long delayed, the French General Henri Giraud might well ride into Rotterdam first.

On the critical sector – the Maas–Waal Canal – the 'Trojan Horse' units had done their job well, initially capturing three of the bridges; but they had been let down by the follow-up formations. That day's verdict by XXVI Corps read: 'The small success of the Gruppe Grave is disappointing. It can be traced to the unexpected strength of the Maas–Waal barrier. An impression that the leadership was sluggish and lacked foresight was confirmed by a personal visit from Ia of the Corps.' This staff officer had found not only slack leadership, but one senior officer of the attacking force sound asleep on the afternoon of 10 May.

A more basic reason, however, was the composition of the Gruppe Grave. It had plenty of fire-power, developed from motor-cycle machine-gun companies, but these were extremely vulnerable even to small arms. The tanks, rationed out in packets of two at a time, did not really constitute a battering ram. A single machine-gun could separate them from their un-protected infantry riding along on motor cycles and bicycles. And their artillery was held up by the nature of the country south-east of Nijmegen, which was hilly, thickly wooded, and traversed only by small country roads or tracks.

The Germans had made good use of this terrain to seep forward across the frontier, unseen, in a stealthy infiltration, avoiding head-on attack on border posts and strongpoints. For the Dutch, it was as though the tide had come in behind them. At Groesbeek, which lay on the routes to Heumen and Malden, they fired a few shots, burnt their documents, and surrendered. At the border village of Wyler, the frontier guard post was first fired on from behind, and when the Dutch tried to get away, they found German tanks between them and the main Kleve–Kranenburg–Nijmegen road.

The task of the Gruppe Nijmegen was to advance along this road and also to the north of it, between Beek and the Rhine at Erlekom. The road ran direct to a traffic roundabout in Nij-megen just south of the river; from this, one road went north across the great Waal bridge to Arnhem, another led south-west to the bridges at Neerbosch and Grave. The de-fences were sited along the road from the frontier post at Beek, with the bulk of them north of the Waal, defending the route to Arnhem.

While German infantry pinched out the road-blocks, a mobile storm troop under Obersturmführer Weiss raced for the great road bridge over the Waal. Its single span, 244 metres long, was the largest of any bridge in Europe at that time. The storm troop was from the armoured reconnaissance battalion of the Waffen–SS Verfügungs Division, which did not operate as a division, but as corps troops for special missions such as this. Avoiding the main road, the handful of tanks and motor-cyclists slipped down country tracks over the 300-foot-high hills near Berg en Dal and entered Nijmegen from the south.

At 0445 hours Dutch time, 50 minutes after crossing the border, they had the bridge in front of them. But they were too late. The 'Trojan Horse' unit that was to have attacked the bridge at dawn from Rhine barges moored in the nearby barge harbour had failed to arrive, and the Dutch had blown the great central span into the water at 0425.

Arnhem is protected by water on two sides – the Neder Rijn to the south and the Ijssel to the east, facing Germany, both rivers forming part of the Rhine delta. It is an extremely defensible position, with high ground to the north and west dominating the flat, low-lying delta plain. In the south, the road and rail-way from Nijmegen to North Holland and north-west Germany are carried across the Neder Rijn on two separate bridges some distance from each other, only the road bridge leading directly into the town of Arnhem. The latter is a single-span bridge carried high up over the flood plain and dykes on a viaduct and is of similar design to the other modern bridge across the Waal at Nijmegen.

To the east, the road and railway lines leading from Germany into the heart of Holland were carried across the Ijssel side-by-side on a many-piered bridge of older design at a village called Westervoort. The old Fort Westervoort, now flanked by more modern casemates, guarded the Ijssel on the Arnhem side of the river. III Battalion of the 35th Regiment of Infantry held this position with 22 Frontier Battalion forming a screen be-tween the Ijssel and the German border.

On the night of 9–10 May the barricades were in place on all roads leading to the bridges. At about 0300 hours, when it was still dark, the sentries on a barricade at Didam, which barred a road route to Westervoort, saw a patrol of uniformed cyclists

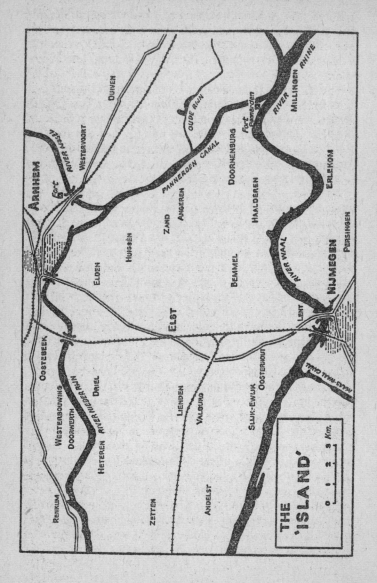

THE 'ISLAND'

0 1 2 3 Km.

ride towards them out of the night. Their officer dismounted and produced a movement order apparently signed by a captain of the Dutch General Staff and directing him to carry out a march exercise through Didam to Apeldoorn via Westervoort.

The barricade commander, a lieutenant of 22 Frontier Battalion, noticed that although the uniforms worn by the military cyclists were apparently Dutch, their weapons were of an unfamiliar pattern. There was something odd about their helmets, too, although these were of familiar shape. In fact, the helmets were not made of steel, but fashioned out of cardboard in amateurish fashion. And, finally, he realized that out of the 28 military cyclists only one man – the leader – actually spoke Dutch! The lieutenant had them arrested and disarmed in front of the barricade, and eventually packed into a bus for dispatch under guard to Fort Westervoort.

But in order to do this, the barricade had to be opened. Before it could be closed again behind the departing bus, the roar of engines could be heard on the frontier road. It was a storm troop detachment from the SS Standarte 'Der Führer', a stream of motor-cyclists leading two tanks. They went straight through the conveniently opened barricade and on down the road towards the bridges. That was at about 0415 hours. It was an exceedingly light but unexpected form of attack, quite unlike a formal infantry assault behind an artillery barrage.

The weight in the German plan on this sector lay along the railway. Two regiments of the German 207 Infantry Division followed up the storm troop detachments, led by three trains – Armoured Train No 7 carrying artillery and machine-guns followed by a troop train holding infantry, followed by yet another train carrying supplies, ammunition, and bridging equipment. The armoured train rolled into Westervoort Station, east of the Ijssel, at about 0440 and thundered on towards the bridge. As it pounded up the viaduct in full view of the defenders on the far bank, the demolition charges were fired from Fort Westervoort. At 0445 the bridges disappeared in smoke, and subsided.

But although the structures were impassable now to vehicles, they still spanned the river and the marshy ground on
both banks. Covered by the guns of the armoured train, the
Germans set up a fire base on the east bank and swiftly mas-
tered the guns of Fort Westervoort. One by one, these fell
silent and eventually only two machine-guns were left, in positions so exposed that the Dutch dared not show themselves but
fired by attaching a length of string to the triggers and blazing
away blind by remote control. So completely did the Germans
win this fire fight, that it took the Dutch garrison a full 15
minutes to surrender; no one dared show himself to put out the
white flag.

The flanking casemates were similarly neutralized by fire,
although they were able to stop the first attempt of the
Germans, at 0800, to make an assault crossing in rubber boats.
But a second attempt succeeded and together with storm troop
detachments that had worked their way over the buckled
girders of the bridges, these attackers succeeded in building up
a bridgehead on the west bank around the battered fort. At
0920 the white flag was seen and by 0930 Fort Westervoort
was in German hands. By 1600 hours they had a pontoon
bridge across the Ijssel, and troops and vehicles were being
pushed across to keep up the momentum of the advance.

Meanwhile, the leading troops had gone clean through
Arnhem and by 1100 were making along the railway embankment for the outlying village of Oosterbeek. Here they
divided, one force heading for Ede, the other striking for Wageningen, and pushing back the Dutch 4th Hussar Regiment,
which had been brought up from reserve, until they were in
sight of the main Dutch defensive position along the high
ground called the Grebbeberg. This, the so-called Grebbe Line,
was a strong position overlooking the valley of the River
Grebbe and shielding 'Fortress Holland' from the east.

As the Germans advanced westward parallel to the Neder
Rijn, their progress was marked by the almost pointless destruction of the fine bridges across it. Both the road and rail
bridges in southern Arnhem were demolished by previously

prepared charges, while the railway bridge at Rhenen was destroyed by Dutch artillery after the charges had failed to explode. The Germans had even got across the Pannerden Canal and penetrated beyond Angeren in the Betuwe, the marshy land lying between Arnhem and Nijmegen.

Thus, the defenders of the north bank of the Waal were hemmed in on three sides. That evening, they destroyed their heavy weapons and ammunition and retreated westward.

CHAPTER FOUR

The Tragedy of Rotterdam

On 13 May 1940 three contrasted groups of people passed through the Hook of Holland, the port at the mouth of the New Maas downstream from Rotterdam. The first party were visitors to Holland – the 2nd Battalion of the Irish Guards, sent to support the Dutch.

At noon, a Dutch party passed them, outward bound for London; this consisted of various members of the royal family, some of whom wanted to go to Walcheren rather than England. The next party to arrive were also outward bound from the Hook for London. They came in at about 1800 hours, and when the Irish Guards saw who they were their decision to sit tight at the Hook was confirmed. For these last arrivals were members of the Netherlands government and diplomatic corps, setting an example that their troops generally did not follow.

If the Dutch government had tacitly admitted defeat in advance of the event, the German government – that is, Hitler – was, at the least, highly nervous and unsure. So much so that on the day following the flight of the Dutch politicians, Hitler issued his Directive No 11. The third paragraph might have surprised the evacuees at the Hook. It read:

On the northern flank the Dutch Army has shown itself capable of a stronger resistance than had been supposed. For political and military reasons, this resistance must be broken *quickly*. It is the task of the Army, by moving strong forces from the south in conjunction with an attack against the Eastern front, to bring about the speedy fall of Fortress Holland.

Hitler was worried about Holland because he was nervous about a French counter-offensive into the southern flank of his push through the Ardennes towards the coast of north-west France, the main aim of Operation Yellow. This preoccupied him for a week. General Halder noted irritably: 'The Führer has an incomprehensible anxiety about the southern flank . . .'

The fall of France did not seem inevitable then, even to the Germans; even Hitler's hope of gaining the coastline from Calais to the Zuyder Zee was essentially defensive. Six months previously, on 23 November 1939, Hitler had told his generals: 'We have an Achilles heel – the Ruhr . . . If Britain and France push through Belgium and Holland into the Ruhr, we shall be in the greatest danger. That could lead to a paralysis of German resistance.'

Such an ambitious stroke was not to be contemplated by the Allies until 1944, but German fears of it in 1940 were real. The German blow into the Low Countries was a pre-emptive strike, but because Allied Plan D assumed that the main weight of the German attack would be there, the actual events in the north so hypnotized the Allied High Command that they did not recognize the massed panzer drive through the Ardennes as the main German effort until they had all their mobile units committed far forward into Belgium and Holland, so that the thrust into France succeeded to an extent far beyond German ambitions.

It was on 13 May that von Rundstedt's armour crossed the Meuse near Sedan and broke through on to the plains of north-east France. In Belgium von Reichenau's Sixth Army had done so well in its drive to Brussels that as a reward for success its armoured corps was to be taken away to reinforce the Sedan breakthrough, leaving only the infantry. Von Reichenau protested angrily, because this would slow his advance, but the decision was undoubtedly correct; Sixth Army had completed its task of drawing the French armour away from Sedan.

Its advance had been facilitated by a swift crossing of the Albert Canal at the outset of the campaign. Some 400 parachutists had captured the two most important bridges at

Vroenhaven and Veltwezelt, although failing to get the less vital bridge at Canne; and an 85-strong force of glider-borne engineers had captured the great fortress of Eben Emael that commanded the canal.

Eleven gliders were used, developed directly from sport gliders, with a flat gliding angle of 1 in 12, which meant that they could be released by the tug aircraft many miles away and make a silent approach to the target; the skill of the pilots, coupled with the use of air-brakes, enabled absolutely 'spot' landings to be made on the roof of the fort. Unlike the paratroop drops, the arrivals were absolutely accurate and there was no audible warning of the attack.

Using special charges, the engineers put the gun cupolas out of action and kept them out of action until the German ground forces arrived. There was very little the 1,200-strong garrison of Eben Emael could do about it, so unexpected were these tactics. Because the Germans kept quiet about them afterwards, the logicians of the British and American press were forced to postulate a mythical 'Fifth Column' and the inevitable 'Dutch officer' was trotted out to explain how German civilians growing chicory in underground caverns had blown up the whole fortress in an instant.

The overall situation on 13 May was that the German main effort (France) was showing all the signs of success; that the armour and some of the air power supporting the advance through Belgium was about to be taken away to support it; and that therefore nothing would be available to help the assault on 'Fortress Holland', which was apparently faltering on the brink of disaster. The flight of the Dutch government at this moment was largely coincidence, but not entirely; they had of course been the target of the airborne landings north of the New Maas, designed to take The Hague.

Not only the date and time of the attacks but details of the operational plans must have been betrayed to the Dutch. Although the refugee government of the Netherlands was to make much of the part played by a supposed 'Fifth Column' in their defeat, they were perhaps naturally rather less free in advertising the advantages in that line that they themselves had enjoyed. In fact, they quite failed to mention it.

The assault by Count Sponeck's force on the Dutch government in its capital had depended on the capture by paratroops of three airfields situated in a rough triangle round The Hague that also gave control over three motorways leading into the city, followed by the landing of two infantry regiments in Junkers 52s on these airfields. They were Valkenburg to the north, near Katwijk-an-Zee; Ypenburg to the south-east on the main Rotterdam road; and Ockenburg (or Loosduinen) near the sea to the south-west.

At Valkenburg a well-dug-in enemy prevented the parachutists from clearing the airfield before the airborne troops arrived; but the pilots landed nevertheless, some with their aircraft on fire, and the infantry went straight into the attack without being able to form up. Against all odds, they took Valkenburg. But the airfield was muddy and, once down, the transports could not leave; soon it was quite blocked by grounded Junkers. When a reinforcing battalion arrived, it was unable to land and some pilots turned back; others made crash landings in fields or among the dunes by the shore. Back in Westphalia, the fly-in of the rest of Infantry Regiment 47 was stopped.

At Ockenburg the first three Junkers carrying men from Infantry Regiment 65 found that they had the place all to themselves (the parachutists having been dropped wrongly at the Hook): but they attacked, with the gunners of the Junkers 52s giving them covering fire. And they also took their objective from an alerted Dutch enemy. But a British bomber attack completed the blocking of the runways, no build-up of an airhead was possible, and this force broke out towards Rotterdam.

At Ypenburg also, because of a faulty drop, there were no parachutists to take on the defenders before the first group of 13 transport planes arrived; 11 of those 13 planes were burning in the air before they touched down, and this airfield also was blocked. The attackers surrendered to the Dutch that evening, but a follow-up force of about 10 planes diverted and made cross-wind landings on the main Rotterdam motorway. From them, some 200 men commanded by the divisional medical officer fought their way towards Rotterdam.

'The landing operations around The Hague must be regarded as a failure,' wrote the historian of 22 Airlanding Division, 'but nevertheless, simply by persevering, 2,000 men chained down three Dutch divisions and completely confused the high command of the Dutch Army.' The division paid a high price for it. Overall, 42 per cent of the officers and 28 per cent of the NCOs and soldiers were killed and wounded in five days.

While operations north of Rotterdam appeared to have collapsed, the vital airhead and airborne corridor between Rotterdam and Dordrecht, under continual attack by the Dutch, was only being held precariously. The area was approximately 17 kilometres long by 10 kilometres wide, and although much of it was bordered by the great waterways of the Old and the New Maas, the German hold was tenuous.

At the north end, the defenders of the tiny German bridgehead over the New Maas in Rotterdam were being steadily whittled down by the Dutch Marines, until at length they had been reduced to only 60 men holding three buildings, some of them on fire. At the south end, the Dutch were counter-attacking their lost bridges, though without much success.

General Student had now arrived at Waalhaven and set up his command post there. As the heavy shells came howling in, sending up clouds of smoke and clods of flying earth, his only comment was: 'Watch it, the English will soon be here as well.'

At about noon, they came. Only six twin-engined fighter-Blenheims to machine-gun the airfield; no bombers, because the British War Cabinet was afraid that in the confusion friendly civilians might be killed by accident. Five out of the six were shot down, three crashing in sight of the airfield, the pilots obviously dead or badly wounded at the controls. From the first, on fire and out of control, a single airman bailed out, his parachute already on fire. Another, one engine blazing, flew right across Waalhaven before crashing into the Rotterdam motor road with a tremendous detonation.

On the river front, Dutch Marines trying to cross the Maas in boats to attack the German airhead were being beaten back by the murderous fire of heavy machine-guns, the Dutch torpedo-boat TM–51 was limping out of action, and the Dutch destroyer *Van Galen* was being dive-bombed by Stukas as she raced up-river towards Waalhaven. Unable to manoeuvre in the narrow waterway, she was holed by near-misses and had to be grounded in the shallows to prevent her from sinking.

For many people in Holland, 10 May 1940 was to be the end of an era, although they did not realize it that morning. Mr W. Brugmans was then a civil servant with his home near the Marine barracks in Rotterdam.

At the north end of the Willemsbrug was a modern bank building, with layers of stone, like a fort (he recollected).

It gave the best possible view over the Willemsbrug and the elevated highway, and was guarded only by a watchman at night, so a group of storm troopers could easily get in. Once in, nobody could get them out again without blowing up the building. There was a delay because the Dutch Marines had to be gathered – some of them did not sleep in barracks, but at their homes in the town – and then they tried to retake the bank, the Maasbrug, and the White House, another high building nearby which the Germans had also occupied.

Anxious waiting was not confined to the Dutch that day. There were not enough transport aircraft to bring in all the troops in one 'lift', a feature that was to mark – and mar – most airborne operations of the Second World War. Prior planning could not predict exactly how many gaps there would be in the formations of transport planes when they returned. There were many gaps, and as the Junkers 52s were refuelled, their crews talked of murderous flak. Losses had been so heavy that 5,000 men of the airlanding division were left stranded on German airfields and never took part in the battle at all. I Battalion, 16th Infantry Regiment arrived over Waalhaven to find the airfield under intense and accurate fire from Dutch artillery hidden among the trees at Kralingen. The area had previously been gridded so that the artillery observers in their lofty perches could bring down fire on any part of it at will. Several of the Junkers 52s were hit and began to blaze as soon as they touched down.

The bulk of the Luftwaffe was engaged elsewhere, so air support was increasingly restricted to supply drops of ammunition only; no food, no petrol, and few air strikes. The breakout by 9 Panzer Division had been delayed by the failure to get the bridge at Grave, and there was no sign of aid from powerful ground forces for three long, anxious days.

Then the first tanks rolled up from the south along the Antwerp road and on into Moerdijk, while Dutch Artillery maintained heavy fire on the paratroop battalion holding the bridges over the Hollandsch Diep. The tanks were French. The spearhead of General Giraud's Seventh Army had crossed Belgium and made contact with the Dutch and were now about to roll up the German airborne 'carpet' from the south.

In this crisis the Germans called up the Stukas, whose basic commitment was to aid the main effort far away in France. Although few in numbers, their great accuracy, combined with a method of radio communication that enabled them to be directed exactly at pin-point targets by the ground forces, made them worth their weight in gold. The tanks were defeated.

The thirteenth of May was the decisive date then; it was the day the Germans broke out onto the plains of France, the day the Irish Guards landed at the Hook to reinforce the Marines; the day the Dutch government fled from Holland via the Hook, the day Count Sponeck's party reached the north of Rotterdam. It was also the day that General Hubicki's 9 Panzer Division at last linked up with the Moerdijk paratroops.

That morning they rolled over the bridge across the Hollandsch Diep and drove down the airborne corridor towards Dordrecht and Rotterdam. By 1300 hours their spearheads had reached Hordijk, the centre of the hard-pressed airhead, and by evening they were in sight of the bridges over the New Maas at Rotterdam.

The thirteenth of May was also the first day of the dialogue between the two colonels – von Choltitz for the Germans, asking for the surrender of Rotterdam, and Scharroo for the Dutch, stubbornly refusing to give in to the weaker force. Undoubtedly, von Choltitz did his best to spare Rotterdam in 1940, as he was afterwards to save Paris in 1944; and Scharroo was equally right to resist him. In Rotterdam, the Dutch Army was not beaten and north of the New Maas the German airborne forces had virtually collapsed.

In his Directive No 8 Hitler had written: 'Neither in Holland nor in Belgium–Luxembourg are centres of population, and in particular large open cities and industrial installations, to be attacked without compelling military necessity.' Up to now, as the RAF official historian put it, 'the Luftwaffe seemed to be operating against military targets in the narrowest sense'. Had Hitler's 'compelling military necessity' now arisen? Clearly it had, and on the evening of 13 May General von Küchler, commanding the Eighteenth Army, the German force attacking Holland, gave the order 'to break the resistance at Rotterdam by every means'. This was passed on to the Dutch by the panzer corps commander, Major-General Rudolf Schmidt, with a warning that failure to surrender 'could result in the complete destruction of the city'. This was a technical exaggeration, as no air force in the world then possessed the power to destroy a city with one blow, even a city as vulnerable as Rotterdam turned out to be. What was very carefully prepared was a 'pattern' bombing raid by 100 Heinkels of Kampfgeschwader 54 operating in a tactical role.

Because of the possibility of the Dutch deciding after all to surrender Rotterdam at the last moment, a recall procedure

was detailed. Oberst Lackner, commanding KG 54, reported:
'On our approach we were to watch out for red Véry lights on
the Maas island. Should they appear we had orders to attack
not Rotterdam, but the alternative target of two English divisions at Antwerp.' Red was an unfortunate colour, as it could
be confused with tracer shells and bullets from light anti-aircraft guns, particularly in the dust and smoke haze of battle.
The Heinkels were airborne from German bases at 1330 hours
German time and due over target at 1500 hours German time
on 14 May.

Since 1040 hours that morning, the great Willems bridge
had been the scene of an unofficial truce, with envoys of both
sides crossing it; first two Germans who were taken through
Rotterdam blindfolded to Colonel Scharroo, then Scharroo's
adjutant to see von Choltitz. Scharroo appeared to be playing
for time, but the Germans radioed to Kesselring's Luftflotte 2:
'Attack postponed owing to parley.' This meant the proposed
tank attack across the Willems bridge, which was to be preceded by an artillery bombardment and the bombing raid at
1500. The recall signal was sent out to the bombers from
German bases, but they were already over the Dutch–German
border, entering hostile territory, and the radio operators had
withdrawn the trailing aerials. This much reduced the range of
the sets and the message was not received. The bomber force
thundered on and dropped its devastating load.

At 1700 hours on 14 May, Colonel Scharroo walked over the
Willems bridge from the burning city and surrendered. At 2030
hours, the capitulation of Holland was announced.

Part II

Target Ruhr

1944

CHAPTER FIVE

Full Circle: 1940–1944

The First Allied Airborne Army was the strategic reserve of the two army groups, one British, one American, which had broken the Germans in Normandy and were now driving forward some 250 miles beyond their beachhead base, towards the Rhine and the Rhine delta. This strategic reserve was to be used to lay an airborne carpet across the three main waterways of the Rhine delta – Maas, Waal, and Neder Rijn – over which a mobile corps spearheaded by an armoured division would advance to the Zuyder Zee and then turn right into Germany, to cut off the Ruhr, thereby bringing German resistance to an end at least by Christmas, 1944, it was hoped.

In essentials, it was a fairly close copy of Hitler's 'Fortress Holland' gambit of 1940, and included many of the same objectives. The only difference was that the axis of the initial thrust was northwards, at right angles to the initial direction of the German axis in 1940; the early objectives were therefore to be approached from the south instead of the east.

The forces employed were to be very much greater, but the clear and logical German command structure of 1940 was lacking. Then, the airborne forces had been under the control of the Luftwaffe, which was directly responsible for the success of the resulting ground battle; hence they supported it to the hilt, taking staggering losses in transport aircraft and laying on Stuka or bomber strikes at the critical moments.

However, the Allied command structure was peculiar, in that the air forces bore sole responsibility when the force was in the air, the military when the force was on the ground. The air forces decided what risks they would run and what objectives they would or would not attack, with regard only to their own interests and not that of the customer, let alone of the battle as a whole.

Although the air forces consisted of British and American components under the command of an American, international rivalries played no visible part; it was the inter-service attitude that was to be disastrous. The inherent difficulties of an Allied command were plain, however, at the very top, with the proviso that this was also very much a matter of personalities and differing abilities.

There were three main bridges to be captured – all of them German objectives in 1940 – and of these the Arnhem road bridge was the third, 'the one bridge too far', as was predicted. The direct parallel lay with the Willems bridge at Rotterdam in 1940 and the precarious bridgehead held by a couple of companies and very nearly abandoned by the Germans as hopeless. The scaling up of airborne forces in the meantime is illustrated by the size of the force detailed to take Arnhem bridge in 1944 – the three battalions of 1 Parachute Brigade.

There were significant differences of doctrine between the German Army and the British Army at that time. The British doctrine stressed the importance of keeping your balance, so that the enemy could not catch you unprepared, while the German doctrine stressed boldness and the deliberate accept-ance of risks. Their idea was that by vigorous and constant attack the defender himself could be put off balance, thereby enabling the attacker to take risks and get away with it. The two doctrines were incompatible. They do, however, serve to explain exactly what happened in 1940, and nothing else does. Both sides fought strictly in accordance with their previously thought-out ideas; and the better idea won.

These contrasts remained to the end of the war, although in less exaggerated form, complicated by additional factors such as the immense amount of actual battle experience accumu-lated by the Germans, offset by the great material superiority of the Allies. In the air, the pendulum had swung completely.

The Allied air forces were so powerful and efficient that the Germans were hardly able to move by day, while some Allied ground units went out of their way to make themselves conspicuous from the air because they feared a case of mistaken identity on the part of their own air force far more than they did an attack by the Luftwaffe; the results were so much worse, in the first case.

By 1944, the panzers had been decimated, the bulk of the railways destroyed, and the roads were scourged by Allied air power. The Germans could move in numbers only by night and at walking pace, and much of their heavy equipment had been lost. The Allied armies on the other hand were more than half mechanized or motorized. That is to say, less than half the troops had to walk, although their supplies were entirely motorized. The opportunity existed, simply by taking away the supply trucks from approximately half the force, to send the other half motoring forward into Germany at 30 miles an hour, or ten times the speed at which the retreating German forces could react. This is certainly what the Germans would have done, had positions been reversed.

But the Germans had a unified command and the Allies had not. Field Marshal Sir Bernard Montgomery had controlled the land battle in Normandy, while the numbers of troops involved were approximately half-British, half-American. But this was only a temporary arrangement for the control of four armies – First Canadian Army, Second British Army, First US Army, and Third US Army. With the arrival of the Seventh US Army, which had landed in the south of France and was now headed generally in the direction of Strasbourg, the majority of the troops would be American (although the vital navy and merchant shipping forces were still largely provided by Britain). By previous arrangement, Eisenhower was due to take over the actual control of the battle, which would now really be controlled by two subordinates – Montgomery, commanding the two armies that made up the British 21st Army Group, and General Omar Bradley, commanding the armies that made up the US 12th Army Group. This was the unsettled and unsettling background for what would be one of the most critical decisions of the war.

On 17 August, immediately after the victory at Falaise in the Normandy breakout, Montgomery suggested to Bradley that both their army groups, consisting of 40 divisions, should drive north, the British for Antwerp, the Americans for Aachen. On 23 August, Montgomery was able to suggest this to Eisenhower, stress that it meant halting many divisions, and point out that a decision based on halting either some British on the left or some American divisions on the right had to be made. Naturally, the commanders concerned were not going to like it, particularly not General George S. Patton, but exactly the same decision had been made by the Germans in 1940, when they withdrew support from Army Group B in the north in order to reinforce the decisive drive by Army Group A through the Ardennes to the Channel coast. Eisenhower simply agreed with everyone, and announced that he was taking over command on 1 September.

Broadly, he had three alternatives – the Rhine, the Ruhr, or Antwerp and its estuary. The Rhine and the Ruhr were offensive concepts with an element of risk. A hold on the entire bank of the Rhine, or the capture of the Aachen–Ruhr area, would cripple Germany economically and might bring the war to an end by Christmas. The capture of Antwerp and the Scheldt estuary would be defensive, giving the necessary port capacities to replace the Normandy beaches and wage a long campaign throughout the winter and spring, deferring victory to 1945. But, although Eisenhower made up his mind on many occasions, and can be quoted as supporting all these objectives, his mind never firmly stayed made up; and so, in fits and starts, his armies tried for them all, more or less simultaneously, and succeeded nowhere. Worse, he had his army and army group commanders snarling at him and at each other.

Meanwhile, the German High Command was beginning to recover from the shock of the apparently fatal catastrophe in Normandy, although some had anticipated it and realized that the war was lost. On 3 September Hitler ordered Field Marshal Walter Model to build up an armoured force to counter-attack Patton's drive; on 4 September Field Marshal von Rundstedt was made commander-in-chief in the west; and on the same day Reichsmarschal Göring pulled 20,000 trained parachute troops more or less 'out of the hat' and offered also to supply 10,000 Luftwaffe men for infantry training. And Hitler was scouring the depots and garrisons of both the Army and the Navy, and even the police and the para-military labour force of the Todt organization, to form new divisions to replace those lost in Normandy. And, because of the immense distances they had advanced, the Allied spearheads had lost some of their impetus.

Nevertheless, all this frantic reorganization took time to effect and the onward rush of the Allied armoured columns seemed irresistible. It was 1940 all over again, but with wild scenes of liberation on the one side and the bitter fury of the defeated on the other.

CHAPTER SIX

Blitzkrieg: September

By September, the Allies were pouring into Belgium, the road convoys stretching back 250 miles and more to the Normandy beaches. And fighting was still going on along most of that 250 miles, large parts of which were 'Indian country', and contained many more German than Allied troops. The hardest – and slowest – going was nearest the sea, on the axis of advance of the First Canadian Army. They were over-running the heavily fortified 'Rocket Coast', where the V-weapons that were bombarding England were sited; and every port had a strong German garrison that did not retreat but hung on with orders to fight to the proverbial 'last round'. Every port, from Le Havre to Dunkirk, had to be either taken by set-piece assault or cordoned off by siege lines. This separate battle of the ports went on throughout September (Dunkirk held out to the end of the war) and absorbed the resources of most of the First Canadian Army, so that only the British Second Army was available for the 'blitzkrieg' role.

Where special conditions did not apply, the British and Canadians ignored even large bodies of Germans left far behind the tank spearheads, and in what was to become famous as the 'Brussels Swan', there was no such animal as a front line. A part of German Army Group B, struggling to get back to Germany, found itself occupying a 'pocket' about 100 miles long, stretching from south of Compiègne to north of Cambrai, while the spearheads of the Second Army were driving for Brussels and Antwerp.

Even so, this was merely an area containing more confused German troops than confused British troops; and while the

British were riding, the Germans were hiding or walking. Similarly, the main axes of advance represented slowly moving traffic jams, in which most of the vehicles were British, although some were Canadian, American, and German. The confusion was made worse by the fact that the maps ran out somewhere north of Beauvais, and a school atlas was a valuable capture.

The blitzkrieg momentarily created a series of ripples that ran through northern France, Belgium, and on into Holland in three days – Sunday, 3 September; Monday, 4 September; and Tuesday, 5 September. They were all mad. This is reasonable, because it is the object of a blitzkrieg to defeat by disorganizing, rather than fighting; although there was fighting, sometimes by rearguards, more often by over-run units as important to the command system as army headquarters.

The ripple that was to reach Holland on Tuesday, 5 September, started at Douai in the very early hours of Sunday, 3 September. General Sir Brian Horrocks, the commander of XXX Corps, had ordered his two armoured divisions – Sir Alan Adair's Guards Armoured and Major-General G. P. B. (Pip) Roberts' 11 Armoured – to over-run Belgium in one bound, and by night. Tanks are vulnerable at night, at least they are when they are static, and it is difficult to see very much out of them even in daylight. Such a night run by a mass of armour was unprecedented and would certainly not be expected by the Germans. But all normal rules were to be disregarded and Guards Armoured was ordered to take Brussels, the Belgian capital, while 11 Armoured was directed to seize Antwerp and its docks, deeper still into Belgium.

The Guards, with the shortest distance to go – 93 miles, by no means all of them unopposed – had its leading brigade on the outskirts of Brussels just before dark on 3 September, having taken 15 hours to cover the distance. As darkness fell, the tanks drove into the city and at first there was no uproar, no reaction. In wartime, there is nothing abnormal about convoys of tanks, armoured cars, and other military vehicles.

But when the Belgians realized what was happening, Brus-

sels went mad. Surging crowds, the women offering kisses and
the men champagne, swarmed on to the main thoroughfares
and swamped the street fighting. At times, advancing columns
of British vehicles were occupying the same street double-
banked with columns of retreating German vehicles, and
neither able to shoot at the other. One furious Guards officer,
secure in the priority of importance rightly according to the
headquarters of 5 Brigade, had only just begun to reprimand the
leading vehicle of a column that was obstructing his path when
one of the occupants replied with a resonant *Achtung!* and a
fusillade of shots followed. Harsher arguments ensued before
that particular traffic jam was cleared.

On 4 September, 11 Armoured Division rolled into Antwerp.
The first Germans they saw were sitting at tables in the out-
door cafés, not even bothering to look up at the sound of passing tracks. The docks of the great inland port on the Scheldt
were taken intact, with all the cranes and other machinery in
working order; enough dock space to solve virtually all the
Allies' supply problems. But the Germans still held the estuary
that led down from Antwerp to the sea. Roberts did not realize
at the time how vital this was, nor, had he realized it, had he
anything like sufficient force to clear the estuary on the Dutch
side.

It is fairly easy to see now, with benefit of hindsight, that
whatever main objective was allotted to Eisenhower's forces,
the capture of the Scheldt estuary should have been a priority
for a subsidiary advance at least. But, of course, only 48 hours
before, even Antwerp must have seemed a near impossible
prize. At least, an Antwerp with the docks intact; for the
Germans had made a sorry mess of Cherbourg earlier, making
its capture by the Americans nearly meaningless. But now, even
so, anything seemed possible — provided the German rout continued.

On the evening of 5 September, Brigadier J. O. E. Vandeleur of
Guards Armoured received orders to advance and seize a
bridgehead over the Albert Canal anywhere on a front of 20
miles. On 6 September the division moved off. By dark the

same day they had a bridgehead at Beeringen. But it was not until 10 September that the 30th US Infantry Division occupied Fort Eben Emael, on the wrong side of the canal, which had been abandoned that day by the Germans because the firing embrasures were still blocked with the wrecked guns that had been put out of action by General Student's glider-borne engineers on 10 May 1940. Oddly, the commander of the German troops holding Eben Emael and the Albert Canal was General Student, with a newly created formation. A fresh battle for the strategic waterways of Belgium and Holland had begun.

The 1944 assault differed in two main ways from that of 1940. Firstly, the axis of advance was roughly north instead of approximately west – a difference of 90 degrees. Instead of advancing along the line of the Waal and the Neder Rijn, the attacking forces would have to cross them. Otherwise, there was not a great deal of difference. The Maas would certainly have to be crossed, preferably at Grave, where the Germans had tried and failed in 1940; and also the nearby Maas–Waal Canal.

In addition, there were two other major canals in Holland – the Wilhelmina and the Willems; and two in Belgium before that – the Albert and the Escaut. The smaller rivers in the path of the advance were too numerous to mention. On the other hand, the Hollandsch Diep at Moerdijk had been much wider than any of these, and the problems set in 1940 by the Old Maas at Dordrecht and the New Maas at Rotterdam, not to mention the Maas at Gennep, had certainly not been less.

The differences lay not so much with difficulties in general but with an alteration in geographical emphasis. The blowing of the great road and rail bridges at Nijmegen and Arnhem had, in the context of a westward advance, denied the Germans nothing of importance in 1940. But to a rapid northward advance, they were essential. The emphasis is on 'rapid', because the bridging of even major rivers is a routine requirement for the engineers of any army. But this takes time, and it also requires the forward movement of large quantities of heavy material.

This brings us directly to the second major difference between 1940 and 1944, and by a long way the more important of the two. The German assault had been launched directly from the German frontier, close to the Ruhr, and with only about 100 miles to go. The Allied assault of 1944 had to be launched from northern Belgium, also with about 100 miles to go. The difference was that in order to get to northern Belgium the Allies had already advanced over 300 miles, most of it within a week, from improvised bases back in Normandy. Their real bases were of course in England and America.

Even the shortest main supply lines started in the London docks, headed south-east towards Margate, doubled back westward past Dunkirk, Calais, Boulogne, Dieppe, and Le Havre to the beaches of Normandy, where all the men and material had to be landed, and then these bumped off by road over an endless succession of Bailey bridges, passing on the way Le Havre, Dieppe, Boulogne, Calais, and Dunkirk, all of them useless except for Dieppe, which was opened on 8 September. The direct sea route was London docks – Antwerp docks, and Antwerp alone had the necessary port capacity. But the German 15th Army still held the coast and the estuaries from just north of Bruges right into Holland.

The effect of all this was apparent in the plans to get a bridgehead over the Albert Canal north-east of Brussels. The purpose of the bridgehead was to concentrate between the Escaut in the north and the Albert in the south all the resources required by XXX Corps for its part in the great attempt to breach the main river-lines of Holland. The CRE (Commander, Royal Engineers) of Guards Armoured Division was Brigadier C. P. Jones (now General Sir Charles Jones, chief royal engineer of the British Army).

His principal difficulty was that he did not have, and could not get immediately over the strained supply lines, anything like sufficient bridging material to span the Albert Canal at any point. The only possibility would be a partially demolished bridge capable of being repaired with the sparse amount of material he actually had. In order to improve the chances of getting such a repairable bridge, Brigadier Jones asked General Adair if he would spread out the reconnaissance troops of the 2nd Household Cavalry Regiment along the whole 20-mile front and to allow the Royal Engineer reconnaissance parties to go forward with each armoured car squadron.

This was agreed, and the armoured cars drove forward into what was obviously 'a deteriorating situation'. This was caused by the arrival of the German 719 Infantry Dvision, which had left The Hague for Brussels on 2 September and, failing to reach the capital before the Guards, had now been given the task of firmly holding the Albert Canal.

As we approached the canal [wrote Brigadier Jones], reports of bridges being blown began to come in and the situation began to look pretty bleak. However, at about 1300 hours, I got a RT message from my reconnaissance party on the right to the effect that it was within sight of Beeringen bridge, which was blown but apparently not completely demolished; that the gap appeared to be 30 feet, but that no close reconnaissance could be made as the far bank was strongly held and covered by fire. But this was too good a chance to miss, so I asked the Divisional Commander to chance his arm and go for Beeringen.

32 Guards Brigade Group was ordered up to carry out the assault crossing, with the Royal Engineer squadrons and all available bridging material of the division close behind them. The attack went in at 1430 hours on 6 September and secured a foothold, about 200 yards in radius, on the far bank of the Albert Canal. By 1730 Brigadier Jones was on the blown bridge with his officers, and glad that he had ordered up all the bridging material. There was one 30-foot gap, but there was also a 110-foot gap. Of the supporting piers, one was destroyed, another damaged.

The weather had broken and the rain poured down from a black and moonless sky; there were also German mortar bombs, shells, and bullets, from very close range, as the engineers worked on throughout the night. Part of their fire was drawn, however, by the actions of some Belgian bargees, who had begun to moor their barges nearby as the basis of a floating footbridge. Brigadier Jones noticed this, thankfully, and sent engineers to help. The decoy worked, and by 0415 hours the next morning, 7 September, a class-40 bridge spanned the Albert Canal at Beeringen.

In the cold light of dawn, that bridge looked 'shaky in the extreme', as Brigadier Jones wrote later. However, by shoring up certain points to reduce vibration, the engineers made the structure strong enough not merely to take the Guards Armoured Division but the whole of the British Second Army besides, plus General Corlett's XIX US Corps.

It was still the morning of 7 September, with the two Guards brigades already across and fanning out and the 8th Armoured Brigade across in support, when the first heavy German counter-attack came in, getting to within 300 yards of the bridge before being stopped. The British noted with surprise that the Germans were actually attempting to advance, something they had not done since Normandy.

The reason was that not merely had the 719th Division come up from Holland, but General Student's newly formed and very formidable 1 Fallschmirm Armee had been brought up to the Albert Canal and the equivalent of two divisions had been thrown in to attack the British bridgehead at Beeringen. The fifth of September had been almost the last day on which there was no German front, merely a stream of disorganized, retreating units shambling back to Germany on foot or in any form of transport they could commandeer.

By Thursday, 7 September, the Germans had a screen along the canal line and were steadily reinforcing it. Many of the units had been hurriedly formed or re-formed in Germany; others came from General Gustav von Zangen's 15th Army, which had been holding the coastal defences in Belgium and Holland. Had the decision been taken to send strong Allied forces round Antwerp along the Scheldt estuary to the sea, these divisions would have been trapped. As it was, they were able to escape across the Scheldt, hold the north bank, and still supply reinforcements to hold the Belgian canal lines. Nevertheless, the British put 11 Armoured Division across the Albert and began to push the Germans back to the next canal, the Escaut.

On 10 September the Irish Guards battle group were probing forward behind the armoured cars of the Household Cavalry, whose task was to reconnoitre routes. Always important for an armoured division, this task was vital when, as now, the Guards had run well off their maps and had only a rudimentary idea of what was in front of them, although they knew they had left a good many Germans behind and on both sides of them.

What happened that evening was not planned. Even the axis of advance was not that which had been ordered, because the rudimentary local motor maps now being used were quite inadequate to indicate where the ground was suitable for tanks and where it was not. Up ahead, the Household Cavalry wirelessed back that they had found a new German-built road, not shown on any map, which ran parallel to the Escaut Canal for a short distance before turning to cross it at a bridge over De Groote Barrier. The bridge was also German-built – a heavy timber trestle affair constructed to replace a bridge blown by the Belgian Army in 1940. It was intact, but strongly held, and eight miles away.

The Irish Guards approached the bridge from the side road parallel to the canal, and stopped to reconnoitre short of the crossroads about 400 yards south of the bridge. The crossroads should have been held but was not, and it looked as if the bridge garrison, with three 88-millimetre guns covered by Spandaus, was on the north bank, and, further, that a slight jink in the approach road to the south would prevent their guns coming into action until an attacking force was close. The Irish had got too far ahead of their own guns to call up artillery support, and the only engineer officer with them, Captain R. D. Hutton, had lost contact during the day with the troops he was supposed to command.

Colonel 'Joe' Vandeleur summoned him and said: 'I am

going to charge the bridge with a troop of tanks. I want you to go with them and make sure the thing's safe.' Hutton replied that he had no engineers with him, and no knowledge of the bridge either. 'Whereupon four weary guardsmen were called for from the side of the road, and that was that!' wrote Hutton afterwards. 'None of them had the slightest idea about demolition technique – especially of the German variety.'

The idea was to give the Germans so little time that they would not be able to blow the bridge until the Guards infantry were across. They would be covered by the fire of the tanks until just before charging the bridge, and two more tanks were to be ready to race across after them. As the tanks opened up with covering fire, they flushed an 88-millimetre gun and its tractor, which made a dash to escape over the bridge and was knocked out while crossing it. Its ammunition truck caught fire, lighting up the scene.

Up went a green Véry light, a signal from the infantry that they had reached the jink in the road 100 yards south of the bridge and that the tanks should lift their fire on to the bridge itself. For several minutes the tanks poured fire on to the bridge; then up went a red Véry. The infantry were at the bridge and the two assault tanks could now race across. As they crashed through the burning wreckage around the disabled 88, the infantry dashed across the bridge after them under a hail of Spandau fire, and flung themselves into the ditches. One of the first Germans to surrender clapped a Guards officer on the back and shouted, 'Well done, Tommy, well done!'

The news of the capture, when wirelessed back to Division, was not believed, and confirmation by independent witnesses was demanded. But once convinced, Division authorized 5 Guards Brigade to cross. For some odd reason, XXX Corps countermanded this order, and the Irish were heavily counter-attacked during the day, but continued to hold on to what was now known as 'Joe's Bridge'. Tactfully, it was never decided whether this referred to Captain Hutton's unit, known as 'Joe's Troop', or to the Irish Guards group commanded by Lieutenant Colonel J. O. E. Vandeleur.

Next day, the corps commander, General Horrocks, arrived in person to tell them that their capture of the bridge had enabled him to bring forward the date of the next great advance. They would have the honour of leading it. 'This last remark took the gilt off the gingerbread,' the historian of the Irish Guards was to comment later. There was an extraordinary idea, prevalent among both generals and patriotic journalists, both British and American, but especially the latter, that there was nothing the soldiers liked so much as a chance of being shot in a good cause.

CHAPTER SEVEN

'Market Garden'

The tenth of September, the day the Guards got a bridgehead over the Escaut, the day the US 120th Infantry Regiment occupied Fort Eben Emael on the wrong side of the Albert Canal, was also the day on which one plan for an airborne assault on Arnhem was cancelled and a much more ambitious airborne plan proposed. Further, it was the day on which Montgomery failed to convince Eisenhower that the First Canadian Army and the 3rd US Army should both be halted, in order that their transport could be diverted to supply one great decisive push by the bulk of the two armies – Second British and 1st US – to break through the Dutch water-lines, outflank the Siegfried Line, and attack the Ruhr.

In retrospect, it can be seen that this decision doomed the operation from the start. Eisenhower did not forbid the attack, he let it go forward, but with insufficient resources, in the hope that the Germans could be kept on the run everywhere, so that all five Allied armies could simultaneously arrive on the Rhine in 1944.

Montgomery accepted the scaling down of support for his plan, but immediately began to press for the date of the attack to be brought forward from the last week of September to an earlier date, because with every day that passed the Germans grew stronger and the attack had correspondingly less chance of success. Eventually, he got a date of 17 September, which allowed detailed planning to begin on 13 September – a very short period for any airborne operation, let alone the greatest airborne operation of all time.

What made this situation more critical than it would

normally have been, was that the controlling organization was
effectively only about a month old. The First Allied Airborne
Army was born officially on 8 August 1944, but was not really
functioning as an entity until some weeks later, and at the time
the operation was to be carried out in cooperation with the
British Second Army, there was not even a direct telephone line
between General Lewis H. Brereton's headquarters and the HQ
of the tactical air force supporting Second Army.

The First Allied Airborne Army differed not merely in size
from the tiny, picked force the Germans had used in 1940. It
was compartmented by different nationalities and services. The
soldiers of three armies were represented. Major General Matthew B. Ridgway commanded the US XVIII Airborne Corps,
consisting of the 17th, 82nd, and 101st Airborne Divisions.
Lieutenant General F. A. M. Browning commanded the 1 British
Airborne Corps, consisting of the 1 Airborne Division, plus
special troops, the 1st Polish Independent Parachute Brigade,
and the 52 (Lowland) Infantry Division, which had been
trained for mountain warfare and was air-transportable, like
the German 22 Airlanding Division in 1940.

The airmen of two air forces were represented. These included the IX US Troop Carrier Command, and two groups of
RAF transports and tug aircraft, numbers 38 and 46. This army
of soldiers and airmen was commanded by an air general,
Brereton, with a good record in the Pacific.

The single-service command structure, which had served the
Germans well in 1940, was missing. Then, the bombers, the
fighters, the transport aircraft, and the parachute troops had
all been members of one service, the Luftwaffe. There was no
built-in split between the aviation general and the airborne
troops, as there was with the First Allied Airborne Army. The
air force commanded while the force was in the air, and the
soldiers took over when they had been landed on the ground.
Nobody had to see it through from start to finish or take entire
responsibility for everything. And there had been no time to
modify existing attitudes.

Nevertheless, the use of this force in some way or other at

the decisive moment was logical; it was the only reserve the Allies had. Now, if ever, was the time to use it. Further, General George C. Marshall, the US chief of staff, and General Henry 'Hap' Arnold, commanding the US Army Air Forces, were pressing for an experiment with large-scale airborne attack deep in enemy territory. Experiment, it would necessarily have to be. The only true comparison was with the exceedingly bold German use of airborne forces, first in the Low Countries and then in Crete.

The Allies had used larger airborne forces in Normandy, but these were intended to be dropped close behind the beaches by night. In fact, they had mostly been scattered all over the place in a chaotic series of drops. One of the few bright spots had been the taking of the Orne bridges by glider-borne troops of the British 6 Airborne Division, landing accurately less than 100 yards away, so that the defenders were overwhelmed before they knew what was happening. Generally, however, the operation had not gone according to plan and the fault lay, one way or the other, with the crews of the transport aircraft. The weather had been gusty and cloudy, making accurate navigation and flying exceedingly difficult – airborne assault is essentially a fair-weather form of attack.

The other factor always present is the flak. Transport aircraft are slow, unarmed, and unarmoured, and in order to drop accurately, the pilots must fly a steady straight-and-level course at dangerously low heights. If the flak is heavy, this requires considerable courage and means heavy losses. Ninety per cent of the first-wave Junkers in 1940 had failed to return. The flak had been heavy and the courage of the pilots high. But in June 1944 a significant proportion of the transport pilots seemed to have flinched, resulting in chaotic drops. At any rate, this was the deduction that must have been made by the planners, although not the sort of thing to be publicized even in peacetime, let alone wartime, when our boys are all brave and the enemy are all brutes.

Very much hush-hush at the time and for long afterwards, but present in many minds, was the fate of a high proportion of the British 1 Airborne Division in Sicily, when at the first sign of flak ahead, the American transport pilots had dropped the British troops, including their general, into the Mediterranean. Although kept out of the press, this story had taken only about five minutes to go round the whole British Army, both overseas and at home; and, most unfairly, this was taken to be a typically American performance. That is, talk big and bolt. For their part, the Americans tended to regard their British allies as rather stolid and unenterprising and this, too, was not without its grain of truth.

But the situation for the forthcoming operation was to stand all preconceptions on their head. In popular mythology, the Americans were supposed both by the British and the Germans to be cowardly; the British were supposed both by the Americans and the Germans to be slow, rigid, and unimaginative; while the Germans were supposed both by the British and the Americans to be plan-happy and essentially incapable of rapid or effective improvisation.

First Allied Airborne Army held a preliminary planning conference on the new operation during the evening of 10 September. It was actually two operations, 'Market' and 'Garden', the first code-name referring to the airborne scheme, the second code-name referring to the plan of the ground forces that were to link up with the airborne troops.

It was similar in conception to the German operation of 1940, but its aims were much wider. The ultimate objective was the Ruhr. But the immediate objectives were to advance to the Zuyder Zee, so cutting off all German troops still in Holland and simultaneously establishing an armoured division on the high ground around Apeldoorn as a springboard for the attack on the Ruhr. In brief, it was a typical 'left hook', designed to swing right round the flank of the Siegfried Line and Rhine defences guarding the Ruhr against direct assault.

The first stage of Market Garden was a three-division airborne assault on the key waterways: the canal and river bridges near Eindhoven were to be taken by the 101st US Airborne Division; the Maas bridge at Grave, the Waal bridges at

Nijmegen, one at least of the Maas–Waal Canal bridges, plus the high ground around Beek, Berg en Dal, Wyler, and Groesbeek were to be taken by the 82nd US Airborne Division; while the road and rail bridges at Arnhem, plus the ferry, were to be taken by 1 British Airborne Division. When Deelen airfield, just north of Arnhem, had been taken, 52 (Lowland) Infantry Division would be flown in. The link-up mission was given to the British Second Army, of which XXX Corps would be the spearhead.

This all sounded very impressive, but it was much weaker than it looked. Indeed, it could succeed only if the intelligence estimate was right – that the screen rapidly being built up by the Germans during the last few days, and in the week still to come, was only a thin crust with very little behind it except chaos and disorganization. In short, the situation as it had existed on 5 September.

There were two main weaknesses – Market had one, Garden had the other. The airborne weakness lay in the shortage of transport aircraft; there were not enough to bring in all three divisions simultaneously. There would have to be two or even three 'lifts' in some cases, all of them liable to delay by the weather.

The weakness of the ground forces lay in the shortage of road transport. Already, in order to keep Horrocks' XXX Corps going, many British divisions had been left behind in France, 'grounded' for lack of transport. Even with the help of some American trucks, they could hardly keep up with a further swift advance of the leading corps, which, having lines of communication 400 miles long, was now about to extend them deep into enemy territory for another 100 miles. The shaft of the spear was going to be very long and very thin, whereas Montgomery's original idea had been for an advance by two armies, one British, one American, supported by all the transport resources of two further armies, one Canadian, one American. The fact that the American army that was to be halted must necessarily be Patton's, played a part in scaling down the power to be put behind the 'left hook'.

Patton claimed that he could go clean through the Siegfried Line, across the Rhine in one bound, and enter Germany; and in the prevailing optimism of the time, even cautious men thought he was exaggerating only slightly. In fact, the Germans had already taken the necessary measures to stop him well before the Rhine. The Siegfried Line was being manned and reserves of armour moved up. This was not known at the time, but it was an obvious counter-move, and it was deliberate.

Equally unknown, but quite fortuitous, was a German order of 3 September issued by Field-Marshal Model. The mauled 5 Panzer Army, then retreating from France, would need to be re-fitted. The 9th and the 10th SS Panzer divisions, which together formed II SS Panzer Corps, would do their re-fitting in the area of Arnhem. The remnants of these two once form-idable divisions, veterans of both Russia and Normandy, there-fore directed their retirement towards Nijmegen and Arnhem.

But hardly had they settled in their new quarters, when on 9 September Model issued fresh orders. 10 SS Panzer Division was to move off into Germany for re-fitting. 9 SS Panzer Division was to transfer its heavy equipment to its sister division. Later, the skeleton of this division would also move to Ger-many, as the basis on which a new 9 SS Panzer Division would be built. These moves took place only at a snail's pace, because of the state of the Dutch and German railways at the time.

The very disorganization of the Germans made the task of Allied intelligence extremely difficult. There were many reports, but it was hard to know what credence to give to each item of information. But already, by 10 September, the day on which Market Garden was approved and the first airborne planning conference took place, Second Army had noted: 'Dutch Resistance sources report that battered panzer forma-tions have been sent to Holland to re-fit and mention Eindho-ven and Nijmegen as the reception areas.'

In the weekly intelligence summary for the week ending 16 September, issued by SHAEF, General Eisenhower's head-quarters, one of these divisions was definitely identified as 9 SS

Panzer Division, the other as probably 10 SS Panzer Division. It was presumed they were to be re-equipped with tanks from a depot at Kleve, the nearest sizeable town in Germany opposite Nijmegen. Lieutenant General Walter B. Smith, Eisenhower's chief of staff, testified after the war that he brought this information to Montgomery's attention, but it was 'ridiculed'.

It may be that Montgomery, having fought so hard for his plan, and being eventually granted it in weakened form, would not have it altered any further; perhaps the in-fighting with Eisenhower, Bradley, and Patton in order to get any sort of plan going at all, had exhausted him. In any event, there is an oddly uncharacteristic lack of thoroughness about Market Garden, over-laying a time-table that allowed nothing for un-expected delays or for anything to go wrong.

Undoubtedly, Montgomery well knew that time was running out for the entire operation; that it should have been launched earlier; but that if it did succeed and Germany surrendered in 1944, not only would many lives be saved but the Russians could probably be kept out of Europe and the future of the entire continent would be determined for the better. It was only a small chance, because the active opposition to Hitler inside Germany had been thoroughly crushed after the abortive revolt of 20 July 1944, and the Allied 'unconditional surrender' policy was well calculated to stimulate German resistance even in a desperate and apparently hopeless situation. But the stakes were great indeed.

If the crowning stroke of the campaign appeared to be a knock-out blow mounted too late with too little, the airborne reserves that were to carry it out had been thought by some to have been offering too much too often. In the space of about four weeks, the First Allied Airborne Army had produced eighteen abortive plans, three of which, although cancelled, had very nearly come off. General Omar Bradley, commanding the US 12th Army Group, was to complain that 'Almost from the day of its creation, this Allied Airborne Army showed an astonishing faculty for devising missions that were never needed'.

Bradley had good cause for his complaint. During the great

exploitation opportunity in late August and early September, his army group experienced a critical shortage of fuel and relied on the services of the transport aircraft to alleviate it. But the aircraft were taken away from him to support an airborne operation instead, so that not only was Patton, his 'star' general, slowed, but the American advance into Belgium side-by-side with the British Second Army was slowed also, to a point where it was lagging badly behind the British. And Bradley, although he favoured a two-pronged attack, did realize the importance of the British drive through Belgium as a part of it.

The infuriating point was that the target of the airborne troops was Tournai and the date set was 3 September. Bradley told Eisenhower that the operation was pointless, his ground forces would have captured Tournai by then. Indeed, they were in Tournai the previous evening and on 3 September Montgomery was complaining about their presence there, as the American columns were obstructing his path to Brussels.

Heavily armed ground forces are generally superior to lightly armed airborne forces, and yet in this instance, because Eisenhower was being pressurized both by Washington and by the Airborne Army, he approved the airborne plan in spite of Bradley's protests, and to implement it took away from him the transport aircraft bringing in fuel. Bradley lost six days' supply, at an average of 823 tons per day, for a gain of precisely nothing.

This vacillation by Eisenhower in turn affected another vacillation. Bradley was continually being pressurized by Patton for the resources that Eisenhower had agreed should go into the northern thrust, and Bradley half-agreed with Patton. He thought there was sufficient force to support both a northern thrust through Holland on one side of the Ruhr and another thrust by Patton's Third Army 'to seize the crossing of the Rhine river from Mannheim to Koblenz', although this involved breaking through the Siegfried Line, at its strongest and deepest point, where it was farthest from the Rhine and the mountain range of the Hunsrück barred the way to the river.

The loss of tonnage over Tournai convinced Bradley that this was now impossible, but nevertheless Patton continued to divert resources to himself, while Bradley looked the other way, apparently because a success in the north would mean headlines for Montgomery instead of headlines for Patton. In this inauspicious situation, the preparations for Market Garden began.

Market Garden was not a plan for a single battle. It consisted of six plans for six battles, all intended to dovetail into each other, and all to take place simultaneously. There were the three airborne battles of Eindhoven, Nijmegen, and Arnhem to be carried out by Lieutenant General F. A. M. Browning's 1 Airborne Corps. There was the battle of the 'corridor' linking all those towns to the Dutch border at Valkenswaard, to be carried out by General Horrocks' XXX Corps. And there were the flanking battles to be carried out on either side of the 'corridor' by VIII Corps and XII Corps, also part of the British Second Army, but as these had very little transport they would move only at walking pace.

Essentially, the four main battles consisted of the movement of many vehicles having varying speeds and operating in restricted spaces.

On the first day, Sunday, 17 September, three separate streams of heavy aircraft would fly from England to Holland. To Eindhoven would go 424 American C-47 transport planes carrying paratroops and 70 Waco gliders towed by British bombers. To Nijmegen would go 480 American C-47 transport planes carrying paratroops and 50 Waco gliders towed by British bombers. To Arnhem would go 145 American C-47 transport planes carrying paratroops, plus 4 Waco gliders, 341 Horsa gliders, and 13 of the huge Hamilcar gliders, towed by British bombers. Approximately 1,880 transports, bomber-tugs, and gliders were involved.

Routes had to be planned so as to avoid any of the three streams passing over heavy flak concentrations, while paying due consideration to the airfields from which the machines would start, the targets on which they would arrive, and the wide turning circles of the transports and bombers for the return trip. For instance, the 480 transports flying from the Grantham area to Nijmegen were 35 minutes long; that is, it took 35 minutes for the stream to pass a given point. They were to fly a tight formation, whereas the streams of glider-towing bombers would necessarily take up much more air space.

These, however, were merely the passenger-carrying machines – the airborne buses. To allow them free passage, it was necessary to knock out many German airfields and flak sites and also to provide continuous escorts along the streams. For these purposes, the US Eighth and Ninth air forces plus the Royal Air Force supplied from England a force of 1,113 bombers and 1,240 fighters on 17 September. This brought the total up to more than 4,200 aircraft of all types, the operations of which were so tightly integrated that the British 2nd Tactical Air Force, based on the Continent, were forbidden to go within 20 miles of the operational areas for some hours before and after the delivery of the airborne troops. Only three years before, heads had been shaken in America at the daring proposal to fly three transport aircraft together and simultaneously drop parachute troops from them, although of course the Germans had already done a good deal more than that.

At the same moment as these streams began to pass over Holland, XXX Corps was to break through the German 'crust' on the border of Holland and Belgium, supported by No 83 Group of the 2nd Tactical Air Force, and start racing for Eindhoven, Nijmegen, and Arnhem, as a prelude to a further bound from Arnhem towards the Zuyder Zee. XXX Corps consisted of Guards Armoured Division, 50th and 43rd Infantry divisions, 8 Armoured Brigade, and the Royal Netherlands Brigade. Because of the low-lying, marshy land to be traversed, for much of the way they would have only one road along which to move, and that road never designed for densities and weights such as these.

Supplies of virtually everything except fuel were cut to a

minimum, particularly ammunition. There was sufficient fuel in each vehicle to take it 250 miles beyond its ultimate destination. Ammunition for the artillery was severely rationed, as was the ammunition for the tanks, on the principle that if a speedy advance is possible, there will necessarily be little fighting.

But one item could not possibly be excluded, and this was a heavy drain on transport resources right back to Normandy. It was perfectly possible that, although the airborne troops took their objectives, the Germans would still blow the bridges in their faces. Therefore a plan had to be made for the most pessimistic forecast – all bridges blown.

Over 1,300 vehicles were engaged in bringing bridging equipment from dumps in Normandy, along the long line of communications, and from the newly opened port of Dieppe. These moved the loads to a major dump at Bourg Leopold, beyond Brussels, where other transport columns were ready to go forward as and when required. To avoid unnecessary use of the roads, the spearhead of XXX Corps, Guards Armoured Division, carried with it only an absolute minimum of bridging equipment.

But should the airborne troops fail to capture the bridges, although succeeding in holding both river banks, four main columns were organized to go forward from Bourg Leopold when called. These consisted of the River Maas Group – 878 vehicles; the Maas–Waal Canal group – 483 vehicles; the River Waal group – 380 vehicles; and the River Neder Rijn group – 536 vehicles. In the optimistic case of all bridges being captured, 766 of these vehicles were earmarked for the bridging of the River Ijssel, beyond Arnhem.

Further provision was made for yet another set of alternatives – possible assault crossings of the Maas, Waal, and Neder Rijn, which would require special units and boats.

And all this had to be improvised from Normandy (where some of the Seine bridges had been dismantled to provide sufficient bridging material), along cratered roads, with only a brief pause, and without the use of intact railways such as would normally handle such loads.

General Bradley was to criticize Montgomery afterwards for demanding too much in the way of American transport resources for Market Garden, and clearly forgot, for he does not mention it, the very distinct possibility of the bridges being blown and the necessity for doing something about it in advance. As his problem was the Siegfried Line and the Hunsrück, this is perhaps understandable; plus the fact that most of the main bridges, although not all, were in fact captured more or less intact.

Montgomery's bridging columns were entirely British, either Royal Engineers or RASC units (Royal Army Service Corps) and vehicles; but had more transport been available, the two flanking corps could have advanced much faster and so prevented the 'Battle of the Corridor', or 'Hell's Highway', as the American official historian calls it, which helped place a brake on the rapid advance to the relief of the paratroops at Arnhem.

A much more imponderable factor was the relative efficiency of the formations involved, British, American, and German. Yet it was an extremely important factor, possibly the most important of all. Assessment is complicated, not merely by national bias, but by formation and unit bias, and, of course, the vast canvas to be considered. However, it is now twenty-five years since these events took place, and the formerly strong loyalties have relaxed sufficiently for many of those who took part to come up with surprising verdicts that would have been violently contested at the time. Battle builds binding loyalties, but objective assessments provide lessons and may save lives in the future.

The advantage of battle experience was with the Germans; their field formations had been fighting continuously for five years, their doctrines had been proved, their organization tested, and their conscript civilians had become professional soldiers. But the fortress divisions that had escaped from the coast had poor-quality personnel, considered as fighting soldiers, that is. They included men of low medical category, including those suffering from stomach ailments who were gathered for administrative convenience in special units, the middle-aged, and the elderly.

American authors tend to describe British units as 'veteran' and US units as 'green', largely because Britain had been in the war longer. In fact, most of the British Army spent most of the war in England, without opportunity to learn at first hand. Only two of Montgomery's 14 divisions had battle experience prior to Normandy, and it was the wrong sort of experience, gained in the desert. The infantry had suffered very heavy losses in Normandy and the reinforcement position was critical – that is, there were no more reinforcements and one infantry division had already been broken up in order to bring other divisions up to strength.

Battle experience generally amounted to no more than two to three months. German experience generally would be an equal number of years. The organization of the armoured divisions had proved clumsy in battle conditions and, as we shall see, the lessons had to be quickly learned and a more flexible mixture of tanks and infantry had just been introduced. The artillery was extremely good, but would be of little use in a lightning thrust along one road.

Airborne divisions normally have little battle experience. One moment they are living in safety and at peace, the enemy no more than a newspaper headline; the next, they are in the middle of an actual enemy, surrounded on all sides, and without hope of immediate relief; and, finally, after a few days or a week or so, they are usually withdrawn from battle. The initial test, without possibility of gradually getting to know the enemy, his strengths, weaknesses, and methods, is severe. But the ordeal is brief and in no way compares to that undergone by the ordinary infantryman, whose chances of survival in the long term are exceedingly small.

The US 82nd Airborne Division was unusual, as parts of it had collected nine months' experience of continuous fighting in various ground campaigns, mostly in Italy, including Anzio. It was probably the best of the three airborne divisions.

The British 1st Airborne Division was part-experienced, but

many of the best leaders had been posted elsewhere, some of the units had no experience at all, and while some were very well trained and led, the general performance was likely to be uneven. Later, the Germans were to comment on it. It was also an unlucky division, many of its units having been dumped into the sea off Sicily earlier. What experience it did have, led to the formulation of a doctrine with which no other airborne division agreed: that it was better to choose a favourable dropping zone some distance from the target than to land disorganized on or alongside the target. Its commander was an infantry soldier of experience, recently appointed, who was in no position to contradict his own 'experts'. It was this division that was to be given the most difficult and dangerous task allotted to any formation during Market Garden, and there was a good deal of foreboding in many quarters.

These facts are no argument against Market Garden as a whole, however. They do not favour the alternative – Patton's drive to the Rhine – because Patton's infantry were poor; even the bakery company of 9th SS Panzer Division had fought them off. Patton's skill lay in finding 'breaks' for his inexperienced troops to exploit, and it may be that all the boastful sound and fury was mainly for their benefit. However, it was to support Patton's drive that Montgomery's original conception had been scaled down; and now, in the third week of September, there were no 'breaks' any more, for anyone.

CHAPTER EIGHT

Escaut to Eindhoven: 17–18 September

The objective of XXX Corps was Nunspeet on the Ijsselmeer. The corps was to get here within six days at the most and hold the area Arnhem to the Zuyder Zee. Arnhem was to be reached in two days. The task of the airborne corps was to seize the river-crossings and nodal points along the axis of advance and thus ensure uninterrupted passage for the tanks and motorized infantry. VIII Corps and XII Corps were to protect the right and left flanks.

The enemy strength immediately in front of XXX Corps was estimated as six infantry battalions supported by 20 tanks and self-propelled guns. As usual with British intelligence, this proved sadly optimistic. The position at Arnhem was not known.

The planning emphasis was on speed. There must be no delay. Nevertheless, among the 20,000 vehicles that were to race forward into Holland were two large and awkward groups – the bridging column of about 5,000 vehicles and the administrative tail of the airborne forces with about 2,000 vehicles. These might have to be called for suddenly and quickly. They were an inescapable result of the problems set by the water barriers of the Rhine delta.

The procession was to be led by Guards Armoured Division, starting from 'Joe's Bridge' on the Escaut Canal. The distance to Arnhem, to be covered in two days, was 70 miles; and the Zuyder Zee lay 30 miles beyond. If this area was gained, the German Fifteenth Army in Holland would be trapped. Undoubtedly, they would try to break out, and the whole of XXX Corps might well be cut off. But the country around Apeldoorn

lent itself to defence and, supplied by air, XXX Corps might
well hold its ground until the rest of the British Second Army
came up. They would be reinforced early by 52 (Lowland) Infantry Division, which would be flown in to the airfield north of
Arnhem as soon as it was captured. Nevertheless, it was an
extremely daring plan, with a very tight time-table, and was
only justified by the tremendous gain at stake – the last chance
for an early end to the war.

The first 70 miles, from the Escaut to Arnhem, was much the
most difficult from the topographical point of view. For most of
the way there was only one practicable road, flanked by
marshy ground, so that the attack would have to go straight up
the road and hit enemy resistance head on. The chances of the
tanks by-passing enemy strongpoints were few and far between, from the beginning. Theoretically, it was an impossible
proposition; but most such propositions become practicable
when thought is given to them and the necessary resources are
available.

Two days before the attack, Lieutenant A. R. J. Buchanan-
Jardine had taken two scout cars of the Household Cavalry
straight down that single road to Valkenswaard and back
again, in a move so swift and bold that the surprised Germans
were in every case just too late in opening fire. His report,
together with what he had been told by Dutch civilians,
showed that the five miles or so to Valkenswaard were held in
depth by tanks, self-propelled guns, and bazooka-armed infantry.

The decision was taken to 'blow' the tanks forward by com-
bining a heavy artillery barrage with pin-point attacks by
cannon – and rocket-armed Typhoons, 11 squadrons of them.
They were the equivalent of the German Stukas of 1940, but
because of their high speed and flat angle of dive, precise target
identification was difficult. Trains and road convoys were one
thing, but concealed infantry and camouflaged, well-hidden
tanks and self-propelled guns were another. Further, soldiers
and airmen tend to think differently and do not even talk each
other's language.

A further decision was made that the airmen would know the ground plan in detail and that RAF officers would control the air attack from the ground, their wireless vehicle being placed beside that of the ground commander. Although both the corps commander, General Horrocks, and the divisional commander, General Adair, had, come up to watch this critical operation, it was actually to be carried out by the Irish Guards group led by Colonel J. O. E. Vandeleur. It was fortunate for him that the necessity of liaison with the RAF kept his head-quarters out of its normal position, immediately behind the leading squadron of tanks.

Two other unusual measures were taken. A bulldozer on a tank-transporter was well up, in case the Germans had destroyed the bridge just outside Valkenswaard, and a 'contact man' from the US 101 Airborne Division was in attendance with a 10-mile-range radio set.

The time set for the attack, early afternoon, was late in the day for such a break-in, break-through, and break-out battle; but this was decided by the airborne timings, which were not exact and depended on the weather, and also on the fact that the Typhoons were from 83 Group of the Second Tactical Air Force, and they were not allowed into the air until all the aircraft of the First Allied Airborne Army had both come and gone and got well clear of the area.

At 1900 hours on 16 September, the weather forecasts being favourable, General Brereton made the decision for the airborne operation to begin at 1300 hours next day, Sunday, 17 September. RAF Bomber Command struck first, during the night, dropping 890 tons of bombs on German fighter airfields, and by one particularly effective raid making sure that none of the new Messerschmitt 262 jet fighters could take off.

On the morning of 17 September, 100 more British bombers escorted by Spitfires attacked three coastal defence batteries in Holland; and later, 816 Flying Fortresses of the US Eighth Air Force, escorted by P-51s, attacked 117 flak positions. September is an awkward month for flying weather, but by 0900 hours the autumn mist and haze had cleared from the airfields in England. At 1025 the 18 transports carrying the pathfinder teams began to take off; these units were to be dropped 20 minutes before the main forces began to arrive.

At 1230 hours on 17 September, General Horrocks received the signal for which he was waiting – the airborne force was on its way. At 1245 their fighter escort appeared, attacking flak positions; and shortly afterwards the southern stream of transports carrying 101 US Airborne Division to Eindhoven, flying very low and slowly, seemingly without end. At 1345 the leading squadron of tanks moved across Joe's Bridge to the start line.

At 1400 the preparatory and counter-battery part of the 300-gun artillery programme began; at 1430 the heavy mortars of the two divisions opened up; and at 1432 the 240 field guns began their rapid barrage fire. That was the signal for the leading tanks to move up to the positions held by the infantry of 50 (Tees and Tyne) Infantry Division. At 1435, the commander of the leading tank, Lieutenant K. Heathcote, ordered: 'Driver, advance!' and the armoured rush was on.

The barrage moved on at 200 yards a minute, and the tanks roared on behind it, towards the frontier of Holland just ahead. The first stretch of ground beside the road was marshy; the next stretch was thickly wooded – good for infantry, bad for tanks. Infantry and armour of 50 Division were to do what they could on either side of the road, while the Irish Guards advanced down the ruler-straight embanked road in the centre. In the smoke and dust of the barrage, the leading tanks several times ran into their own shell-fire and this saved them.

No 3 Squadron, supported by the infantry of No 1 Company, reported: 'Advance going well.' But behind them, just as they crossed the frontier, the German gunners they had bypassed came to life. Amazingly unshaken by the fire of 300 guns, they opened up with deadly accuracy on the following squadrons. In two minutes, nine tanks went up in flames – half a mile of roadway was littered with their burning hulks. As the survivors leapt from the turrets they were cut down by small-arms fire.

The following tanks edged into what cover they could find, while the infantry riding on them were off in an instant and into the ditches. There was no telling where the fire was coming from until Lance Sergeant Cowan's tank spotted and knocked out a self-propelled gun and took the crew prisoner. Having seen so many of their friends killed only minutes before, they were in a bad temper and the German prisoners talked, pointing out the positions of the various guns. Now was the time for the Typhoons, circling above in their 'cab rank' and waiting for orders. In the next hour, they flew 230 sorties in support of the Guards who by 1730 had the bridge just outside Valkenswaard, and the burning town just after dark.

The streets were filled with Dutch civilians shouting themselves hoarse, Germans still fighting, Germans trying to get back to Germany, and Germans coming in to help the garrison, including two men on bicycles who had been sent to get news of the American parachutists near Eindhoven. Shortly afterwards, the German commander at Eindhoven telephoned a message to the commander at Valkenswaard, telling him to hold on, and this message was duly delivered by the mayor's clerk to Guards' HQ.

The Guards then opened up contact with Eindhoven via the Dutch telephone operators, but all that could be learned was that the Germans still held it and there was no sign of American parachutists. On the other hand, the Guards had definitely identified their immediate opponents as I and III battalions of Fallschirmjäger Regiment 6, plus two battalions of 9 SS Panzer Division, the latter being quite unexpected.

A night advance of the type which had been possible on several occasions during the Normandy break-out was no longer so, and this was only partly due to unfavourable terrain. The main reasons stemmed from the basic drawbacks to the blitzkrieg technique – while ever-lengthening lines of communication tend to attenuate the attacker's striking power, the defender is simultaneously being driven nearer and nearer his base depots, dumps, and reinforcements, and taking desperate measures to improvise fresh units. In the case of Market

Garden, the attackers were driving into a narrow salient between Germany itself on the right hand and the 250,000
German fortress troops in coastal Holland on the left hand.
Speed was vital, but both terrain and the enemy were likely to
impose delays.

News of the results of the airborne landings was important
to the ground forces, but at 2100 hours on 17 September
Guards Armoured Division was still relying mainly on inter-
cepted enemy broadcasts, which implied successful drops. The
air force reported that all bridges on the main axis of advance
were still intact and unblown at 1500 hours, but anything could
have happened after that. Late in the evening it was reported
that 101 US Division had taken its objectives between Eindhoven and Grave, and that 82 US Division had captured the great
Maas bridge at Grave, as well as bridges over the Maas–Waal
Canal, but had failed to reach the Waal bridges at Nijmegen. 1
British Airborne Division was close to the Neder Rijn bridges at
Arnhem and holding one end of the road bridge. It was not
clear whether or not the Waal and Neder Rijn bridges had been
blown.

The mounting of such an airborne operation in daylight had
been considered very risky, and the soldiers had had first to
win a battle with their own air arms in order to get a daylight
operation at all. Up to and including Normandy, the Allies had
used the cover of night for all large-scale airborne operations.
This was the first time that they were to attempt anything
comparable to the German invasion of the Low Countries in
1940, and the planners had steeled themselves to accept losses
of transports and gliders of up to 30 per cent. If this occurred,
far fewer aircraft would be available for the second and third
'lifts' and the supply runs; and reinforcement and supply of the
airborne troops would be slowed. If losses were higher than
estimated, then some of the reinforcements would never even
leave their airfields; like the Germans in 1940, there would be
no aircraft remaining with which to fly them into the battles.

But the results were astounding. Losses of transports and
gliders en route were only 2·8 per cent of the force employed

on the first lift. Similarly low were the losses of bombers and fighters. The American official historian calculated the total number of aircraft sent off as 4,676 transports, gliders, bombers, and fighters, and states that only 75 failed to get through to their targets. From the air point of view, the operation had been a brilliant success, as well as the largest of its kind ever carried out up to that time or afterwards.

From the soldier's point of view, the accuracy achieved in the drops was astounding; without exception, the best ever of any operation or exercise. The US 101 Division reported a 'parade ground jump'; the US 82 Division reported 'without exception' the best landings they had experienced; and the landings of 1 British Airborne Division were almost 100 per cent. More than 20,000 parachute and glider-borne troops had been landed behind the enemy lines in less than an hour and a half.

But in what really counted – the capture of the Rhine bridges – the seeds of disaster were already sown. Only the Maas bridge at Grave was securely in Allied hands. This was the nearest of the three major bridges. But resistance at Nijmegen had proved too strong for the Americans, and the town itself, both river banks, and both Waal bridges were firmly held by the Germans. The airborne plan has been criticized as being partly responsible. At Arnhem, certainly because of a defective divisional plan and not because of initial strong resistance by the Germans, the rail bridge over the Neder Rijn had already been blown, but only after a long delay had the paratroopers managed to reach the north end of the road bridge. That delay was to be critical, because the Germans managed to rush reinforcements across it to Nijmegen before the British paratroops cut the road at the north end. So one end of this bridge was now British, the other end German.

After Normandy, the Guards Armoured Division had reorganized in a less musclebound way, so that it now consisted of four battle groups controlled by two brigade headquarters. Under 5 Brigade were the Grenadier Group and the Coldstream Group, usually known as 'Group Hot' and 'Group Cold', and under 32

Brigade were the Irish Group and the Welsh Group. Each battle group consisted of one armoured battalion and one infantry battalion of the same regiment, which always worked in cooperation.

The new organization of the division was sufficiently flexible to make full use of the blitzkrieg technique when the terrain allowed. By far the fastest method of advance is on a number of parallel routes and not on a single road, which tends to become one large, non-fighting traffic jam, although it is easier to control. Once beyond the marshes and woods of Valkenswaard, there appeared to be opportunities for an advance along more than one road, and on Monday, 18 September, as soon as the mist cleared, the armoured cars of the Household Cavalry were sent out far ahead to reconnoitre the routes for the tanks, which were given two main axes of advance – north to Eindhoven and east towards Leende, Geldrop, and Helmond.

There were no real motorways in the area; most roads were country roads spanned by country bridges, the capacity of which was not known. Nor were the opposing German units known, let alone their dispositions, except for reports by Dutchmen that proved far more reliable than information previously obtained from Frenchmen and Belgians, who almost invariably multiplied the Germans by ten. The Guards had got into the habit of automatically dividing such 'statistics' by five, and so were not used to the coldly detailed accuracy of some Dutch civilian reports. But the Dutch could report only what was already in the area; they could not know of fresh German units about to enter the battle.

The Allies had been doubly unfortunate to begin with, in the choice of their main opponents. Most of the German forces came under Army Group B, commanded by Field Marshal Model, and one of his senior commanders was General Student. Model had the nickname of 'the Führer's Fireman', gained on the Russian front, where he had a reputation for dealing coldly and effectively with apparently disastrous situations. And Student was the pioneer of airborne forces, the original expert on their strengths and weaknesses. Even so, German reaction might not have been so rapid and effective had not these two outstanding commanders been convinced, literally from the first minute, of the seriousness and extent of the Allied attacks.

Model's headquarters were in a country hotel just outside Arnhem, beside the dropping zones of 1 British Airborne Division, and he escaped from the hotel only just in time, his servants leaving a trail of burst suitcases behind them as they fled. Very shortly afterwards, the field commandant of Arnhem, Major General Kussin, was shot dead. Student's headquarters were at Vught, just south of 's Hertogenbosch, giving an unrivalled view of both streams of transports passing south and north. It was clear that this was no feint, indeed Student's main sensation at the sight was envy – what could he have done with resources like that?

Two hours later, the operation order for Market Garden was lying on his desk – taken from the body of an American officer in a wrecked Waco glider that had crashed nearby. Student was not too surprised at this carelessness; it had happened to him in 1940, when, against all orders, a German officer had carried his own operations order into battle and it had fallen into Dutch hands.

The German appreciation was that XXX Corps was the main enemy; if that corps could be slowed, stopped, or cut off, the lightly armed airborne troops would become merely a minor nuisance. This was based on their own experience of such operations and was undoubtedly correct. Therefore, on the first day they reinforced Nijmegen and began to take measures to bring pressure to bear all along the flanks of the Allied operation, as far south as the Escaut Canal bridgehead.

On 18 September, 50 British Infantry Division held off the bridgehead attacks, but farther north around Veghel German probing attacks began to come in, light at first, and nervously conducted, because the Germans did not know the enemy situation either and were afraid of being caught and crushed by the British armour while dealing with the lightly armed Americans. Later, when their own armour arrived, they became much more confident; the heaviest fighting took place some days later.

This then was the situation when the Household Cavalry moved out of Valkenswaard on 18 September. The countryside being wooded and the morning misty, they tended to bump opposition at close range; this varied from a case of one Panther and two self-propelled guns to many cases of bazookas fired by determined infantry from the hedges. The tactics were for the surviving cars of the squadron to 'loop', with one troop going west and one troop going east in search of an easier passage that ended, often as not, in a bridge too light to bear even the weight of an armoured car. Nevertheless, by continually dodging down side roads, one or two troops of the regiment were almost bound to get through. Two did in fact manage it at widely separated points, though eventually the major effort was made on the main road to Eindhoven. The opposition broke at about 1800 hours on 18 September, and Brigadier Jones radioed for the bridging equipment. The Americans by then had cleared most of Eindhoven, and the Guards drove straight through without stopping until they reached Zon, where the bridge across the Wilhelmina Canal had been blown. Although their formal objective for 17 September had been merely Valkenswaard, they had hoped to reach Eindhoven on the first day and link up there with the Americans. But no one had got to Eindhoven on the first day, and the link-up had not occurred until the evening of 18 September, approximately one day behind time.

The American failure to capture the bridge at Zon now caused further delay, but this was mitigated by the speed with which the canal was bridged. Brigadier Jones reached Zon before the bridging convoy, which arrived at 1930, and promised the divisional commander that the first vehicle could cross at 0600 hours next morning. The estimate was not quite accurate. The first armoured car rolled over the new bridge at 0615 hours on 19 September, followed by 5 Guards Brigade.

With most of the key points along the road held by Americans, Nijmegen was now only a few hours' drive away. But probably because the area of 101 US Airborne Division was comparatively secure, General Brereton was to divert to it resources actually intended for 82 US Division, which needed them far more. Possibly correct from the aviation point of view, this further emphasized the inherent imbalance of the air plan. The more exposed the division, the less it got in the way of air transport, reinforcement, and supply. 1 British Airborne Division at Arnhem, 70 miles from the Escaut, was given so little that it was flown-in in dribs and drabs, a procedure that has been described as like feeding Oxo-cubes to a lion one by one. Now 82 US Airborne Divison at Nijmegen was to be cut down in favour of 101 US Airborne Division, which, at Eindhoven, was a mere dozen or so miles from the Escaut bridge-head.

To make matters worse, the weather clamped down and nearly half the reinforcements either returned to England or were lost. This was particularly serious, because it was mostly artillery units that were affected; of 66 guns dispatched to help the paratroops repel heavy attacks, only 36 guns arrived, and these were all the lighter pieces up to 75 millimetres. The Luftwaffe, however, was less affected by the weather and put up 125 fighters, so that the advancing columns had clear evidence that things were going wrong. This was to make the subsequent battle for Nijmegen extremely bitter.

As the result of a bad plan, 1 British Airborne Division at Arnhem got itself involved in street-fighting and the resulting delays allowed the Germans to send reinforcements south over the road bridge on 17 September which were to intervene with decisive effect against the 82nd on the Sunday evening; and the subsequent disintegration of the British division was to allow the Germans to send further reinforcements south over the road bridge to hold up XXX Corps.

The 82nd had some advantages over the 1st British. They got a much larger share of the available lift, and the bulk of the division, less one regiment and the bulk of the artillery, came in to Nijmegen together; however, had they been heavily counter-attacked by tanks, the diversion of the bulk of their second lift to the already secure positions of the 101st might have had awkward results.

S—RFRB—E

Although they did not have such heavy anti-tank guns as the British, there being no American gliders large enough to carry them, the 82nd had a great advantage in communications – their radio sets worked. But the real American superiority lay in the smooth working that comes only from long experience under the same leaders, a principle that applies to every kind of organization, warlike or peaceful, from banks to parachute brigades.

There was one other major difference that was profoundly to affect the fate of both divisions. This lay in the intelligence estimates of the enemy forces available for counter-attack near the drop zones. Both were wrong, but wrong in profoundly different ways. Although SHAEF had heard reports of two SS Panzer divisions being stationed near Arnhem, this information was quite definitely not available at the level of the division concerned; the British did not expect to meet armour in any quantity.

On the other hand, unsubstantiated reports of a massive build-up of German armour in the Reichswald Forest, bordering the American drop zones south-east of Nijmegen, had come from Dutch sources. There was one mention of 1,000 tanks. And even if the tried and tested method of dividing by ten was employed, this still gave 100 tanks; and against parachutists minus most of their artillery such a force could be formidable.

According to the American official history, this information became 'a major and pressing element in the predrop picture of German forces'. Therefore, in considering the operational decisions, it must be borne in mind that the British planned in the belief that they would not meet armoured forces, while the Americans planned on the basis that they might encounter substantial numbers of tanks.

It must further be remembered that this was 1944, not 1940. The Dutch had had no tanks, no self-propelled guns, and only a handful of armoured cars. Indeed, the self-propelled gun was a war-time development, largely improvised by putting a large-calibre gun on the chassis of a tank designed to take a much smaller gun in a revolving turret. The gun of an SP would not traverse 360 degrees, so it was not a tank; it was merely an efficient method of getting a large gun to go cross-country and into action. In 1944, the artillery component of armoured divisions normally consisted of such mobile tracked and armoured guns.

In one respect only were the British and American plans similar. The object of the whole operation was to gain control of the road from Nijmegen to Arnhem by capturing the Waal bridges at Nijmegen and the Neder Rijn bridges at Arnhem; but no attempt was made by either division to seize these bridges instantly by *coup de main*. It will be recalled that the Germans had tried (and failed) to take these identical objectives in 1940 by variations of the 'Trojan Horse' theme; and that those bridges that were really vital were taken by simultaneous attack from both ends, as at Moerdijk, or by seaplanes actually landing in the river, as at Rotterdam. This was the original book of airborne warfare, as written by General Student. Why were these lessons disregarded?

As far as the 82nd were concerned, Major General James M. Gavin was a firm believer in the principle of landing on both sides of a bridge, as close to it as possible, even if this meant heavy losses; because landing far away and then walking up to the target was bound to mean even heavier losses, and probable failure. For this reason both he and other commanders in the 82nd had doubts, to put it mildly, about the chances of British success at Arnhem.

But as far as the 82nd was concerned, the real threat was believed to lie in the Reichswald, and not on the 'Island' between Nijmegen and Arnhem. Gavin thought so himself, and Browning agreed. An armoured attack out of the Reichswald would take the entire Market Garden operation in flank; not merely Gavin's division, but XXX Corps as well. This was the underlying appreciation.

Equally important was the fact that, as the Germans had found in 1940, the Nijmegen area was awkward to attack, in that a concentration of force would achieve little except the blowing of the bridges by the enemy, and that the solution, if there was one, was to scatter the attack force in terms of space so as to attack as many different objectives as possible at the same time. This was Gavin's solution, too, although his means were different; and, like the Germans in 1940, he had insufficient resources to attack simultaneously at all points and was therefore compelled to draw up a priority list, on which the Waal bridges came bottom.

In 1940, the Germans had wanted the high ground south-east of Nijmegen, at least one bridge over the Maas–Waal Canal, the bridge over the Maas at Grave, and, if possible, the road bridge over the Waal. They had taken the high ground easily, and simultaneously three bridges over the Maas–Waal Canal at Heumen, Malden, and Hatert (but losing Malden to counter-attack), had failed to take the vital Grave bridge, and failed at the Waal bridges also, although these were not vital.

Gavin saw the situation in almost exactly the same light and these were his objectives also. He got the high ground, the bridge at Heumen (which he calls Molenhook), and the bridge at Grave on the first day, doing much better than the German 254 Infantry Division in 1940, because Grave bridge over the 800-foot-wide Maas was much more important than any of the bridges over the 200-foot-wide Maas–Waal Canal. Although he had the advantage of airborne troops, whereas the Germans could call only on a handful of ersatz 'Fifth Columnists' from Special Battalion 100, Gavin was not operating next door to the borders of the United States, his division was 60 miles or so inside enemy territory with lines of communication that were exclusively airborne. This meant that for re-supply and re-inforcement, he had to have an airhead.

His solution was to site this on the high ground between Nijmegen and the Reichswald, which he regarded as the key to the whole area. The 300-foot elevations here dominated both the Waal and the Maas–Waal Canal, and also blocked off any attack from over the German border, either from the Reichswald itself or along the Kleve–Kranenberg road that fringes

Holland at Wyler and runs at the foot of the high ground through the border at Beek directly to the road bridge at Nijmegen. This was to be the eastern flank of his division.

The western flank lay around the bridge at Grave, and the Maas–Waal Canal ran almost north–south and almost through the centre of the divisional area, so that at least one bridge there had to be taken to ensure the internal communications of the division. Compared to these objectives, Gavin judged the Waal bridges less vital.

Although he considered several plans for taking the road bridge from the area of the airhead, if conditions allowed, no forces were available to drop on either side of the road bridge, or even merely on the Lent side of the river, where the ground favoured defence and was difficult for tanks. The objection was that if the bridge was taken but the high ground lost, the bridge was useless because it was dominated by the high ground. Remembering the possible threat from the Reichswald, plus the difficult country to be traversed by XXX Corps, the 82nd had to be prepared to fight a heavy battle alone for possibly three or four days.

Although the area of the Market Garden operation was generally unfavourable for armoured warfare, it was 'preeminently suitable' for airborne forces, in Gavin's opinion. 'Parachutists can land in pretty rough terrain. Their greatest obstacles are tall timber and deep marshes and flooded areas.' This gave considerable flexibility to the attack and to the selection of the airhead, which should theoretically be sited actually on the main target so that reinforcements and supplies go directly to where they are wanted within an area that has to be defended anyway for tactical reasons.

Gavin's choice was in accordance with his principle, whereas the 1 British Airborne Division plan breached it entirely, their drop zones being far from the target and of no tactical importance, so that they had to fight two battles instead of one over a much larger area than necessary, with far fewer forces than Gavin had. It is hardly surprising that resupply to their airhead failed, because the delivery of this vital tonnage by air is always difficult. The enemy may be taken by surprise by the initial landings, but expects the follow-up; and in this case, as German units were still holding out in the Pas de Calais, they would receive early and accurate warning of all the succeeding lifts as they crossed the coast.

The first lift consisted of 482 transport aircraft carrying the 504th, 505th, and 508th Parachute Infantry regiments as well as HQ units, plus 50 gliders carrying mainly HQ units plus the 80th Antitank Battalion for defence of the landing zones. The total of personnel was 7,477. Next day, the second lift, consisting of 450 gliders carrying mainly artillery, were to land inside the airhead on the hillslopes from Wyler to Mook – that is, within the tactical perimeter already encircling the top-priority target of the division. The two regiments that landed there on 17 September were to undertake two additional tasks – the capture of bridges over the Maas–Waal Canal and a quick dash to the Nijmegen road bridge, if it could be managed.

Colonel Reuben H. Tucker's 504th Regiment had the task of dropping to the west of the Maas–Waal Canal and taking the big Maas bridge at Grave. Of his unit at that time, he wrote:

The 504th Regimental combat team that jumped in Holland were all veterans of Sicily and approximately 9 months fighting in Italy to include Anzio from D-Day, 22 January 1944 to 23 March – no breaks. It might be well to point out that many of us commanders felt that General Urquhart's troops stood a good chance of much trouble since they were jumping so far from their target, the bridges at Arnhem. Open space or not, we always planned to jump right on the target. The Div Comdr – General Gavin – told me he didn't care how I did it, but to get the bridge at Grave. I ordered E Company to jump on the south end of the bridge and the rest of the battalion on the north end. We had no clear DZs but landed on houses, churches, roads, ditches and wherever we came down – but no open fields. As a result of this direct action the 504th had control of its targets by 1800 hours, 17

September – four hours from the time we jumped from our planes.

This was a really big prize, the bridge at Grave that the Germans had failed to get in 1940, thus forcing a time-wasting diversion of 9 Panzer Division in its drive to link up with the corridor of airborne troops holding the key bridges from Mo-erdijk to Rotterdam. But the 504th had other subsidiary targets – the bridges over the Maas–Waal Canal at Heumen, Malden, Hatert, and Neerbosch (which the American histories call Honinghutje).

Hatert was attacked by elements of both the 504th and the 508th, as were the Neerbosch bridges the following day. But the Germans blew both these bridges, although demolition was not complete at the northernmost and Neerbosch would be repairable. To the south, Malden bridge blew up in the faces of the attackers, but once again, as in 1940, the complicated lock-bridge at Heumen, the most southerly of all, fell intact to the assault.

At the airhead there was almost no opposition as yet, merely cautious German reconnaissance followed up on the second day by attacks from units put together in a couple of hours from soldiers on leave, convalescents, Home Guards, etc, who had been told that the Americans had no artillery – indeed, the normal first reaction to an airborne landing. The Americans were probably better informed than the Germans, because they had a Dutch captain with them who immediately after landing found a civilian telephone and started to make a number of calls asking for information. Someone suggested by-passing all these Dutch civilians and putting through a personal call to the Führer himself, who would surely know best of all. After dark on 17 September General Gavin was startled to hear the loud wail of a locomotive whistle, as a train drove through his air-head less than 100 yards away and carried on merrily into Germany, without a shot fired. The next one was not so lucky.

Also on the evening of the first day, the first attempt was

made on the road bridge at Nijmegen by a platoon from the 1st Battalion of Colonel Roy E. Linquist's 508th Regiment. The Dutch had reported that it was guarded by only 18 men. Because their radio failed, they simply vanished as far as Gavin was concerned. Later in the evening, Gavin ordered the complete 1st Battalion to try for the bridge. Members of the 'Underground' promised to lead them there and said also that they knew the location of the building in Nijmegen that housed the apparatus for setting off the demolition charges. Companies A and B led off after dark, with Company C in reserve; B got lost, but A got as far as the main roundabout in the city centre, Keizer Karel Plein, before coming under fire.

The 'Underground' vanished, as they so often did on these occasions, and General Gavin thinks that his men may have been betrayed to the Germans. However, it is just as likely that the 'Resistance fighters' were boastful riffraff with a liking for self-importance; there were many of these in the occupied countries, as well as better men.

As Company A were forming up to attack, a German motor convoy drove up through the streets on the opposite side of the roundabout and stopped. The unit may have been the armoured cars and armoured half-tracks of the reconnaissance unit of 9 SS Panzer Division, which Oberst Walter Harzer, commanding the remnants of this division, had sent across Arnhem bridge before the British were able to reach it and temporarily stop traffic. They were to reinforce SS Battalion 'Euling', already in Nijmegen, which had just previously been transferred from the 9 SS to the 10 SS Panzer Division. It will be recalled that the latter was to be brought up to strength as soon as possible, while 9 SS was to be reduced to a skeleton and then transferred to Germany for complete re-building.

On 17 September, it was no longer a division and was referred to merely as the 'Battle Group Harzer'. However, it was able to play a decisive – indeed the decisive – part in blocking Market Garden because Harzer was an energetic and canny officer who in true army style was holding a larger amount of effective armoured fighting vehicles than he was showing on his returns. The result was that the German armoured forces sited near Arnhem and Nijmegen on 17 September were larger and more effective than even the German High Command was aware.

The 82nd had a long, lightly held, sensitive front in the area of the airhead. The slopes and meadows nearest to the German border were fairly open, giving good fields of fire; but to the west of them were woods that could hide an army. If the Germans once got in there, it would be impossible for the troops available to get them out. It was a maze of trees and forest.

On 18 September the Germans launched their first dangerous counter-attack, over-running a company of the 508th holding the drop zone of Wyler where, a few hours later, the 450 gliders of the second lift were due to land, followed within minutes by the supply drop. It would take about one-third of the force to collect those supplies. The Americans re-grouped to counter-attack only just in time, but although they drove the Germans off the landing zones, these were still under German small-arms fire. It was not until the morning of 19 September, a day later, that the leading units of XXX Corps linked up with Colonel Tucker's Regiment at Grave.

CHAPTER NINE

1 British Airborne Division: 1–17 September

In the first month of its existence, the First Allied Airborne Army had produced eighteen separate plans for possible operations and had carried out none of them. The 1 British Airborne Division had been required to produce sixteen. In many cases, they were cancelled at the last moment, after the planning had been completed, the units moved to their airfields, 'sealed', and briefed.

The effect of this on the planning staff is difficult to imagine, unless one has had similar experience of cancelled operations. The enthusiasm that comes from belief begins to wear off, particularly where the operation involves a high element of personal risk for the planners, who will themselves be dropping into enemy territory. The subconscious excitement cannot be sustained for too long, and in the absence of this, the keen edge of urgency is blunted.

The last detailed and accurate picture of enemy disposition, received mainly from Dutch sources, had been prior to the Normandy invasion in June. Since then, the Arnhem area had been in turmoil with no clear pattern apparent. The only known fact was that the Arnhem training area had a barracks capacity for 10,000 troops. There was a report of 10,000 troops concentrated at Zwolle, well north of Arnhem, which, if correct, might represent the evacuation of the Arnhem barracks, or alternatively, one or two battle-scarred panzer divisions re-forming. Zwolle was 35 miles from Arnhem. But of recent, direct evidence of German troops in the Arnhem area, there was none.

The strength of the British force depended not on the size of the division, but on the size of the lift. There was a shortage of transport aircraft, most of which were American and had to be borrowed. There were 157 transports available for the first lift, compared to 482 for the 82nd and 436 for the 101st US divisions. The number of gliders was much larger, 320 as against 50 and 70 for the two US divisions respectively, but these took up far more airspace than did the transports and therefore could not achieve anything like the same concentration.

The most effective comparison, however, lies in the number of infantry battalions in the first lift. Both American divisions landed almost complete in front-line infantry, with three regiments each, of three battalions per regiment. The British division had in the first lift only two brigades, of three battalions each. The second lift was to bring in another British brigade, while the third lift was to bring in the Polish brigade.

To put it another way, 1 Airborne Division was to land in the following proportion: one-half on the first day, one-quarter on the second day, and one-quarter on the third day. This is what contemporary airborne people call feeding Oxo-cubes to the lion, one by one. The division would never strike as a division, even if the weather was favourable throughout, which, in September, was most unlikely.

Worse still, the divisional plan arranged to split the two brigades involved in the first lift. The targets of the whole operation – the bridges – were to be attacked only by the three battalions of the 1 Parachute Brigade. The gliderborne infantry of the 1 Airlanding Brigade were to hold the non-tactical drop zone eight miles away for the following lifts, and so would contribute nothing whatever to the success of the first day's operations. In sum: the attacking force on 17 September was not 1 Airborne Division but merely 1 Parachute Brigade.

This extraordinary situation arose through the muddled command set-up, the division between the soldiers and the airmen, further addled by most incompetent intelligence work and photographic interpretation.

The obvious place to land was on target – by the riverside and on both sides of the bridges if possible. But this was vetoed by the airmen on two grounds: heavy flak on the 'Island' plus routing difficulties. It the transport stream turned south after the drop, they would be likely to run into the stream coming back from Nijmegen, and if they turned north they would be flying over the Luftwaffe airfield of Deelen where flak was also believed to be strong. If correct, the flak argument was a reasonable one, for heavy flak meant heavy losses of transport aircraft, which in turn meant reduced strength available for the following lift.

These flak reports were in fact pessimistic. But even if they had been correct, the obvious counter was air attack, particularly by Typhoons, the flying artillery of the time. The Second Tactical Air Force, who already knew the area well, could certainly have dealt with the flak but were not allowed to operate because of a veto from HQ First Allied Airborne Army, in case they got in the way of their operations. This is, of course, ridiculous, but such was the position at the time. It was later altered.

Just possibly the argument with the airmen might have been taken further, but the 'Island' was reported unsuitable for the dropping of parachutists and the landing of hundreds of gliders. As regards parachutists, this was unspeakable nonsense, particularly at the south end of the road bridge. Further, a fair number of gliders could have been landed there, or even landed on the water in the shallows of the south bank of the Neder Rijn. There was nothing whatever to prevent a reasonable force, either of parachutists or gliderborne troops or both, from actually landing on target.

The north side of the road bridge presented a slightly more difficult problem, but hardly insuperable, because the road continued off the bridge on to a long straight ramp, an ideal landing strip, and it was surrounded by reasonably open spaces. It will be recalled that the German pilots of the Junkers 52s had of their own volition made emergency landings on main roads when the airfields were blocked, and a three-motored transport aircraft is a much more awkward landing proposition than a glider, as it has a much longer run and even a slight accident may cause it to catch fire.

Landing in daylight, it should have been possible for the gliders to put down, not only close to the bridges, but along the main road from Nijmegen to Arnhem. Here the country favoured the infantryman rather than the tank; and, indeed, the defence generally. None of the effective German counter-moves that were in fact made would have been possible had this been done. The link between Nijmegen and Arnhem would have been severed in the first half-hour, and by occupying a position that was of tactical value to Market Garden as a whole.

However, convinced that they were lucky even to obtain a daylight drop from the airmen, who up to now had always insisted on the cover of night, Urquhart accepted the second-best solution and chose dropping and landing zones on the heathland west of Arnhem, which were near perfect for their purpose. The drawback was that they were between seven and eight miles from the targets – the bridges. The initial landings might achieve surprise but the subsequent attack on the bridges was almost bound to be expected and opposed.

To cut down this delay to the minimum, it was planned to send Airborne Reconnaissance Squadron racing to the bridges in their armoured jeeps, followed by 1 Parachute Brigade and a strong force of engineers, mostly on foot, and towing the heavier loads behind them on small hand trucks. This was a risky procedure, but more serious was the splitting of the first two brigades to land.

The dropping and landing zones had to be protected for the following lifts on D plus 1 and D plus 2, 18 and 19 September. Only an optimist could consider that the defensive role was tactical, although the divisional plan envisaged 1 Airlanding Brigade on the drop zones forming the left flank of a box, with the 4 Parachute Brigade, when it arrived on 18 September, forming the north line of the box on the high ground behind Arnhem, and the Polish Parachute Brigade, when it arrived on

19 September, forming a line south of the bridges on the 'Island'.

Arnhem was, after all, an important German training area capable of holding a minimum of 10,000 troops; and it was to be attacked on the first day by only some 3,000 lightly armed men. Airborne troops were not the surprise weapon they had been back on 10 May 1940, with an unknown potential. The Germans had not merely carried out the pioneer work, they had studied the answers, too. It really does seem that someone should either have produced a better plan or scrubbed the entire operation.

General Urquhart was not really in a position to do this, because he had never before taken part in an airborne operation. His experience had been in the desert and in Italy as an infantry brigadier, and he had not taken over the division until January 1944. His predecessor, General Eric Down, was a most experienced airborne soldier whom the War Office had sent to India to raise a new airborne division there.

By September, Urquhart had realized that there was 'a certain naïveté in upper level planning,' when for Operation 'Comet' 1 Airborne Division alone were to take the crossings of the Maas, the Waal, and the Neder Rijn.

Two of his juniors, Brigadier Shan Hackett and the Polish General Stanislaw Sosabowski objected, the latter violently, interrupting Urquhart's explanation of the plan with, 'But the Germans, General, the Germans!' Comet was to become Market Garden, using three airborne divisions instead of the single one originally proposed, in itself an apt comment on planning at the level of HQ First Airborne Army.

At lower level, the trouble was age. Tony Hibbert, the brigade major of 1 Parachute Brigade, feels that he could do very much better now; he was then too young to stand up to older senior officers if he felt that a plan was unsatisfactory, as this one was. The bridge problem should have been re-thought, instead of merely taking the word of RAF bomber pilots about the flak, and tamely going elsewhere. If necessary, the brigade should have been dropped on the houses by the riverside.

The formation which was to fight the real battle of Arnhem was both well trained and experienced; but what it was being asked to do was to walk through a built-up area for many miles before reaching its target, in the middle of a town containing barracks for 10,000 men. The brigade itself was about 2,000 strong, and without heavy weapons or vehicles.

There were two alternatives: to advance the battalions into the town one after the other, on the same road, a method that gives concentration and control but is necessarily slow; or to advance the three battalions in line, on three separate roads, which means faster progress when unopposed but is basically weaker, because in a built-up area, as opposed to open country, the battalions are unable to help each other. On the other hand, although one or even two battalions may very well be stopped, one is almost bound to get through to the objective. This was the plan adopted, and this was what happened. The brigade fulfilled its task, but the force that reached the objective and occupied it consisted of a single battalion; the others were held up, for good, in the built-up area.

In sum: it was not 1 British Airborne Division that attacked the bridges at Arnhem; it was not even 1 Parachute Brigade; but merely the 2nd Parachute Battalion, and not all of that actually reached the bridge. Instead of a complete division, the striking force consisted of only about 600 men. This was the inevitable result of decisions taken higher up.

On 13 September, Major Hibbert had written the brigade operation order. There were two targets – the main road bridge (code 'WATERLOO' bridge) and the German pontoon bridge just to the west ('PUTNEY' bridge). The brigade was not concerned with the less important railway bridge ('CHARING X') still farther to the west. The targets were to be seized by 1 Airlanding Reconnaissance Squadron in their armoured jeeps, which would cover the seven or eight miles at high speed. The three marching battalions would follow after them, 2nd Battalion on the right, nearest the Neder Rijn, 3rd Battalion in the centre, 1st Battalion on the left, nearest the hills to the north.

The 2nd Battalion (under Lieutenant Colonel J. D. Frost) was to form an L-shaped defensive position, the lower stroke being on the south bank of the river covering the approaches to both bridges; it was to be accompanied by a detachment of Royal Engineers with three flame-throwers. The 3rd Battalion (Lieutenant Colonel J. A. C. Fitch) was to assist in the capture of the main bridge ('WATERLOO'), and then face east. The 1st Battalion (Lieutenant Colonel D. T. Dobie) was to occupy the high ground north of Arnhem, thus denying the enemy direct observation over the town and also out across the 'Island' towards Elst and Nijmegen. The effect would be to form a kind of brigade 'box' around the town, very thinly held.

On the second day, they were to be reinforced, particularly to the north, by 4 Parachute Brigade; and probably on the third day the Polish Parachute Brigade would land south of the bridges, move over them, and take up positions to the east. 1 Airlanding Brigade had the task of holding the airhead out on the heathland to the west of Arnhem from D-Day on. XXX Corps was to arrive within two days, if possible, and 52 (Low-land) Division was ready to be flown into Deelen airfield, some seven miles north of Arnhem, when that was captured, to assist in the drive to the Zuyder Zee. A great deal depended on the weather, and on Saturday, 16 September, Major Hibbert noted: 'Weather report good, hopes for op very high.'

The operational timings for the drops on the 17th were important and deadly. In the nature of things, they were not exact. Nor were the flight paths. Officially, there were two main airstreams, one to the south of Antwerp and one to the south of Rotterdam. General Gavin, headed for Nijmegen, found himself a spectator of the 101st's drop on Eindhoven before the pilot corrected for drift.

The 82nd's airstream was nearly one-and-a-half hours long. The northerly stream carrying 1 British Airborne Division was much longer and slower, because of the glider element. Transports carrying paratroops can fly a tight formation, whereas gliders are towed some distance behind tug aircraft struggling along at just above stalling speed. On 10 May 1940 the

Germans had attacked with 11 gliders, carrying only seven or eight men each; 1 Airborne Division's first lift included 358 gliders, some of them enormous and capable of carrying the largest anti-tank guns.

Consequently, it could not be said that the division landed at any particular time, but merely that the pathfinders of the Independent Company started to jump from 12 aircraft at about 1200 hours; and that the main stream began to arrive at about 1300 hours, divided into a parachute contingent and a glider contingent. The latter, being slower, had started first, its rear elements being rapidly overtaken by the leading elements of the paratroop aircraft.

The Germans had already reacted when some parts of the division were still crossing the Channel. The route over the sea was marked by ditched aircraft and burning flak ships, the first casualties on both sides having been incurred hundreds of miles from Arnhem. The route over the land was outlined by flak, but not very much of it, and the activities of the fighters as they dived on the flak positions.

It seems likely that it was not the main landing, but the arrival of the pathfinders in 12 Stirlings somewhere about noon that interrupted Field Marshal Model's lunch at the Tafelberg Hotel in Oosterbeek. This was the forward headquarters of Army Group B, securely situated behind three main river-lines – Maas, Waal, and Neder Rijn.

Model seems to have been under the impression that it was an attempt to capture him and that he only just managed to escape 'through the eye of a needle'. He packed one suitcase and dashed for his car. Within a few minutes it was pulling up outside the Feldkommandantur in Arnhem. Here, Model informed the area commandant, General Kussin, that airborne landings had begun two or three miles west of Oosterbeek and that the news should be radioed to Hitler at the Führer HQ in East Prussia. Model then drove on to Doetinchem, east of Arnhem, where General Bittrich, commander of 11 SS Panzer Corps, had his headquarters.

At 1340 General Bittrich began to issue orders: 9 SS Panzer

Division was to send its armoured reconnaissance unit to Nijmegen via Arnhem. The bulk of the infantry, formed into
'alarm units', were to carry on westward through Arnhem to
oppose the airborne landings directly. There were only a handful of armoured vehicles with them, and 9 SS was no longer an
armoured division in any sense of the word, but merely Battle
Group Harzer. It numbered only 3,500 men scattered widely in
billet as far away as Zutphen and Apeldoorn, some 15 miles
north-east of Arnhem.

The 10 SS was stronger and sited in the border area between
Germany and Holland. This division was ordered to concentrate, then move on Nijmegen via Arnhem. Its task was to
occupy the road and rail bridges over the Waal and hold a
bridgehead south of Nijmegen, taking under command all
German troops already in the area. The nearest unit was Major
Euling's 11 Battalion of SS Panzergrenadier Regiment 21,
which crossed the Neder Rijn at Pannerden and linked up early
with the 750 German troops then in Nijmegen.

In short, Model and Bittrich had decided within the first
hour or so that Nijmegen, and not Arnhem, was the point that
required urgent and powerful reinforcement.

The historian of 9 SS Panzer Division, who fought at
Arnhem, states that after Model's 'mad drive' from Osterbeek
to the Feldkommandantur, he 'scraped together' for the Battle
of Arnhem 'a very poor defensive force'.

The only unit in position to act quickly was Sturm-
bannführer Sepp Krafft's SS Panzer Grenadier Depot and Reserve Battalion 16, at Oosterbeek. It was a battalion in name
only, and numbered 12 officers, 65 NCOs and 229 soldiers, and
as its commander reported, 'was mainly composed of half-
trained 17–19-year-old personnel, forty per cent of them
graded as unfit for action'. But, he added, 'We knew from experience that the only way to draw the teeth of an airborne
landing with an inferior force, is to drive right into it. From a
tactical point of view, it would have been wrong to play a
purely defensive role and let the enemy gather his forces un-
molested.'

At 1345 Krafft ordered the 2nd Company to make a probing attack while the remainder concentrated or reconnoitred in the Wolfhezen area, close to the drop zones and between two possible routes of advance into Arnhem. Neither of these routes was near the river.

Initially, these 300 men, most only partially trained and many marked for light duties only, represented the Germans' largest and finest force immediately available for the defence of Arnhem. The rest were the scraping of the defeat in Normandy. In the first 24 hours or so, 48 prisoners were interrogated by the British. They proved to have come from 27 different units, some unarmed. Twenty-four hours later, the number of different units totalled 42, including coast artillery and the German Navy. Among the first prisoners were one Japanese civilian, one female auxiliary in uniform, and one 'gentleman of the road' (i.e. a tramp). To describe this sort of opposition as 'poor', smacks of understatement. It seemed as if the most optimistic rumours of German weakness were correct. Further, the two brigades were arriving at the drop zones with a perfection never before achieved and virtually without interference from the enemy. Indeed, it might have been an exercise, except for the smoke still rising to the north from Deelen airfield, lately bombed.

Even so, it took some time for units to assemble and it was 1530 before 2 Parachute Battalion moved off on foot towards the bridge some seven miles away. At 1630, 1 Parachute Battalion started on its walk towards the high ground north of the town, and at 1700 the 3rd Battalion, advancing into the centre of the town, between the two other battalions, first met opposition.

General Urquhart, finding that the armoured jeeps of the *coup-de-main* party that was to race for the bridge were missing, and that his wireless sets were not working, got into a jeep and drove after Frost's 2nd Battalion in order to tell him personally that he would have to take the bridge on his own, and to hurry. But as the 2nd Battalion proved to be somewhat spread out and trying to infiltrate past an armoured car, he

merely left a message for Frost and drove off again to look for
Brigadier G. W. Lathbury, commanding 1 Parachute Brigade,
who was with the 3rd Battalion.

While Urquhart was racing about, far from his HQ, trying to
find out what was happening and to influence local events personally, his opposite number, General Kussin, the commandant
of Arnhem, was doing exactly the same thing. At 1715 he drove
into Wolfhezen and conferred with Sepp Krafft. Kussin told
Krafft that he had just visited one of his battalion's sentry posts
farther west; that it was 'manned by the sick, convalescent and
odd details of the battalion', and that 'all was well'. Krafft urged
Kussin to return to Arnhem by a detour to the north, but Kussin
was in a hurry and continued along the Wageningen–Arnhem
road. A few minutes afterwards, Kussin ran into a skirmish
between B Company of 3 Parachute Battalion and a German
force consisting of infantry and two armoured cars. The cars
had easily knocked out the company's 6-pdr anti-tank gun, because it was being towed and so could not be got into action
swiftly, and as the leading platoon had no Piats, they were now
without an effective counter-weapon. Kussin was killed by wild
and undisciplined British machine-gun fire.

The general's death made very little difference, except to
Major Ernst Schleifenbaum, from Siegen, who was his chief
operations officer, for Field Marshal Model rang up and told
him: 'You are responsible that we hold Arnhem,' Schleifenbaum wrote a few months later that he had 'felt giddy' at the
thought, as the situation was 'a pretty thorough mess-up'.
Next morning, however, he felt that the situation was under
control, as indeed it was, as a result of measures taken during
the night.

At 1800 hours, the armoured cars and half-tracks of the
reconnaissance battalion of 9 SS, nearly complete, raced into
Arnhem and tore across the great road bridge, heading south
for Nijmegen and the decisive intervention there. Although
firing was going on, and some German units blew up their
stores, Frost's 2nd Battalion had not yet reached the bridge.

At about 2030 hours, German infantry from Nijmegen ar-

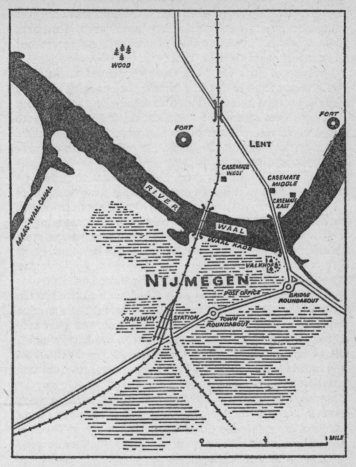

rived at the south end of the bridge, and minutes later, A
Company of 2 Parachute Battalion reached the houses at the
northern end to find German vehicles still crossing it. Half-a-
dozen parachutists could have had the bridge for the asking
any time between noon and 2000 hours. It was not even prepared for demolition. Now no one had it, for the span itself was

no-man's-land. Counting from the time of arrival of the first pathfinders, the Germans had been given more than eight hours in which to react. In their disorganized state, even this had not been quite enough.

Neither the British nor the Germans arrived at their opposite ends of the bridge in a bunch, but straggled out; and there was a brief burst of firing across the span that wounded the commander of the SS detachment coming from the south end. Like so many Dutch bridges, it was much larger than, say, its equivalent over the Thames. In order to clear the low-lying ground on the approaches, which flood in winter, the roadway at both ends was carried up on a massive ramp for a considerable distance before meeting the great upflung arc of steel that actually spanned the width of the river in its normal state. The open girderwork gave very little cover for infantry, and to take one end of the bridge by sending men across from the other end was a short form of suicide. This fact dictated the pattern of the ensuing battle.

At 2045 hours a platoon from A Company led by Lieutenant J. H. Grayburn tried to dash across, but lost eight men in the first few seconds after covering only 50 yards. The fire came mainly from an armoured car and also light flak guns in a pillbox actually on the bridge. The survivors ran back to cover, followed by Grayburn, who had been wounded in the shoulder. This ended the first attempt by the leading elements of the 2nd Battalion.

Meanwhile, numbers of assorted troops were moving towards 'Waterloo' bridge. These included parties of Engineers and Royal Army Service Corps amounting to about 100 men, medical personnel, motor transport, some 40 German prisoners, and a bevy of Dutch guides.

The latter halted for some time, arguing among themselves as to which was the better of two roads, and as neither of these roads was shown on the British military maps, the discussion was wearing for the British, particularly as the sound of fairly general firing was coming from the north, where Krafft's men, supported by a few armoured vehicles, were contesting the advances of the 1st and 3rd battalions. This left flank of the 2nd Battalion's advance was vulnerable and open during the march to 'Waterloo', and some platoons were in fact swallowed up by it, so that even to this day it is not known what happened to them.

On the right flank, which lay on the river to the south, there was intermittent firing from the direction of 'Charing X', the railway bridge. The northern end was held by a small detachment of Germans manning three flak guns, the south by a demolition team of under a dozen men. It was the objective of a platoon of engineers from 9 Field Company, but C Company of 2nd Battalion attempted to take it on their way into Arnhem. At 1830 hours there was a loud explosion, and one section of the bridge collapsed into the Neder Rijn. One route to the south bank had been closed. When B Company arrived at 'Putney', the pontoon bridge, they found that the centre part was missing. A second route to the south bank was closed.

Darkness came soon after 1930, and C Company took a wrong turning into the town and disappeared, being cut off there for good. It was impossible to creep forward stealthily and infiltrate towards the bridge, because, as Major Hibbert wrote, 'although we were taking every precaution to be silent, every few yards Dutch civilians would come rushing out of their houses shouting their welcome at the tops of their voices'.

Nevertheless, Brigade HQ had got to within 500 yards of the northern end of 'Waterloo' by 2045, the time of Lieutenant Grayburn's first unsuccessful attempt to seize it. Hibbert knew by now that they were not going to get any immediate help from the remainder of the brigade. He had got through by radio to Lathbury at 1930, and had been told that the 1st Battalion was trying to by-pass trouble near Wolfhezen, while the 3rd Battalion had run into considerable opposition and would have to halt for the night.

Captain D. J. Simpson, with ten engineers, was bringing up the rear of Brigade HQ. When he arrived,

The position at the north end of the bridge was that an assault had just been made and had failed. The battalion was re-forming for another attack, this time with the assistance of two sappers with a flame-thrower. The attack went in and was a great success. The pill-box, which was the mainstay of the defence, blew up with a great roar. The whole area was as light as day and the remaining Germans came running from the bridge silhouetted against the flames from the pill-box. The north end of the bridge was ours.

Two attempts were made to secure the south end by crossing the river. A patrol was sent to B Company with orders to cross by barge, but could not find B Company; and there appeared to be no barges. The brigade defence platoon was told to cross by boat, but could find no boat. Then, quite unexpectedly, Major Lewis' C Company of the 3rd Battalion joined Frost's men from the north, having got into the town along the railway line. This welcome accession of strength to a force of around 400 men, of whom less than 300 were infantry, proved to be largely an illusion. While Major Lewis was giving orders, one complete platoon vanished. Another platoon was ordered to occupy a house just north of the bridge, and they were never seen again. The third platoon suffered severe casualties while moving into another building. Clearly, they were no match for these particular German troops at house-fighting by night.

At Brigade HQ, all wireless contact had gone completely, even though they had the sets in an attic with aerials sticking out of the roof. There was not even a whisper on the large 76 set, although the small 22 set was receiving 2nd Battalion loud and clear. As their HQ was only 30 yards away, the unassisted human larynx would have done just as well. The set owned by the engineers in a building farther away could pick up Brigade only intermittently, and the only transmissions they could receive with fair regularity were those of the BBC Home Service, with London telling the world about the battle of Arnhem.

During the night, the defenders holding positions in the houses immediately to the north of the bridge were to be cut off from the rest of the division by more than a wireless failure. The Germans, having virtually no wireless sets left after the debacle in Normandy, relied on the civilian telephone network to gather the nearest units for an immediate counter-stroke. Their moves, therefore, were based on much better information and were much better coordinated than those of the British. And the whole of II SS Panzer Corps had undergone thorough training in anti-parachute work prior to the Normandy landings.

Very rapid switches of command were smoothly executed. The reconnaissance unit of 9th SS, which had gone to Nijmegen, was transferred to 10th SS; and the reconnaissance unit of the 10th was sent to help the 9th. This was commanded by Major Brinkman and was given the task of closely encircling and attacking the 2nd Parachute Battalion's small perimeter in the houses north of the bridge.

As we have seen, they were more skilled at this sort of work than were the British, who simply sat in their houses and waited to be attacked, and almost certainly they were much less weary and thirsty than the paratroopers, who had been without rest since the early morning and had had nothing to drink for eight hours or more. The houses were close together, and they simply moved forward in the darkness across the gardens, covered by bushes, until they could fire through the windows, in some cases by resting their machine-guns on the windowsills. In short, they made silent advances right up to their enemy before opening fire.

While this close encirclement was going on around the northern end of the bridge, the remainder of Harzer's force, under Major Spindler, formed a blocking-line right through Arnhem to the river west of the road bridge. They faced west, to oppose any further advance of British units into the town towards the bridge.

So, while Brinkman's force faced into Frost's perimeter around the bridge, Spindler's force had their backs to the bridge and faced outwards towards the bulk of the British troops trying to get into Arnhem – that is, the remainder of 1

Parachute Brigade. The blocking-line was weak at first, and by no means continuous, but reinforcements had already been summoned by telephone and it became continually stronger.

Harzer, meanwhile, had been whipping up reinforcements and putting them into the positions where they would do most good. The little armour he had consisted mainly of half-tracked infantry carriers, but at midnight on Sunday he received news of actual tank reinforcements. Hauptmann Knaust, commander of the Bocholt training and depot battalion for armoured infantry, the panzer grenadiers, reported that his unit would reach Arnhem early on Monday, 18 September, bringing with them ten training tanks, vintage roughly 1940. Harzer directed them to join Brinkman's group at the road bridge as soon as they arrived, because it was imperative to reopen the bridge to traffic. It was the natural main axis of II SS Panzer Corps for the Battle of Nijmegen.

Field Marshal Model had expressly ordered that neither the road bridge at Arnhem nor the road bridge at Nijmegen were to be blown up, as both were vital to the operations of his corps. Until Arnhem bridge had been well cleared of the British, reinforcements and supplies for the 10th SS would have to cross the Neder Rijn on the ferry at Pannerden and then use minor roads to reach Nijmegen. It was a poor route, not really capable of handling masses of heavy material. Therefore, as long as Frost's men hung on to the bridge, they were directly affecting the Battle of Nijmegen in favour first of Gavin's 82nd US Division and later of XXX Corps as well.

At dawn, two platoons from B Company broke through the German ring near the pontoon bridge and reached Frost, a welcome reinforcement. At about the same time an artillery officer, Captain Harrison, succeeded in making a lone journey in the opposite direction. His object was to bring the guns of 3 Battery forward to Oosterbeek, from where they had the range to fire on the area around the bridge. This was important in the early stages, because Harzer's artillery initially amounted to only four 2-centimetre and two 8·8-centimetre flak guns, although a mortar battery was on its way.

At 0800 the Germans made a rush for the bridge from the south end, firing all guns. Once the span was crossed, the ramp was covered and overlooked by the houses alongside it, in which Frost's men and Brigade headquarters had established themselves. In addition to Piats, they had just completed the siting of four six-pounder anti-tank guns, high-velocity weapons. The Germans had to run a real gauntlet, in what were basically vulnerable vehicles — armoured cars, open half-tracks, and unarmoured trucks.

The Royal Engineers were in the Van Limburg Stirumschool on the opposite side of the road to the Brigade HQ building and a little farther north, but still overlooking the ramp leading down from the bridge into Arnhem. They could do nothing about the armoured cars, but the open half-tracks were targets for everything, including grenades; and when one was brought to a standstill, the passengers were shot down as they tried to get out. Seeing what was happening, the commander of one half-track turned off the ramp and took a path leading directly under the walls of the school. Captain E. M. Mackay, in charge of the Royal Engineers party, heard the clanking of its tracks below his window, and stuck his head out to look. Five feet away, the half-track was passing, with the German commander looking at him. The German grinned and got off three shots with his Luger, smashing Mackay's binoculars, before the engineers shot him down and the half-track, out of control, crashed into the wall of the school.

The ramp was now partially blocked by a disordered zig-zag column of stranded or blazing vehicles. The attempt to break through had taken about an hour, and its failure was marked by increased mortar fire and shellfire from the German positions on the south bank of the river around the bridge, and by British shellfire in reply.

As early as 0730, General Urquhart had been officially reported at Division as 'missing', although in fact he was merely with Brigadier Lathbury and out of wireless contact. But during the day, the report became literally true. Both Urquhart, the divisional commander, and Lathbury, his appointed successor, were cut off in a house with a German self-propelled gun outside the door. No one now commanded the division, and there was an argument between the two remaining brigadiers, Shan Hackett and Pip Hicks, as to who should take over.

This was the day when the Dutch message reached the 82nd US Division at Nijmegen: 'Germans winning over British at Arnhem', and it was true and could not be remedied. German reinforcements were coming in faster than British reinforcements, the available troops were too few for their tasks of holding the bridge, holding the dropping zones, holding the areas for the supply drops, and attacking north of Arnhem. This day the landing of reinforcements was delayed from the morning to the afternoon, because of bad weather over the airfields, and the supply dropping zones were mostly held now by the Germans. Eventually, the decision was taken to send two more battalions to try to reach Frost at the bridge, but they could not get through.

Both in Arnhem and in Nijmegen, contemporary Dutch narratives published during or just after the war express nearly speechless indignation at the barbaric horror of the Germans, in that they deliberately set fire to houses in both towns for purposes of illumination at night. We should of course all be incoherent with fury if it was our house that was being burned down wantonly by foreign troops. In fact, it was not wanton at all, and it was done by both sides. Major Hibbert, who logged the battle at the bridge from first to last, noted at 1700 hours on Monday, 18 September:

As it got dark it was decided to set light to several wooden huts round the bridge in order to keep the area illuminated and so prevent German movement and infiltration over the bridge. This was highly successful and kept the whole area as light as day. The Germans too seemed to have the same idea and proceeded to set fire to most of the houses outside the perimeter. In the process they set fire to the house next door to Brigade HQ and only by the action of very energetic fire-fighting squads on each floor was Brigade HQ saved.

On Monday, the Germans had first tried to rush the bridge and when that failed began to press in on the perimeter from the east, in order to drive the paratroops to the west, away from the bridge road. That is, they were attacking roughly from the area of the power station near the waterfront, on the Nieuwekade, in the general direction of the Rijnkade and the church of St Eusebius, as this would open the road for heavy reinforcements to pour south across the bridge for the Battle of Nijmegen.

On Tuesday, instead of attempting to rush the bridge from the south, they brought up guns and a few tanks to bombard the paratroops on the north bank of the Neder Rijn; they continued to drive from the east with infantry, more tanks arriving during the day; and they adopted the policy of methodically burning the defenders out of their houses, one by one. The attack began at about 0700 and meanwhile the German guns on the south bank opened fire. Methodically and systematically, they began to shell all the churches in Arnhem; this was a great relief to the paratroops who, up to that moment, had supposed that their steeples were occupied by German artillery observers.

During the morning and again during the afternoon, the Brigade HQ sets picked up XXX Corps (although they could not get Division). First, there was a Canadian voice, apparently transmitting less than 20 miles away. Eventually Hibbert got a message through that they were holding the north end of the bridge and how soon could help reach them? The answer was: We are putting in an attack on Nijmegen bridge at 1200 hours, and hope to be with you soon. The last message was at 1700 hours; it was still 'soon', but it sounded as if the bridge attack had failed (which was the case).

During the daylight, the Germans made two attempts to get artillery close up to the British positions around the bridge, and both failed. Several Mark IIIs were roaming about the area, pumping shells into the houses at will, out of range of the

Piats, and usually beyond effective rifle range. Tanks are not really effective for fighting in built-up areas, because they can only operate in penny packets and being blind when closed down, the commander has to have his head out of the turret. The attack is slow, cautious, and can have only one end – the defenders will be burnt or blown out of the houses they hold.

At noon, with 'tanks coming up in relays from the waterfront', the engineers listening in the school to the BBC news broadcasts heard that 'everything was going according to plan and that relief was imminent', according to Captain Mackay's contemporary narrative. Later, 'I turned on the six o'clock news and learnt with amazement that we had been relieved,' he wrote.

Help was in fact at hand – for the obsolete Mark III training tanks from the Bocholt depot. At 1930 hours the first of a number of Tiger tanks, weighing over 60 tons, came rolling down to the ramp from the north. They were armed with 88-millimetre anti-aircraft guns, a long-range, high-velocity weapon of extreme accuracy and penetrative power. They were probably from 506 Heavy Tank Battalion, recently formed in Germany, which had been promised to Harzer the previous day.

With their enormously long gun in a hand-operated turret, seven-inch-thick frontal armour, and poor mechanical reliability, they were far more formidable in defence than in attack. Two or three Tigers, in the right sort of country, could hold up an Allied armoured division. For short-range work in a built-up area, they were less effective than the American Shermans or the British Churchills, and their crews handled them gingerly. Nevertheless, that 88 was a nasty gun.

Captain D. J. Simpson was with the Royal Engineers in the school building, one of the first targets.

The Tiger rolled slowly up the ramp until it was opposite the north-west corner of the school at about 25 yards range. Its massive 88-mm gun turned steadily until it aimed at our northern room. It seemed to spit a shell at us and a six-foot hole appeared in the west wall. Again it fired, this time at the southern leg, and another piece of wall disappeared. Contrary to our expectations the Tiger turned its gun south and backed down the ramp. Apparently it was a little nervous of staying in one spot too long and that was the last we saw of it that night. We now had no shortage of loop-holes and the men took up their positions with all available ammunition and explosives. We thought that they must surely attack in strength and try to finish us. The only sound now was the crackling of the fires, the occasional crack of a rifle and the noise of heavy guns miles to the south of us. We had so few men now (4 killed and 27 wounded out of 50) that we all needed to be awake. Our boots made so much noise in the quiet night that we raided the remains of the linen cupboard and bound our boots with blankets, sheets, and even with ladies' stockings. Our nerves began to show the tremendous strain. The men's faces, in the flickering light of the fires, looked terrible – their eyes red from want of sleep, three days' growth of beard, blackened by fire fighting and whitened again with thick plaster gave them the grimmest of appearances.

On Tuesday, 19 September they were still acting offensively. Tanks and armoured cars were stalked with Piats and damaged or knocked out. A house was lost, and then retaken. But the houses that were burned over their heads were unapproachable, and slowly they were driven north, away from the bridge, except for a party that got underneath and fought on from there.

On the morning of 20 September, Brigade had at last contacted Division on a 22 set, and Urquhart and Frost were able to talk. The division commander, who had escaped from his temporary imprisonment, congratulated Frost and his men and asked them to hold for the arrival of XXX Corps, without help from the rest of the division, which was stuck in the Oosterbeek area.

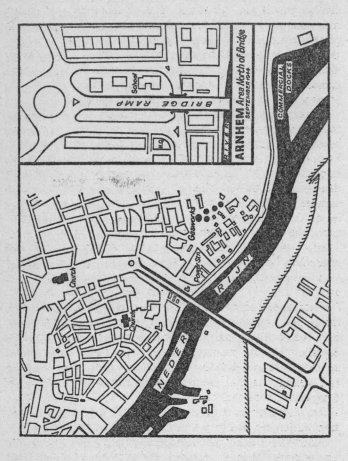

ARNHEM *Area North of Bridge*
SEPTEMBER 1944

Frost said his own position was 'satisfactory' for the time being, but that he needed food and ammunition at once, also a surgical team. Urquhart suggested that he might ask the local civilian population to bring in food, ammunition, and stores from the supply containers, which had fallen in the wrong place the previous day. Frost replied that the battalion was in the middle of a devasted area, with no one else living there except a large number of aggressive Germans who had them completely surrounded, and that it was impractical for civilians to wander to and fro carrying supplies for the British.

Brigade then passed back their estimate of casualties inflicted on the enemy by a force that probably never numbered more than 500 men and considerably fewer now: 8 halftracks and armoured cars destroyed, 6 Mark IV tanks destroyed, 20 to 30 lorries destroyed or damaged, 1 Tiger tank damaged, 300 to 400 killed or wounded, 120 prisoners. The number of prisoners was known to be correct, but as the first 80 of them had been sent to the civilian prison on Sunday night, they must have been freed soon after.

Frost was badly wounded early in the afternoon and shortly afterwards General Urquhart came on the air again from Division. His message was that the bulk of the division was being attacked from both sides, east and west, and that far from Division's being able to come to the help of the 2nd Battalion at the bridge. Division would probably have to call for support from the 2nd Battalion. Major Gough replied for Frost that 2nd Battalion were in 'great spirits' and could easily hold out for another 24 hours. Hibbert noted that this was indeed the general feeling, but that the facts hardly supported it: A and B companies driven back almost to Brigade HQ, 50 per cent casualties, six-pounders under short-range rifle fire, no more Piat ammunition left, and very little small-arms ammunition.

Shortly after dark, the Brigade HQ building was set on fire. This was very serious, because there were 250 wounded men, British and German, in the cellars. An attempt was made to move them to another building, but this was fired also before much could be done. Further, many of the wounded required much more than first aid. Consequently, a truce was arranged; and in the confusion, when no one could fire at anyone else, the defence more or less dissolved.

In retrospect, Model's decision to leave the bridge intact was correct for Arnhem, wrong for Nijmegen. But if Frost's battalion had not held on for so long at Arnhem bridge, Model might have been right about Nijmegen also, for then he would have been able to reinforce quickly with heavy units. As it was, Euling's battalion, plus the original garrison, had held out there in defence of the town and the bridges from the evening of the 17th to after nightfall on the 20th. For exactly the same length of time as Frost, that is, and at the same time. And these two battles had decisively affected each other.

Now that the real battles for Arnhem and for Nijmegen were over, the 'Island' was to become the next battlefield.

CHAPTER TEN

The Battle of Nijmegen:
19 and 20 September

Operation Market began at approximately 1300 hours on 17 September with the opening of three simultaneous battles at Eindhoven, Nijmegen, and Arnhem. Operation Garden began at approximately 1430 hours with the advance of the Irish Guards on Valkenswaard. The first day was therefore in reality less than half a day by the clock, and in terms of actual daylight only some six hours long, sunset on that day being at 1847, last light at 1941 hours.

If 1 British Airborne Division was to be relieved within 48 hours, XXX Corps would have to reach Arnhem bridge by late morning or early afternoon of 19 September. There were hopes that it might be possible for the Coldstream Guards to reach the Zuyder Zee by the evening of 19th, and thus complete the first part of the whole operation.

In the considered view of Colonel A. N. Breitmeyer, who was at the time intelligence officer of the 2nd Grenadier Guards, this was 'an ambitious plan depending on all links falling into place according to schedule, but had we got the high ground in the Apeldoorn area nothing could have stopped us'. The Grenadier Guards Group were to be in the van of that advance, taking over from the Irish Guards who were to break through the thin 'crust' of German resistance in the initial stages. But no real break-through took place, partly because the German 'crust' was thicker and rougher than expected, partly because the going was bad and favoured the defence, partly because the attempt to go round the enemy opposing the advance up the main centre line failed when it was found that the bridges would not support the weight of a tank, and partly because support from the 2nd Tactical Air Force was not available on the second day.

Between Zon and Grave, however, a distance of some 25 miles, American paratroopers held all the bridges. The leading troops of the Household Cavalry left Zon at 0615 on 19 September and reached Grave two hours later, just after 0800, easily outdistancing the tanks. The armoured cars pressed on to within two miles of Nijmegen and found that the road bridge over the Mass–Waal Canal at Neerbosch was too badly damaged for immediate use. With the help of the Americans, they reconnoitred a diversionary route to the intact bridge at Heumen. The 2nd Grenadier Guards reached Grave bridge at about 1000 hours and halted short of it. Breitmeyer, as intelligence officer, went forward with his CO to meet General Browning; and then they were all sent on to General Gavin's HQ in the woods south of Nijmegen, where a combined plan was drawn up.

By now, the Grenadier Guards should have been nearing Arnhem bridge, but were in fact some eight miles short of Nijmegen bridge; and Arnhem bridge lay about ten miles beyond that by road, although the direct line distance was shorter. And, although Arnhem bridge was still held on the north side by the remnants of 2 Parachute Battalion, Nijmegen bridge was held on both sides by Euling's SS Battalion. Three attacks in two days, carried out by the Americans at strengths not exceeding that of two companies, had failed to get anywhere near the bridge.

Both Browning and Gavin considered that it was more important to hold the high ground securely than to risk losing it by attacking the bridge in strength. No serious German attack from the Reichswald had yet materialized, and all the reported German 'tanks' had proved to be 2-centimetre flak-guns mounted on armoured half-tracks. The first dangerous attack was not to occur until 20 September, but at the time no one could know that.

An important element in the planning on this day was the bad weather over England and the Channel. The fly-in of a glider infantry regiment to reinforce the 82nd was cancelled and so too was the planned drop of the Polish Parachute Brigade at Arnhem. The 82nd did receive a supply drop, but the aircraft flew high and the loads were scattered, making the task of collection more lengthy than usual. As this normally involved a third of the men already landed, it was a more than usually serious dilution of strength at a critical time.

By early afternoon the Guards were closed up behind the Americans in the southern outskirts of Nijmegen; the armoured cars of the Household Cavalry had got as far to the east as Beek, where from an American position on the high ground they could observe the road bridge, which was still intact. Indeed, it was far more heavily defended than it had been in 1940, when the casemates, pillboxes and trenches had not been backed by artillery.

88-millimetre guns sited 400 yards north of the Waal were firing on the Americans, who were unable to reply. Two Daimler armoured cars elevated their two-pounder guns to extreme range and drove the crews of the 88s out of their emplacements. Then a single 88, farther away, opened up; but this was quelled by calling up the divisional artillery and giving them the map reference. They hit with the first salvo, aided by the excellent defence overlay maps that pin-pointed all known enemy positions most accurately. The Germans then moved up four 105-millimetre guns and opened fire. To this there could be no reply, because ammunition was 'desperately short' and the little left was wanted to support an attack now being planned. Meanwhile, the armoured cars engaged the casemates sited north of the bridge, which were within their range, before withdrawing at about 1600.

The Dutch 'Underground' played an important part in the decisions made that day, through the Dutch liaison officer with the 82nd, Captain Arie D. Bestbreurtje. The historian of the Irish Guards wrote:

The Dutch Resistance gave rather confused information, but they were emphatic about two things: That the German demolition control centre was in the Post Office, and that the road bridge could not be blown anywhere because a youth called Van something had cut the lead from the Post Office to the bridge, or alternatively, that the 'Underground' had removed all the explosive charges from the bridge. This story was rather doubtful. Why should the Germans blow the bridges from the wrong side, and did they never inspect or test their preparations? But however doubtful, the story could not be ignored.

Therefore, the decision was made to make a quick dash with combined forces for three objectives – the road bridge to the east, the railway bridge to the west, and the post office in the centre of the town and almost midway between the southern approaches to both bridges. Each task force was to be composed of mixed British and American units, led by guides from the Netherlands Interior Forces.

The eastern force, which was to take both the post office and the road bridge whose demolitions it was supposed to control, consisted of the tanks of 3 Squadron, 2 Grenadier Guards, and the infantry of 2 Company, 1 Grenadier Guards, plus Companies E and F of the 2nd Battalion, 505 Parachute Infantry.

The western force, which was to take the railway bridge, had five tanks from 3 Squadron of the 2nd Grenadiers, led by Captain J. W. Neville, a platoon of infantry from the 1st Grenadiers travelling in three carriers, plus Company D of the 2nd Battalion, 505 Parachute Infantry, commanded by First Lieutenant Oliver B. Carr, Jr.

The eastern column moved off at about 1600 hours for yet another attack on the road bridge, the fourth in three days. All went well until the leading tank, commanded by Lieutenant J. Moller, came in sight of the traffic roundabout 300 yards south of the bridge. Then it was immediately knocked out by an 88, and Moller was killed. Other Shermans tried to ease past the blazing hulk and were in their turn either knocked out or damaged. The American paratroopers under First Lieutenant James J. Smith got to within a hundred yards of the roundabout, then had to withdraw.

For the rest of the afternoon, they left the streets and tried to get forward by moving along the rooftops and blasting a way through houses, but were unable to reach the roundabout. Indeed, they made absolutely no impression on the German defences, which consisted of loopholed houses and slit trenches dominated by the Valkhof.

This site had originally been chosen by the Romans as the key to Nijmegen and had been fortified by the Second Legion; then by Charlemagne; then by Frederick Barbarossa; and now the remains of Barbarossa's fortress afforded cover to anti-tank guns and infantry of the Waffen SS amply equipped with automatic weapons. The bridge roundabout, the Keizer Traianus Plein, gave radial fields of fire down all the approach roads at its south-eastern corner.

However, in the centre of the town, the post office was captured. 'There was nothing in it but civilians in the cellars and dead Germans behind the counters,' wrote the Irish Guards historian. There was no sign of any demolition mechanism connected with the bridge, but as the building was excellently placed, it was chosen as headquarters for the remainder of the battle of Nijmegen, which was to be controlled from there.

The railway bridge party under Captain J. W. Neville assembled in the lane outside the town, and he recalled that

Our party had been given a guide, a Dutchman who spoke very little English. Nevertheless, by following his instructions we were able to reach our goal, which otherwise would have proved extremely difficult. The paratroops rode on the backs of the tanks and we set off with the infantry carriers disposed between the tanks, keeping about 40–50 yards between each vehicle. I myself rode in the middle, giving instructions concerning the route on the wireless. This went well out to the west, with the result that the railway bridge was approached from its western side. To begin with, the advance was comparatively uneventful, with occasional shots from buildings. In at least two cases, civilians opened fire. The principal trouble came from a house in which there were several Spandaus, and these were knocked out with the 75-mm gun from the leading tank. At this stage we expected the opposition to increase, but it would appear that they were in isolated houses, for the last 400 or 500 yards before we reached the railway line was comparatively uneventful. No doubt the Dutch guide had some part to play in this result.

The column halted at a crossroads while the leading tank reconnoitred. Looking back along the route they had come, Neville saw a Panther tank cross the road at the nearest intersection, headed for the scene of the shooting, with the crew apparently so intent on the place where the column had last been in action that they were in fact looking the wrong way.

About 200 yards from the southern end of the bridge, Neville called a halt and went forward with the American officer. The railway line was carried up to the bridge on a long embankment, not negotiable by tanks, but there was one point where the road beside the Waal passed under the embankment. As they subsequently discovered, on the other side of the embankment was a ramp that led up to the railway line and the bridge. On the side facing them, however, were many dug-in positions for heavy machine-guns and anti-tank guns, firing over an open space about 100 yards across.

As the light was beginning to fade, we decided upon an immediate attack. The plan was simple, if unimaginative. Three tanks were to charge the opening in the embankment while the other two gave covering fire. At the same time the Americans, aided by the infantry carriers, were to gain the embankment to the south and drive out the machine-gunners from the flank. Alas, the plan did not work. As soon as the leading tanks moved forward across the open space, they came under heavy artillery fire from a battery on the north bank of the Waal. Clearly, these guns had been calibrated in advance. The leading tank was hit and destroyed immediately, and the next was hit immediately afterwards. All but one of the crew in the leading tank were killed and my own driver, contrary to orders and with misplaced bravery, jumped out of my tank and went to the rescue of those trapped. As a result, two crews were rescued but my driver sustained serious burns. Our attack had lost its impetus and the lot of the Americans was no better. They came under exceedingly heavy machine-gun fire, not only from the embankment in front, but also from Germans who were by then on all sides. The Germans also had the support of two self-propelled guns, which appeared through the tunnel in the embankment and were engaged by our tanks. By this time it was dark, and since we had failed to make any impression on the defences, I decided to call off the attack during the night.

We withdrew about 100 yards and commandeered several houses to form a temporary headquarters. There were about six seriously wounded men who probably would not have survived without medical treatment, whom I decided to send back in a carrier. The Americans, despite the reverse and a few casualties, were still quite unmoved. We placed our three remaining tanks in strategic places and everyone else took cover in the adjoining houses. The American commander, who was otherwise a most cooperative man, refused at this stage to have anything to do with sentries, on the grounds that his men needed 'a good night's sleep'. Despite some forceful words from me, he remained adamant. To protect themselves against surprise attack, their so-called 'sentries' slept behind the doors, so that any intruder would have to wake them up before getting in. My own expectation was, that we would be rushed during the night; and at frequent intervals we could hear the Germans moving around us. Looking back on it in the light of what happened next morning, it is obvious that the Germans, far from making a plan to attack us, were withdrawing.

As at Arnhem, so too at Nijmegen the Germans selected a small proportion of houses and public buildings for burning, so that the streets would be brightly illuminated for their anti-tank guns and automatic weapons. Darkness was dangerous, as under its cover infantry might be able to creep forward and rush them from close range. The same principle applied to Captain Neville's tank, similarly blinded by night; and indeed his small force, having simply driven past a number of German-occupied buildings on their way to the railway embankment, had in fact lodged itself among the German defenders. He was understandably anxious at having Germans behind him, and the Germans were equally concerned at having been apparently cut off from their main force and, in particular, the escape route over the Waal offered by the railway bridge, upon which a so-called 'hare track' had been constructed.

That night, the pocket panzer division, which had hurriedly been re-routed from Aachen, got to within sight of the Bailey bridge spanning the Wilhelmina Canal at Zon and was firing on the command post of the 101st US Airborne Division until Major General Maxwell Taylor himself brought up reinforcements and drove them back. This attack caused some chaos among the drivers of the supply-column vehicles, one of which was burning brightly on top of the Bailey bridge.

Worse was to come farther south at Eindhoven, where a cluster of parachute flares bursting out over the town signalled an attack by about 100 twin-engined bombers, which dropped their loads systematically and accurately, some of them diving to within 300 feet of the columns of vehicles slowly passing through the town. In ten minutes it was all over, and 18 Royal Army Service Corps trucks had been destroyed.

But the chaos created was out of all proportion. The first half-dozen trucks to sustain direct hits held artillery ammunition, which began to burn and explode. The next line of vehicles to go up held fuel, and from them the flames spread to trucks loaded with small-arms ammunition. The road was strewn and blocked by wreckage. An officer of the Household Cavalry, Captain Profumo, rapidly mustered all available Dutchmen to help clear the debris; and the column got on the move again. But the loss of so much ammunition, at a time when there was a severe shortage in Nijmegen, could not be made good immediately.

By dawn on Wednesday, 20 September, the supply column had reached Grave bridge. It had started from Bourg Leopold in Belgium the previous afternoon and included 800 vehicles as well as a number of anti-aircraft guns, bridging equipment, and engineer units. Two troops of roadbound armoured cars provided only illusory protection from flank attacks to such an unwieldy convoy, and the commander of a part of it decided to halt for the night rather than risk the Panthers still roaming about. Major Ward, the armoured car escort commander, fell out with him over this, and carried on through the night with the remainder of the column.

In the darkness, aided by a divisional sign that was pointing the wrong way, he took a side road leading to Heesch, where the Germans were reported to be in force, and had the column turned round rather than risk so many vulnerable and valuable vehicles. It was with bent wings, dented radiators, and drivers falling asleep at the wheel that the head of the column reached Grave bridge, where three Focke-Wulf 190s attacked it.

The sudden reappearance of the Luftwaffe, even in small numbers, seemed an omen of change; and was due to the peculiar Allied command system that achieved a general denial of tactical air support to the whole operation, while managing at the same time to give the Luftwaffe local air superiority, although the German planes could be numbered only in hundreds, while the Allies counted by thousands. Adverse weather also played a part, but only a small part, in this surprising reversal of conditions in Normandy. Consequently, the ground troops had to rely largely on their own efforts and had nothing like the close air support given by the Germans in 1940 to both their airborne troops and the ground forces moving along the corridor from Gennep to Moerdijk and Rotterdam. The almost complete absence of help from 'flying artillery' was a major factor both for the landed airborne divisions and the troops and supplies moving up along the corridor to their aid.

During the night of 19–20 September, a number of plans had been devised by various people, with many blank spaces to be filled in at the last moment, agreements secured, arrangements made, and so on. No doubt the urgent necessity of crossing the Waal and relieving the visibly wilting Arnhem bridgehead helped these negotiations to go smoothly. Considering that the plans entailed the dovetailing of British tanks, infantry, engineers, and artillery with American paratroopers, engineers, and artillery, plus the Netherlands Interior Forces, in a complicated four-pronged attack of the utmost danger and difficulty, this was truly remarkable.

The previous precedent – that of 10 May 1940 – indicated that the bridges would be blown. All through 20 September 1944 it was expected that the bridges would go up at any moment; and the nearer the attackers got to the bridges, the greater became the likelihood.

Consequently, one-half of the plan was an assault crossing of the Waal west of both bridges by Colonel R. H. Tucker's 504th Parachute Infantry Regiment. This in face of fire from the artillery component of the 9th SS Panzer Division, now under command of the 10th SS, which Oberst Harzer described as possessing 'tremendous fire-power, from almost entirely armoured vehicles, handled in the most clever and flexible manner, which until Battalion Euling cleared out of Nijmegen prevented the Americans from gaining a bridgehead'.

To oppose it, a hundred British and American guns were to be brought up, plus the tank guns of the Irish Guards, and these were to 'shoot' the American parachutists across the Waal. Consequently, Brigadier C. P. Jones, Commander, Royal Engineers of Guards Armoured, received a telephone call early on the 20th: 'Have you got any assault boats?' To which he replied: 'Yes – 32 serviceable.'

Having set the wheels in train, he drove over to Gavin's HQ. 'I found that they proposed to carry out an assault crossing of the Waal, in the power station area, with the idea of taking the bridge defences in the rear, in conjunction with an attack by the Grenadier Group from the south on to the near end of the bridge, a formidable project,' he noted soon after. He offered them rafts and Royal Engineers to ferry their anti-tank guns across, and this was accepted. Then he hurried off to make sure that all this equipment would actually be there by early afternoon, although the exact site for the crossing had not then even been selected.

Colonel Tucker had been told what he was in for the previous day at 2100 hours by his divisional operations officer, and that he was to contact General Horrocks next morning and 'iron out as smooth an operation as could possibly be done'. Consequently, while Brigadier Jones was ironing out the assault boat problem at the American HQ, Tucker was at the British HQ, from where he went forward with Colonel Giles Vandeleur (commanding the Irish Guards tanks because Colonel 'Joe' was ill) in his reconnaissance car as

neither of us was sure as to where the crossing should be made. I had warned my battalion commanders the night before what to expect, but basically I want my 2nd Battalion to form a base of fire along the river bank. The 3rd Battalion was to lead the assault, followed closely by the 1st Battalion. The 3rd Battalion was to fan out to the east, getting about 1,000 yards north of the Nijmegen highway bridge. The 1st Battalion was to fan out to the west, maintaining contact with the 3rd Battalion and form[ing] with them an arc around the northern exits of the bridge. A short order, but you must remember these battalion commanders had been with me in combat for more than a year. They understood me and I them, and all their officers and men. With the advice of my combat engineer company commander, I picked the crossing site when we had reached the river bank and could see the tiny beach available for launching our boats. They were British engineer assault craft which carried 16 men, propelled by paddlers; they did not arrive until 30 minutes before we were to jump off, and our troops had never seen them before, but they would be steered by our engineers.

The Grenadier Guards of 'Group Hot' had been notified that their task for the 20th would be the clearing of Nijmegen, without reinforcements, because the 325th US Glider Infantry Regiment had been unable to land, owing to bad weather. The two Grenadier COs, together with the CO of the 2nd Battalion, 505th Parachute Infantry, had worked out a combined plan by 0400 on the 20th.

Instead of putting in their main attack along the south-east road to the bridge via the 'bridge roundabout', where they had been held before and where the Germans were well prepared to meet them, they would instead attack from the west towards the Valkhof. This meant methodically clearing the town to procure enough space for the final assault on the Valkhof and the bridge it guarded, and also protecting the western flank.

Captain Neville's force, still surrounded by Germans near the railway embankment, was ordered by wireless to clear the town near the railway bridge. Pressure was to be maintained towards the 'bridge roundabout' and Hunner Park, but this was not the main assault. The culmination of these concentric attacks was to be the rushing of the road bridge, or an attempt to do so, and the bridge approaches were to be kept under continuous fire from the 25-pounder field guns, using the ammunition just brought up by the Eindhoven convoy.

The attack began at 0830 from the big 'town roundabout', the Keizer Karel Plein, from which the roads radiated north-east towards the fire-swept open ground at the southern end of the road bridge, which, reading from left to right, consisted of the Valkhof, Hunner Park, and the 'bridge roundabout', all heavily fortified and entrenched.

This was not a job for an armoured division, and not all the tanks were, or could be, employed. Basically, in street-fighting only the two leading tanks in any one street are of any use, as they alone can fire; apart from which, they are vulnerable both to short-range bazookas fired from houses on their flanks and to anti-tank guns firing down the street in front, and if snipers can keep the tank commanders' heads down, the vehicles are almost blind. Consequently, the battle was fought mainly by the infantry of the 1st Grenadiers, supported by the tanks of 2 Squadron, 2nd Grenadiers.

At first, the attack went well, each section of the town being cleared methodically by one party of infantry, another party waiting behind them to leapfrog through the next section. under cover of their fire and that of the tanks, towards the Valkhof and Hunner Park, while the 2nd Battalion of Colonel Vandervoort's 505th Parachute Infantry, also supported by Guards' tanks, pressed forward from the south-east towards the right-hand objective, the 'bridge roundabout'.

Some two and a half hours after the combined British and American attack had begun in the centre of Nijmegen, General Eugen Meindl's II Fallschirm Corps put in a seven-battalion attack at two points on the long perimeter held by five battalions of the 82nd US Airborne Division. At Mook and Riethorst in the south, dangerously close to the vital intact bridge at Heumen, the German parachutists came in under a hail of 88-millimetre shells and Nebelwerfer bombs against the American parachutists, and drove them back. Gavin called on the Coldstream Guards for tank support, and got it.

But the more immediately dangerous attack was that southeast of Nijmegen, which re-took Wyler and Beek and drove the American parachutists back up the hill to Berg en Dal. From here, one can walk into Nijmegen, and the Germans very nearly did. The American commander, Colonel Lou Mendez, by shifting his platoons about quickly, managed to conceal the fact that there was a gap a few hundred yards away through which the Germans could have strolled into Nijmegen along a route leading to the 'bridge roundabout'.

General Gavin only heard the details of his own attack to get the bridge at second-hand, the next day, and explained to me:

On the afternoon of the assault crossing of the river, the 82nd Airborne Division became deeply involved with a German attack coming from two directions. One German force over-ran the town of Mook and another over-ran the town of Beek. From mid-afternoon until long after dark, I was almost totally preoccupied with shifting reserves, visiting unit commanders, and seeking to stabilize that side of the Division area.

The attack of Colonel Tucker's 504th Parachute Infantry across the Waal west of both bridges was timed for 1500 hours, covered by a smokescreen to be put down previously by the 25-pounders of the Leicestershire Yeomanry. This was vital, because the launching beach was in full view of the Germans on the Lent side of the Waal, and the Americans had never seen the boats before and would have to be taught how to use them before they could embark.

The opposition was not a matter of small-arms fire, but of the mobile artillery of 9 SS Panzer Division plus flak emplacements. How accurate these guns were was shown when one of the Royal Engineer trucks carrying six out of the 32 assault boats promised by Brigadier Jones to the Americans tried to get to the site by moving out on to the road parallel to the river. In an instant there were only 26 boats instead of 32, and the number of trucks had been reduced by one.

At 1430 the tanks of 2 and 3 squadrons of the Irish Guards moved slowly into position, the former having good fields of fire but being as exposed as the Americans to deadly accurate shellfire, the latter having less good fields of fire but being protected by rubble. At 1455 the British and American guns put down smoke on the far bank, before lifting to fire high explosives on the German positions farther back. The Americans carried their assault boats down to the river and then gathered round Major Thomas of the Royal Engineers for a brief lesson in boatmanship. Then they launched them and scrambled in, packed so tightly that they could hardly move. Under the weight, some of the boats grounded again in the shallows at the water's edge, and some men had to get out, push, then scramble in again.

Colonel Tucker was now at the top of the power station with his radio man and Colonel Giles Vandeleur, who was to control the fire of his tanks. General 'Boy' Browning was there as well.

The entire crossing area was spread out below us [recalled Colonel Tucker]. The first wave of the 3rd Battalion (Major Julian A. Cook) raced through a hail of lead across the beach area, loaded into the assault boats, and set out for the other side, roughly 400 yards away. There was direct fire from Germans 88s, flak wagons, 20 mm canon [sic], MGs and rifle fire kicking up splashes in the water beside the boats. Some men were hit, direct, others blown into the water, but those still able to used their helmets and even their hands to paddle furiously towards the shore. Of the 26 boats that made up the initial wave, only 11 were in condition to return.

The Irish Guards historian wrote: 'Each boat took twenty-five minutes to cross and return. No praise is too high for their courage, especially that of the second and third waves, who stood on the bank watching the fate of the first.' The smoke-screen was blown away by a fitful wind and the packed, burdened infantry jammed in their frail canvas craft were exposed nakedly to the enemy guns.

Fortress West, from which much of the German fire was coming, was speedily overrun by the men from those boats which got safely across. In 1940 it had been used by the Dutch merely as a barracks; the Germans had since installed 20-millimetre flak guns and machine-guns on top of the building, but from the Irish Guards it was not getting 'particular attention – even armour piercing shot to keep the defenders' heads down,' wrote this historian.

Colonel Tucker had told the tanks to shoot anywhere, any time at anything. His troops he said, would fire amber Véry

lights if the fire was coming too close to them. No Véry
lights ever went up, not necessarily because the Irish
Guards' shooting was so good – though, of course, it was –
but because all the Véry cartridges had got wet in the crossing.

The American units had got totally scrambled in the crossing, and at first no units existed, merely bunches of men, many
of them strangers to each other, determined to get forward.
The Irish Guards were running out of ammunition, and some of
the Browning machine-guns were actually 'running away' – that
is, having become so hot from almost continuous firing, they
would not stop until the last cartridge had been fed in. It was
hard to make out where the Americans were, particularly as
Colonel Tucker had gone over to lead from up front.

At four o'clock Major Tyler saw figures moving on the
railway bridge and reported that he could distinguish American uniforms or, maybe, German [wrote the historian of
the Irish Guards]. Being over-excited, he said a different
thing every minute, and so did every other tank commander.
In fact, no one could possibly tell at that distance, through
the smoke and girders. But at five o'clock the American Command Post said that their troops controlled the northern end
of both bridges.

This piece of information confused a good many people in
Guards Armoured at the time, has been accepted by most historians, British and American, ever since, and as it could not
possibly be made to fit other information in my possession,
was a source of puzzlement to me, too. The favourite version,
British in origin but copied by American historians also, is that
an American flag flying in fact from the railway bridge and put
there by Colonel Tucker's men, was mistaken for an American
flag flying from the road bridge, which report caused the
Guards tanks to charge the road bridge.

The basic fact appears to be that Captain Neville's party got

the road bridge early on the 20th, but being cut off physically
and their wireless sets suffering from the same sort of trouble
as was being experienced at Arnhem, were unable to tell
anyone. As Neville's force consisted of both American and
British infantry, as well as British tanks, it may well have been
that an American flag went up on the railway bridge as an
alternative means of signalling.

From mid-afternoon of 20 September, the Battle of Nijmegen is
best considered as a triangle north of Nijmegen. Its base was
the south bank of the Waal, running from east to west from the
'bridge roundabout' through Hunner Park, the Valkhof, along
the Valkade to the railway bridge, and past the railway bridge
to the power station on the west by the Maas–Waal Canal.

The left-hand, or western side of the triangle was the line of
advance of Colonel Tucker's 3rd Battalion, which was striking
right-handed to the north-east across the 'Island' towards the
third bridge – the bridge that, north of Lent, carried the railway line to Arnhem over the main road to Arnhem.

The right-hand, or eastern side, of the triangle was that
same Nijmegen–Arnhem road that began at the 'bridge roundabout' and was carried over the river by the largest single-span
bridge in Europe.

At that point the river was 550 metres wide, and the bridge,
supported by four piers, had a centre span 244 metres long
over the deep water in the middle of the Waal. As the road at
both ends of the bridge was embanked, in effect that road was
carried almost in a straight line and high above the level of the
surrounding countryside for a distance of 1,300 metres – or
something like three-quarters of a mile.

The critical time was around 1800 hours, three-quarters of
an hour before sunset. Having begun to cross the Waal at 1500
hours, Colonel Tucker's 3rd Battalion had not turned due east
and made directly for the northern ends of the rail and road
bridges; instead, they had driven inland to the north-east,
gaining a deep bridgehead.

The Germans defending the road bridge were about to be

caught in a trap that would snap shut as soon as the Americans had cut the Nijmegen–Arnhem road at the apex of the triangle, the bridge beyond Lent, 1,500 yards north of the Waal.

Meanwhile, the battle around the southern end of the road bridge was reaching its climax. Field guns and mortars had been hammering the dug-in defenders all day; in the later stages these were backed up by tank guns. The final assault began at 1530 hours, with very little time for planning; but the Germans had not expected an attack from the south as well, and two platoons of the Grenadiers crawled up the embankment at one point, cut the wire on top, and got into the Valkhof.

After costly hand-to-hand fighting, the Grenadiers established themselves on the eastern edge of the fort and were then able to fire on the bridge and on the Germans dug in around the bridge embankment to the south. In the centre, with more heavy losses, the Grenadiers managed to work their way through the blazing streets until they could fire on Hunner Park, backed up by the tanks, while simultaneously the Americans were beginning to wear down the defenders of the 'bridge roundabout'. As the historian of the Grenadiers wrote: 'At this point all serious German resistance seemed to crack. They were overwhelmed by fire.'

CHAPTER ELEVEN

Across the Bridge: Nijmegen, Evening, 20 September

Guards Armoured consisted of the Grenadiers, Coldstream Irish, and Welsh Guards. They were the blade of a narrow-pointed spear with a very thin, long shaft behind them stretching back to Eindhoven, a corridor in many cases little more than one road wide. The Welsh Guards were back at Grave, guarding that vital bridge that was in effect the base of the spear-blade. The Coldstream were acting as armoured reserve to the long perimeter held by Gavin's 82nd, and were in action at a number of points on the 20th where the attacking Germans of Meindl's corps had either driven back the Americans or were threatening to do so. The Irish Guards were using their firepower to cover Colonel Tucker's regiment attacking over the Waal. The battle inside Nijmegen was being fought by the Grenadiers alone, aided by one American battalion. The battle that day, of attack and counter-attack, ran in a great half-circle round Nijmegen, and by now the British Forces, even more than the American, were well under-strength, having had no replacements for their casualties for a longer time.

The armoured reserve in Nijmegen consisted of No 1 Squadron of the 2nd Grenadiers, commanded by Major J. Trotter, with Captain Lord Peter Carrington as second-in-command. Late that afternoon Major Trotter called an 'orders' group in the doorway of a Nijmegen hotel. We know what those orders were, because Sergeant P. T. Robinson had to make a statement a day or so later, which was written down by a sergeant-major.

His orders had been to take the bridge at all costs to enable us to link up with the American paratroops who had previously crossed the Waal approximately one mile west, and were believed to be clearing north of the bridge. No 1 Troop was selected to lead the Company over the bridge in one mad rush in the hopes of contacting this force to form a bridgehead.

Robinson was the commander of No 1 Troop which consisted of four tanks, all with 75-millimetre guns except for Robinson's, which had the deadly 17-pounder. As second-in-command of the squadron, Lord Carrington would cross immediately after Robinson's troop and try to control the operation as a whole. There would also be one light reconnaissance car carrying Lieutenant Jones of the Royal Engineers, who wrote:

At about 1630 hours I got into a house on the river bank, and saw the huge bridge, with someone from our side shooting straight down the line of it. I tried, with binoculars, to see if there were any demolition charges, but there were none visible. I left the house and went up behind the forward company to see how close they had got to the bridge. They had just lost their company commander in addition to a lot of men and were in no condition to push on much farther, so I decided to go back. When I got back to my car at about 1800 hours, I found an urgent order from OC 14 Fd Sqn to report to the roundabout near the bridge at once. I arrived at the roundabout at 1820 hours and found a troop of 2 Gren Gds tanks lined up ready to rush the bridge. The OC told me that the Americans were reported to be on the far side of the road bridge and that I would be going with the troop of tanks ... It transpired subsequently that the American signal to indicate that they had reached the north end of the railway bridge was misinterpreted to mean that they had reached the north end of the road bridge. This mysterious mistake had the fortunate effect of speeding up the operation!

Colonel Tucker's men had not then cleared back as far as the road bridge, or anything like it, although they had patrols criss-crossing the area; there was no American flag flying from the north end of the road bridge – and no one at the south end thought there was. Indeed, the Grenadiers very well knew who then held the north end of the bridge.

According to Sergeant Robinson's contemporary statement, zero hour was 1813. He then led his troop slowly forward on to the bridge. They could hear very little inside the machines, because of the noise of the engines and tracks. Immediately behind him was Lance Sergeant Billingham's tank. 'It was not quite dark as we went over,' recollected Lord Carrington. 'What struck me was the absence of anyone, either at our side of the bridge or on the other side. This I found intimidating. There was tension behind the emptiness of it. We knew there had been fighting for this place for a couple of days, and that this assault was the culmination.'

As Robinson's Sherman nosed its way on to the bridge and came into view of the far bank, Johnson in the tank behind saw an 88-millimetre shot strike the road in front of the 'point tank', not hitting it directly, but damaging it and putting the wireless out of action. As Robinson threw out smoke and reversed, the 88 changed target to Billingham's tank, and this time Johnson saw the flash of the gun firing. The gun itself he could not see because it was positioned in front of a burning house that was pouring out smoke to the west of the north end of the bridge. Johnson got off four rounds in that direction, but it was probably Sergeant C. Pacey's tank that hit. Anyway, the 88 stopped firing.

All four tanks reversed off the bridge, and because the wireless of his own tank was out of action, Sergeant Robinson dispossessed Billingham and took over his tank, so that Johnson now had Robinson as his tank commander. Robinson had heard very little of the firing as long as he was in his tank, but as he ran from one to the other he was aware of tracer bullets going past him in the fading light, and yet another 88 opened up. Over the radio, the CO was ordering the attack to go in at all costs.

Sergeant Pacey's tank moved forward again, followed by
Robinson, into a hail of fire only half-perceived inside the
tanks. Three anti-tank guns were firing on them from the east
and a further two from the west side of the bridge.

We had barely travelled 50 yards [stated Robinson], when
a Panzer-Faust struck a nearby girder. It seemed that projectiles were coming from every angle, yet strangely we remained intact. Not only was the bridge defended from both
flank and front, but we suffered repeated attacks from the
air in the form of men hanging from the girders and dropping
grenades, while snipers endeavoured to keep us running
blind.

Both Pacey's and Robinson's tanks opened fire with their
Brownings, raking the bridge girders around and above them.
Enemy dead and wounded began to fall out of the girders on to
the roadway 'like ninepins', and the anti-tank shot was coming
in so fast that it seemed like small-arms fire, hitting everything
except the tanks. 'I swear to this day that Jesus Christ rode on
the front of our tank,' declared Johnson.

At the far end was a road-block that could be negotiated
only by turning the tanks broadside on; and it was covered by
an anti-tank gun. Pacey stopped his tank, and was passed by
Robinson, going flat out. As they came out from behind the
road-block, Johnson saw the gun at the side of the road, about
50 yards away, about to open fire; he opened fire first and
destroyed it with three shots, the Sherman charging the gun
and going over the bodies of the crew. Still flat out, tracks
splattered with blood, flesh, and bits of uniform, they careered
down the ramp from the bridge, Robinson bellowing into his
microphone for the rest of the troop to keep up. 'He has a
voice like a bull,' wrote Johnson, 'and that, I think, annoyed me
more than anything. It was coming through my earphones like
claps of thunder.' In fact, only Pacey was left. The other two
tanks had been hit.

Then, as they came to a wide tree-lined avenue where the

road curved, Robinson spotted a self-propelled gun. It fired one shot, and missed. Robinson never gave it time to fire another. The tank slowed, Johnson swung on to the target, and then began pumping in high explosive as fast as the loader could run the shells into the breech.

Directly opposite was a church, with German infantry swarming in and out. Johnson opened fire with the turret Browning, until Robinson told him to stop and use the 75-millimetre gun instead. Shot after shot went in, until the church burst into flames, lighting up the avenue like day and showing more infantry beating up the line of trees. Again, the tank switched target, before moving on again. 'If you see anything move, shoot it!' was Robinson's motto, and when after travelling about three-quarters of a mile they saw a railway bridge loom up ahead, they went under it slowly, tensed for anything. Nothing happened, until the avenue took a wide sweep to the right.

We went round about 15 mph, machine-gunning as we went [wrote Johnson]. Suddenly there were two terrific explosions right on the front of the tank. The blast from them came down the periscope and into my eyes and I thought for a minute that I had been blinded.

Robinson had seen a number of men jump into a ditch, and this was what he was firing at. In return, they had thrown two grenades at the tank, causing

so much smoke and dust that I was compelled to halt until it subsided. Suddenly, I saw one American paratrooper whom I beckoned over, and then from nowhere there suddenly appeared a further thirty of his comrades, who gave me a most royal welcome, climbing all over my tank. It was the first time I had ever seen a tank kissed, whilst frankly I too felt like kissing them.

It was now completely dark, and although British tanks had

crossed the bridge it was not in British hands. The crews of the
tanks that had been hit had bailed out and were taken prisoner
except for Lance Sergeant Knight, who lay down and shammed
dead, not a very difficult thing to do in the circumstances. A hit
on a tank by an explosive projectile that does not penetrate can
cause the crew to black-out momentarily. Anyway, Knight lay
in a ditch by the north end of the bridge while what felt like
half the German Army walked over him. One gave him a deliberate kick, and grunted, 'Todt,' satisfied that he was dead.
When they had gone, Knight found that one of the two
knocked-out tanks was still a 'runner' and brought it up to
Robinson's support afterwards, crewless.

Lord Carrington had followed Robinson's troops across,
passing a burnt-out tank on the way, and reached the far end,
where the road led down from the bridge on a long ramp. There
were still Germans milling around, one of whom fired a bazooka at him, so he stayed there and for a short while, which
seemed terribly long, his tank was the British garrison of the
bridge.

What were needed were not tanks but infantry. It is necessary to get inside a tank to appreciate how blind the occupants
are, even in daylight. In darkness, a tank is simply a sitting
target for infantry, who can work close with impunity to fire
bazookas or drop grenades down the turret hatch, if this has
been kept open for the commander to look out. For this reason,
tanks usually withdraw at night, or if they have to stay forward, are closely guarded by infantry. But the infantry of the
Grenadiers were still scattered in their firing positions amid the
blazing ruins of Nijmegen, and there was 'an ugly period of half
an hour when we didn't know what was happening,' said
Colonel Breitmeyer. Robinson's troop had simply disappeared
over the Waal into the night, and only Lord Carrington's tank
was in contact. Two companies of Irish Guardsmen were sent to
join him, but it was 45 minutes before they could get there.

Lord Carrington was now released from his position and
could try to join Robinson. Up to now, he had no idea why he
had not been hit. 'I can only imagine the whole thing was luck.

There was no real reason why it should have succeeded.'
Travelling fast to avoid the bazooka shots fired at him, he
'zoomed' down the road to join Robinson, where the situation
was very tense.

The tanks could not go on because of the darkness, and they
could not go back because they had to hold the road at all
costs. The Germans were all around them, and the Americans
were low on ammunition. Already, one American officer had
considered the position hopeless and had thought it would be
necessary to surrender. Robinson had replied that although
two of his tanks had been knocked out, the remaining two were
still runners, and so he could not surrender. He let the American use his wireless to contact Guards Armoured.

Then, Johnson wrote,

> We were joined by Lord Carrington, making a total of three
> tanks, and like that we stayed all night with never a wink
> and our nerves like razor blades. Our idea was, for the
> Yankees to take up ground positions a few yards from the
> tanks and give us some sort of protection during the night.
> Tanks are useless in the dark. But the Yanks had other ideas
> and took up positions the other side of the railway. That was
> no earthly use to us at all, so we got the Brownings out of
> the tanks and put one at each corner of our little square.
> The enemy was so near at times, we heard him talking.
> Anything that moved had had it. We just waited for him to
> come and finish us off, but the fool never came. He never
> realized there were only three tanks holding that road to
> the bridge.

Meanwhile, back at the road bridge, Lieutenant Jones was
completing the 'delousing' process in the dark, now aided by
the whole of his troop. While doing it, they took 81 prisoners
hiding behind girders or in the large compartments built inside
the tops of the concrete bridge piers, 'all of whom were in a
very bad way indeed'. But Jones had followed immediately
behind Sergeant Robinson's troops in his reconnaissance car,

and as the last tank slewed through the gap in the road-block
he stopped the car near the northern end of the bridge, for this
was where the wires leading from the charges to the control
point should be, logically, and in fact proved to be.

The first thing I saw was about half a dozen wires on the
footway at the side of the bridge. These I cut. I walked up to
the roadblock and saw about ten Tellermine 35 in a slit
trench near it. These were obviously designed to close the
block. I removed the igniters and threw them in the river.

Jones then walked back along the bridge towards Nijmegen
and found a set of charges lying on the footpath just north of
the second pier.

These had been designed to cut the concrete roadway, but
had never been placed in position and were quite safe. I went
to the west side to see if there were any charges underneath
the bridge corresponding to those on the deck.

A German prisoner volunteered to show Jones where the
other charges were; they were all placed so as to blow the
concrete roadway north of the centre span. Jones removed the
detonators and declared the bridge safe.

In coming to a judgement as to the importance of the capture
of the bridge, it must be remembered that it was Guards
Armoured Division that had made the wild night drive through
the German rear areas to Brussels only a few weeks before. If it
had been possible to repeat this feat on the 'Island', they would
have done it; but it was not possible, owing to the unsuitability
of the terrain and the shortage of well-trained infantry with
supporting artillery.

It is also as well to remember the Germans. Judging that
except for those at the road bridge, the British parachutists at
Arnhem were not worth bothering about, they had concentrated on reinforcing Nijmegen with units of 10 SS Panzer

Division as fast as they could be ferried across the Neder Rijn at Pannerden.

In the marshy terrain of the Betuwe between Arnhem and Nijmegen, infantry and guns were more important than tanks, and it was with these principally that they had already formed a screen at Ressen, south of Elst, facing towards the Waal. This was to have been merely the preliminary to an attack to clear the British and Americans out of Nijmegen. But few pontoons were available and ferrying was a slow business.

The consequent delay was a direct result of Colonel Frost's hold on the northern end of Arnhem road bridge, which for more than three days had closed to the Germans the only good route to Nijmegen. The British defence of Arnhem bridge had collapsed only an hour or so before the first two British tanks raced across Nijmegen bridge, and the way was open to the Germans to reinforce rapidly in the Betuwe. But with the capture of the bridge intact, their last chance to re-take Nijmegen had gone. And the bridge was intact, largely because Field-Marshal Model had wished to use it for his own attack.

General Bittrich stated:

> After reconnoitring the bridgehead I suggested to Field Marshal Model that the Nijmegen bridge, which had already had a demolition charge in position, should be blown up. Field Marshal Model rejected this suggestion ... arguing that the bridgehead might be the point of departure for future attacks towards the south.

Arnhem road bridge had not been prepared for demolition, and at the end some of Frost's men gave their lives uselessly in trying to prevent what they thought was a last-minute attempt by the Germans to blow it up, actually the last thing the Germans wanted.

The capture of Arnhem bridge intact was Harzer's primary objective. Even Nijmegen bridge was prepared only for part-demolition. There was no intention of dropping the entire structure into the water, as the Dutch had done in 1940, but

merely to blow a large gap in the roadway north of the great
centre span, so that if the bridge was recovered it would be
repairable. The man who saved Nijmegen bridge for the Allies
was therefore Field-Marshal Model.

As Colonel Breitmeyer pointed out, in strict military logic
the bridge should have been blown, regardless of Model's
order, as soon as the Grenadiers had taken the Valkhof and so
commanded its approaches. The confusion of the Germans, and
the number of different units by then well mixed up, probably
prevented this. 'It seemed to me,' said Breitmeyer, 'that there
was no one person on the spot, on their side who was capable
of taking a decision. Its capture, in the event, meant very little,
if anything. The bridge was not much used after, and so all that
hard fighting was for nothing.'

CHAPTER TWELVE

The Betuwe: 21 September

The 21st of September was the day on which Market Garden was irretrievably finished. This was not apparent at the time, certainly not immediately, because communications were so poor that the commanders had insufficient information, particularly as to the situation in Arnhem. On that day, a number of separate movements were taking place that were to prove immediately decisive.

The most important movement, we can see now, was that of the Wossowski Battalion of recruits and NCO instructors from the Hermann Göring Division, which had started their cycle-ride from Katwijk-an-Zee to Arnhem on Sunday, 17 September. On 20 September, they had been combing through a woodland area by the Ede–Arnhem road where paratroops were supposed to be, and had found only dead men.

At dawn on the 21st they took their place in the western cordon formed by a rag-bag of units provisionally known as 'Tettau's Division', (after its commander) which was not a division at all, lacking all organization and equipment, including even field kitchens. Many of the 'battalions' in the 'division' were not battalions either, but merely collections of refugee soldiers from the debacle in Belgium and Holland who had been stopped by the field police and sent to a collecting centre.

In such a 'division' the young recruits of Wossowski's command ranked as 'elite troops', and no doubt this was why they were directed down a country road from Wolfhezen towards the 100-foot-high hill of Westerbouwing, overlooking the Neder Rijn ferry, and also overlooking the long, sausage-like perimeter now held by the airborne troops west of Arnhem.

After riding down the road from Wolfhezen towards Oosterbeek, they turned off on to a narrow forest track and stopped,
still sitting on their bicycles, in no recognizable military formation, and 'quite unworried', according to one of the
NCOs, Herbert Kessler.

> There was no trace of the enemy anywhere, when suddenly,
> from the flank, we were attacked by murderous machine-
> gun fire. Some were hit before they had time even to throw
> themselves to the ground, let alone take cover. On the left of
> the path was a hedge and low trees, and at their edge the Inn
> Westerbouwing with an observation tower in which the
> enemy had obviously sited a defensive position. From there,
> the English must have watched our unit approach, brought
> machine-guns into position, and opened fire. When we had
> got over the first shock, the order came through: 'Company
> attack – attack!' The heavy train had already set up their
> MGs and were busily returning the fire. The soldiers snapped
> out of their surprise and started to go forward into the brush
> and open fire, so that we could not hear our own weapons in
> action. In this way, single groups penetrated the low wood,
> moved towards the hotel, and occupied the building in which
> the enemy still was. The first prisoners were taken in the
> observation tower and sent to the rear. Superficially, the first
> sight of the enemy soldiers confirmed that these were indeed
> elite troops, fellows tall as trees, well fed, and excellently
> equipped.

Regrouping around the hotel, the Luftwaffe soldiers then
carried the attack forward towards Oosterbeek itself, and the
heights of Westerbouwing were securely in German hands.

The hill overlooked the low-lying polderland on both sides
of the Neder Rijn, at Oosterbeek and far over the Betuwe, so
that the roads leading to the ferry site from both banks of the
river were clearly commanded. This ferry site was the objective
of British and Canadian Engineer units that had just moved up

Pillbox of the Maginot Line, 1940

Dutch defences, 1940

German airborne attack on The Hague, 1940

The German Army crosses the Rhine: May 1940

Nijmegen Road Bridge, 1940

Arnhem Road Bridge, 1940

Blitzkrieg, May 1940: parachutists rush the bridge from both ends simultaneously

Dordrecht Bridge, 10 May 1940; Germans holding the bridge

Left: Nijmegen Road Bridge, 1944; British Army transport crossing.
Right: A German Mark 14 tank knocked out at Arnhem Bridge, 1944

Nijmegen Rail Bridge, 29 September 1944

'London Bridge' over the Rhine at Rees

Rhine bridging: Emmerich, 1945

Hohenzollern Bridge, Cologne, 1945   Remagen, 1950

Scottish troops cross the Rhine, 23 March 1945

Remagen Bridge, 1945

Arnhem and the Neder Rijn: mid-1945

from Bourg Leopold to Nijmegen. The original orders were to build class-40 rafts on the Betuwe side of the river in order to ferry tanks across to the north bank. Eventually, they rolled across Grave bridge, but instead of proceeding immediately to the ferry opposite Westerbouwing went into a staging area on the outskirts of Nijmegen. In front, Arnhem was still unattainable; and behind, the road had been cut.

The two flanking corps had barely reached Eindhoven, so a 30-mile stretch of highway was wide open to any sort of attack. A concerted assault from both sides of the corridor was being planned by the Germans for the following day, but many of the attacks were almost accidental, and the 101st Airborne were too thin on the ground to do more than mount a mobile defence as the supply columns moved up in two lines, the vehicles jammed nose to tail, the traffic movement being interrupted from time to time by German traffic movements taking place at right-angles to the British line of advance, as German units escaping from Belgium and Holland collided with it and were forced to fight their way home.

On the morning of 21 September, the battle was still going on inside Nijmegen. Although the bridges had been taken, only a part of the town had been captured. At dawn, the armoured cars of the Household Cavalry moved off for the small bridgehead in the Betuwe, in order to assist the Irish Guards on the main Arnhem road and also to probe for weak spots on the flanks. They failed to find a way through the defences the Germans had established, and so there was nothing for it but a head-on attack by the tanks directly down the road to Ressen, Elst, and Arnhem, where the armoured vehicles on the raised road had to advance on a one-tank front, perched up like coconuts to be knocked off by the anti-tank guns already placed there in readiness.

The hasty nature of the operation, due to its urgency, played a major part in taking away what little chance there was of success. The situation (we now know, but it was far from clear to those concerned at the time) was not unlike that at Valkenswaard. The single good road. A determined enemy with anti-tank guns and infantry, plus tanks, sited in orchards on either side of the road. And again the Irish Guards attacking with the support of Typhoons, plus infantry from another division, backed by artillery.

But this was not a set-piece attack, it was improvised at the end of a long line of communications. The losses sustained by the Irish Guards at Valkenswaard and after had not been made good; they were seriously under-strength. The arrangements for Typhoon support to blast the enemy guns and armour were haphazard, particularly the wireless link, which failed; artillery support was not immediately available and when it did become available later, was pathetically weak. The additional infantry were not British, but American airborne, who were not allowed to take part in the armoured advance; and there were some misunderstandings between them, because British tanks and American paratroopers had not been trained to work together.

The 10th SS Panzer Division 'Frundsberg' held an east–west-aligned blocking position, facing south to Nijmegen, astride both the main road and the secondary roads (which were unsuitable for tanks). Later in the day, so that Frundsberg could give undivided attention to the spearheads of XXX Corps, Harzer formed a north–south-aligned blocking position to the west, facing west, with the miscellaneous units that were now part of the 9th SS Panzer Division 'Hohenstuffen'.

The German defences were then L-shaped, with the upper stroke of the 'L' on the Nijmegen–Arnhem railway embankment, the lower stroke consisting of SS troops blocking the main approach and with their screens out as far as the Waal in the south-east corner of the 'Island'. When the leading Irish Guards tanks drove over the bridge at 0300 on 21 September, there was virtually no information to be had from the Americans as to what lay ahead, and even adequate maps were lacking. In a properly prepared attack, defence overproof sheets were issued, showing the enemy positions in detail, down to individual machine-gun sites. But this takes time, and there was no time.

There had been much criticism of the lack of urgency in XXX Corps, made mainly at the time by 1 Airborne Division, who thought then that they were taking on the bulk of the German forces and could not understand why the spearheads were not simply driving down the road; and did not realize that the main German effort was being made, not at Arnhem, but to the south at Nijmegen. The airborne were not fighting two panzer divisions; the only panzer division worthy of the name was the 10th SS, and they were mainly concerned to stop the spearheads of XXX Corps. This criticism was based on incomplete information and is not now normally made in airborne circles. However, neither the Irish Guards nor the American airborne were entirely happy with their own efforts to get forward that day.

The advance towards Arnhem was slower than it should have been for a variety of reasons, and there have been accusations of negligence and sluggish reactions made on both sides. Exhaustion, over-extended supply lines, and lack of adequate air support all contributed to gradual loss of impetus.

The only available infantry division – the 43rd Wessex – was with its 5,000 vehicles stretched out all the way from Nijmegen to Eindhoven in the confusion of the fighting along the centre line. It may perhaps seem unfair to give the 'casting vote' to the Germans, but Oberst Harzer, a panzer leader of great experience, was on this same day confronted with a similar problem – the unsuitability of the Betuwe for tanks; and on the following night, what happened to his Tigers at the hands of the 43rd Infantry Division spelled out in capitals the valid reason why the Irish Guards had waited for daylight before attacking.

They were still attacking, under a pathetic artillery barrage, when the final airborne reinforcements for Arnhem arrived – the 1st Polish Parachute Brigade – little more than 700 strong, the last Oxo cube for the lion. Half the transport aircraft had lost their way in bad weather conditions, or been shot down, before this forlorn little band arrived.

The first Dakota transport planes were sighted at quarter past four and the Germans greeted them with a heavy barrage of flak which swept up to meet them from positions half a mile ahead of the leading Irish Guards tanks and 'D' Squadron cars [wrote Major Orde]. The pilots, undeterred by the bursting shells, deviated neither right nor left, but flew straight on with extreme gallantry. Many planes could be seen to have been hit and crashed before attaining their objective. The others, enveloped in bursting shells and appearing to the ground onlookers to be extremely cumbersome and slow, carried on.

The air forces were now paying in full for having refused to risk flak losses on the first day when this would have been justified by the immediate capture of the bridges; or rather, the aircrews were paying for a decision taken much higher up. And the Luftwaffe were making them pay with fighters as well as flak, for in spite of concentrated attacks on the German aircraft industry in 1944 by both the British and American air forces, German aircraft production had reached its highest peak of the war. In this month, September 1944, the Luftwaffe received 3,013 single-engined fighter aircraft, newly built or repaired.

All at once the air seemed filled with hundreds of parachutes like so many swinging mushrooms floating slowly down to earth. One failed to open and plummeted to the ground. The rest disappeared behind the horizon and the village of Elst [wrote Major Orde]. The ground battle, which had appeared to halt momentarily to gaze skywards at the arriving Poles, was quickly jerked back to its own sphere of action by a thud, followed by the crackle of exploding bullets, as yet another Irish Guards tank was hit and burst into flames. Traffic piled up behind the stricken Sherman and although several other tanks tried every trick they knew to get off the road and continue cross-country, they only succeeded in getting themselves hopelessly bogged down. Infantry was the one hope of forcing a way up the road to Elst, and they could only achieve their object if supported by an adequate artillery barrage.

The feeble shelling that day was due to an ammunition shortage caused by the cutting of the 'corridor' from time to time, and this was due to become absolute the next day.

The Poles should have landed at Driel, not at Elst, so that they could cross the Neder Rijn by the ferry into the airborne perimeter at Oosterbeek, under the hill of Westerbouwing. But the hill, held only by a platoon of the Border Regiment, had been captured that morning by Herbert Kessler's company of the Wossowski Battalion. The Poles had been dropped half a day too late, and in the wrong place. And by landing successfully near Elst, nor far from the main Nijmegen–Arnhem road, they had proved wrong the experts who had declared that the terrain on the Betuwe was unsuitable for parachutists.

But, at the same time, they had not proved right the experts who had declared that the flak defences on the Betuwe were too heavy. Most of the guns had only just come into position, rushed there from the Ruhr; and, while the landings on 17 September came as a complete surprise, not to say shock, to the Germans, on the 21st they were receiving advance warning by radio from their coastal fortesses in France and Holland of the incoming fleets of vulnerable transport planes.

The Germans were alarmed by the Polish landing, by accident so near to the main Arnhem–Nijmegen road; Model and Bittrich did not realize it was an error, they thought it was an attempt to cut the road and to move into the rear of 10 SS Panzer Division, which was holding a blocking position against the advance of XXX Corps.

Harzer was given the task of stopping the expected eastward attack of the Poles, and he encountered exactly the same problem already met by the Irish Guards at Ressen. 'Unfortunately, the terrain round Driel did not permit the use of tanks, otherwise we would have managed to scatter or destroy this Polish parachute bridge before nightfall,' he was to comment.

The solution was infantry, and it was mainly with infantry, German and Dutch, that he set up on this day the 'Barrier Unit Harzer', which took over a north–south defensive line along the Arnhem–Elst railway embankment. The result was to relieve the immediate pressure on the airborne perimeter around Oosterbeek, and to provide a start-line for an attack across the Betuwe towards Driel.

After taking Westerbouwing early in the morning, Herbert Kessler's company had carried on the attack, and by noon was 'completely shattered', according to notes he made at the time.

> Fighting amongst the trees made it particularly difficult to recognize the enemy. Snipers up in the trees caused considerable losses, enemy automatic weapons changed their positions frequently and it was therefore very difficult to silence them and there were more losses.

Half the company of some 300 men were dead or wounded by nightfall, and after they had gone into reserve that evening

> the English supply planes arrived and disgorged their loads. There was no clear front line and this caused a large percentage of the parachutes to come down in the German positions. The soldiers became their own suppliers and were not dependent on the unit kitchen any longer. The best and finest tinned foods, things of which one dared only dream, complemented by cigarettes and chocolate, rained down on us. We even found a folding bicycle and, to make things complete, a copy of the London *Times*. We were flabbergasted!

Re-supply of the Germans by the British and American air forces had become routine, almost from the first, because the airhead was much too large to be held for long. And because the Allied air commanders had refused to take merely theoretical heavy losses in order to establish a realistic perimeter around the bridges, they now took actual losses that were even heavier in a cause that was lost, and in doing so helped the enemy more than their own troops.

Lieutenant Colonel M. S. Packe, service corps commander of the airborne, estimated afterwards that of the 1,431 tons of supplies dropped by the RAF, less than 200 tons were recovered by the British. The rest went to the Germans. This was a direct result of a perimeter too large to be held.

CHAPTER THIRTEEN

To Driel: 22 September

'Without meaning any offence to General Urquhart, I feel that he stuck too stubbornly to his orders. German paratroopers would have occupied the entire town of Arnhem on the first day. That would have made the attempted counter-attacks less simple. In the event, he played into our hands by staying at Oosterbeek.' So Oberst Harzer wrote in answer to various queries I put to him. This mistake, he explained, gave him time to collect his units around Arnhem in an orderly manner, reinforce Nijmegen, and then turn against the airborne perimeter at last and give

the troops of Urquhart real hell. And apart from that, I had moved a 'Barrier Unit Harzer' into the marsh between Nijmegen and Arnhem, so that the attack to the north was indeed not a pleasant walk for the 43rd British Division. There was very little they could do to launch an attack, because it was possible to move only on top of the dykes.

This is the position as it really was, on the German side. But it was not apparently the picture as seen by Second Army intelligence at the time. That, as ever, was incredibly over-optimistic. In his history of the Household Cavalry, Major Orde quotes the narrative of his CO, Colonel Abel Smith:

Late in the evening of the 21st the following orders were received by 2 HCR: *'Intelligence believes that the enemy will withdraw during the night. 43 Infantry Division will relieve the Guards Armoured Division during the night, and con-*

tinue the advance next day. One Squadron of 2 HCR will advance to Arnhem, covering 43 Division at first light.' On receipt of these orders I immediately drove off to 43rd Division Headquarters as the Intelligence appreciation of the enemy intentions seemed extraordinary. The enemy had fought most tenaciously all day, and if they could hold us a little longer, the airborne troops would be doomed. The G1 was soon found. He was not yet in the picture, having only just arrived to take over. The Divisional Commander had gone to bed, giving orders that he was not to be disturbed.

Colonel Abel Smith therefore passed on the order, with an amendment that showed his own doubt in the belief that the enemy would withdraw. His narrative continues:

It was appreciated that the enemy could hold all the direct routes to Arnhem; therefore patrols would in the first place move east and west along the north bank of the Waal in the hope that the enemy would not expect us in that direction. Should either patrol get through, after two or three kilometres, it would move north to the Neder Rijn.

The Household Cavalry had tried precisely the same gambit on 21 September, and failed. There was really no reason why they should succeed on the following day. But on the 22nd, luck was on their side. September is a month for mist, haze, and fog, and at dawn the north bank of the Waal was shrouded in a thick mist – impossible for aircraft but perfect operating conditions for probing patrols of armoured cars.

Even so, the troop that tried to infiltrate to the east was soon held up by an anti-tank gun screen near Bemmel. Captain Wrottesley's troop, which moved west along the north bank of the Waal in visibility of about 50 feet, passed through the defenders' screen without incident, although they could hear the Germans talking.

Only one German was actually seen in the fog, and because it was important to keep silent, he was not fired at. At about

0800 hours, the armoured cars had linked up with the Poles south of the Neder Rijn near Driel. There they remained, to act as wireless link and to help the Poles hold off Harzer's men, who from their defensive blocking position along the north–south railway line were now sending out patrols preparatory to an attack. 'The Polish general was charming but quite fanatical, and if he had thought it the least possible would have asked us to fly our armoured cars into battle!' commented Lieutenant A. V. Young.

Major Peter Herbert, commanding C Squadron, had decided to reinforce Wrottesley with Lieutenant Young's troop before the fog lifted. They took the same route, going about six miles to the west along the banks of the Waal, then turning north and on coming to the Neder Rijn turning east towards Driel.

'Things were exceptionally quiet at this time,' wrote Young. 'We passed several Mark IVs which we liked to presume at the time had been knocked out, but these we discovered later from Peter Herbert proved to be very much alive!' The Germans did know that these armoured cars were British, but the fog was still thick and the vehicles were out of sight before a gun could be swung on to them.

Having reached Driel, Young then went off with one other car to reconnoitre possible crossing-points of the Neder Rijn, fought a German patrol, picked up three parachutists, and captured a map belonging to the river engineer at Driel. His wirelessed reports, together with those of Captain Wrottesley, were the first definite and detailed news to be received of the British position in Arnhem since Market Garden had begun.

And then the fog began to lift.

As it did so, C Squadron HQ and Lieutenant Hopkinson's troop were passing through the leading elements of 43 Division, which had come into the bridgehead during the night, their carriers and trucks parked beside the road. The route ahead, said Lieutenant Young, consisted of 'very, very narrow country roads, in the main sided with ditches, which you will appreciate is very difficult operating country for armoured fighting vehicles'. Young's troop had made it. The remainder got no further than the village of Osterhout, for as they emerged from the forward positions of the infantry, the mist began to clear and within a few minutes normal daylight conditions obtained.

Unfortunately, the optimistic intelligence appreciation, apparently borne out by reports of the ease with which two troops of armoured cars got through to Arnhem, misled Major General Thomas, the commander of 43 Division. It seemed as though immediate and vigorous action might secure a breakthrough, while a delay could be fatal. He therefore cancelled his fire-plan, which would have required time to execute. But the intelligence estimate was false, and the success of the armoured cars a result of good fortune. Further, the division had not yet been able to deploy as a division because of the traffic jams in the 'corridor', and even if all of it had been in Nijmegen, the bridgehead over the Waal was still far too small.

The attack on Osterhout was therefore made by a single company of 7 Somerset Light Infantry, part of 214 Brigade, commanded by Brigadier H. Essame. His brigade was to come into the bridgehead over the railway bridge, while 129 Brigade was to enter the Betuwe over the road bridge to support the direct road approach to Arnhem via Ressen and Elst. This brigade was still strung out along the road to Nijmegen and even 214 Brigade in the lead had not yet had time or space in which to deploy. The battalion following the Somersets was 5 Duke of Cornwall's Light Infantry, and they spent the morning waiting their turn in the streets of Nijmegen.

The story is best told in a contemporary narrative written by Lieutenant Colonel George Taylor, who commanded the Duke of Cornwall's Light Infantry that day, and whose job was to pass through the Somersets after they had taken Osterhout.

One of the difficulties that had to be faced up to at this period was the limited amount of artillery ammunition available. For this reason the 7th SLI had to spend a great deal of time finding out exactly where enemy strongposts were located before the precious artillery ammunition could be

used. The methods left to do this quickly are generally limited to attempting to draw fire by feint attacks or the use of
fighting patrols. There is, of course, always the hope that the
fighting patrols will suffice to dispose of the enemy. This,
however, is seldom realized in practice. Once an enemy is
finally 'dug in' then to attack him without firm support is a
form of suicide. At Osterhout the enemy resisted tenaciously, and Major Sidney Young, the best company commander in the unit, was killed. It became obvious to the CO
of 7 SLI, Lieutenant Colonel Borrodaile, that a battalion
attack with full scale artillery support would be necessary.
This attack by the Somersets was fixed for 1600 hours. In the
early afternoon, the 5th DCLI moved over the railway bridge
into an assembly area behind the big embankment. At about
this time, a Staff Officer of XXX Corps came forward and told
me that news had been received that the 1st British Airborne
Division were in a desperate position and that the DCLI
must link up with them that night. Two Dukws carrying
ammunition and medical supplies were given to the battalion
to be delivered to the airborne troops. The great risk of the
operation was obvious to all. However, it was made clear to
all concerned that the stakes were so great that nothing was
to be allowed to stop the 5th DCLI and the tanks of 4/7
Dragoon Guards.

The plan devised by Brigadier H. Essame was designed to
open the way 'brutally and effectively' with a 40-minute barrage from the divisional artillery, a medium regiment, a heavy
battery, and the brigade mortars. This was the time to spend
what little there was in the way of ammunition. Then the 7
SLI were to break through Osterhout, the DCLI were to pass
through them, and while part of this battalion held the flanks,
and while the Germans were still off balance, the remainder
were to mount on the tanks, carriers, and other vehicles for a
headlong dash to Driel.

Under the cover of a heavy artillery barrage, the 7th

Somersets swept over the embankment to the attack [wrote
Colonel Taylor]. Soon, news reached us of their success and I
gave the command, 'Advance'. Prisoners, many of them
wounded and a pitiful sight, were being brought in by the
Somersets as our 'B' Company felt its way forward through
the shattered village. Rumours of enemy tanks caused them
to move off the main road and go through a tangle of gardens
and orchards, which caused a slight delay . . . But no sign of
the enemy, so I told them on the wireless, 'Push on, change of
plan, seize "D" Company's objective,' as this would save
time. Then through the village came the head of the main
body of the battalion and it began to form upon the road
north-east of Osterhout. Before it lay a fleeting chance.
Would it be possible to make it before the enemy recovered
his balance? Disturbing news was received that two enemy
tanks could be seen about 1,000 yards away. The plan was
reshaped and I ordered, 'Ignore them, mount your tanks and
carriers.' Speed was more than ever essential, for the enemy
would move his reserves to close the gap. Also, night was fast
approaching and in the dark it would not be possible to move
more than a mile or so. The vital minutes were flying. I threw
off my equipment and ran to the slow, plodding platoon,
galvanizing them into action, as they came forward from the
village. Soon they were all mounted on tank, carrier, or
towed anti-tank gun.

The four infantry companies were split up between two distinct groups of vehicles, the leading column consisting mainly
of armoured vehicles and anti-tank guns, the rear column being
made up mainly of 'soft-skinned' vehicles and anti-tank guns.

Off the battalion moved, trucks clanking, motors roaring –
dashing headlong [wrote Colonel Taylor]. Ignoring the
danger of ambush and mines, they were soon in the streets
of Valburg. The Dutch inhabitants, somewhat astonished at
this eruption of armour and men, went wild with joy, shouting and cheering till their lungs almost burst, as the column

moved quickly on. The light was fading rapidly as the head
of it reached Driel, the leading tank being blown up on a
mine at the entrance leading to the village. The journey of
about ten miles had been completed in under thirty
minutes.

What they had done, after 7 SLI had torn a hole in the
southern blocking position held by 10 SS Panzer Division, was
to ride right across the front of 'Barrier Unit Harzer', with their
eastern flank open to attack which was not long in coming.

The sound of battle could not be heard behind the armoured column, and very shortly afterwards a DR came up
to the command carrier and reported to me that enemy
tanks were attacking the soft vehicle column. He had been
standing at the cross-roads between Valburg and Elst to
direct traffic and, seeing some tanks approach, had signalled
them on. A few seconds later, to his horror, he saw the dark
German crosses on the tanks. Fortunately, his motor-cycle
was just round the corner, facing the right direction, and
running to it, he moved up to Driel with all speed to report. I
realized that, in the darkness, the troops of the soft vehicle
column would have a very good chance of holding off the
tank attack, and I turned my attention to the problems of
linking up with the Airborne troops and delivering the two
Dukw-loads of supplies.

A first-hand account of conditions in Arnhem was received
from two staff officers of 1 Airborne Division, Lieutenant
Colonels Charles Mackenzie and E. C. W. Meyers, who had just
rowed across the Neder Rijn in a reconnaissance boat and were
on their way to contact XXX Corps. They had had no news of
Frost's battalion at the bridge for 24 hours and assumed correctly that he had been overwhelmed.

Colonel Taylor's first thought was to re-take the road
bridge, but further discussion convinced him that it would be
impossible, and he decided to concentrate on getting men and

supplies across the river, while firmly holding the south bank. In the event, only about 60 Poles got across. The transport consisted of six reconnaissance boats and one RAF dinghy, soon reduced by two reconnaissance boats. The airborne engineers had intended to pull them back and forwards across the river on signal cable, on the same principle as a ferry, but the current was too strong and the cable broke. The two Dukws never reached the water. They were big, awkward vehicles – in effect, amphibious, open-topped trucks – and although they handled quite nicely in the water, the mist, the darkness, the mud, and the constricted roads defeated their drivers. They ended up in the ditch short of the river, hopelessly bogged, defeated by the flood plain of the Rhine.

In fact, the German armoured column was moving very cautiously, with their own infantry right beside them in immediate contact, as Company Sergeant Major Philp of the Duke of Cornwall's Light Infantry discovered. His carrier was unable to keep up with Major Parker's jeep, the vehicle immediately ahead, and Philp saw it pass a tank that he presumed was British. 'When I was within a hundred yards,' he wrote, 'I saw that there were a column of tanks and, more important, they were all marked with the black cross.'

It was a traffic misunderstanding of the worst sort. The small carrier could not stop, but charged on; two of the German tanks politely pulled over to the side of the road; but the third did not get out of the way, and the carrier skidded to a standstill, head-on to the German tank and touching it. The tank commander leaned out of the tank and began to remove his goggles, whereupon Philp shot him. Both tank machine-gunners opened fire, but one gun was mounted too high and the other too low to hit the crew of the carrier, so they bailed out. As Philp stood up, in order to jump over the side of the carrier, he hit his head on the barrel of the 88-millimetre gun of the tank. Then he and his crew drived straight into a mud-filled ditch overgrown with reeds: 'From this ditch I observed five Tiger tanks on the road above us, and about a dozen enemy infantry on the road about one hundred yards away.' In the

failing light, they escaped along the ditch and reported the
position of the tanks to the oncoming 'soft' column, which
detoured round them and reached Driel safely, leaving an infantry company to hold the road.

Major Parker, assuming that the tanks would return to Elst
for the night rather than remain in contact with infantry in
the darkness, decided to set up an ambush for them at a convenient crossroads.

I gave orders for complete silence [he wrote], and no small
arms rounds to be fired unless attacked by infantry, because
of the flash; Piats to be fired in a volley of three when given
the order. No firing to take place until the leading tanks had
hit the mines [which they had laid across the road]. We then
heard the Tiger tanks shooting up 'B' Company, and as this
was happening, a German motor-cycle combination came up
the road from Elst, presumably to contact the tanks. He
blew up, literally, on our '75' mines. Next, we heard the
tanks returning, headed by a DR. He also blew up. The leading tank was firing Véry lights every thirty seconds, to light
the way. It was fairly obvious that they were 'windy'. There
were five tanks. As the first tank reached the '75' mines, I
gave orders for groups two and three to fire. There was a
tremendous explosion and six Piat bombs hit the tank. This
put him completely out of action. The next tank hit the
mines, and received the same treatment. The third tank
tried to back out, but hit a string of mines which had been
pulled in behind it, came to a halt on the initial explosion,
and, every time he tried to move, another mine went off.
Private Brown went within a few yards before he fired his
Piat; the tank was knocked out, but so was one of Brown's
eyes. As he was put on the jeep and just before he lost
consciousness, he said, 'I don't care – I knocked the so-and-
so thing out.' It was his first action. The two remaining tanks
completely panicked and tried to back out in a hurry. They
both ditched themselves, the crews escaping into the wood.
CSM Philp then made sure that every tank was incapable of

further action, by dropping grenades down the turrets.

When the Poles first arrived in the airborne perimeter, some mistakes occurred, aided by the fact that their berets were grey, not red, and possibly a little trigger-happiness. Lieutenant G. A. Paull, an anti-tank gun troop commander, wrote

> There were many cases of mistaken identity, resulting in exchanges of fire between friendly troops. A Polish officer came to me in an understandably agitated condition and in broken English said, 'Our men are shooting each other.' Some sense of sanity in this respect was fortunately restored before getting too serious.

Having been baulked in his attempt to get supplies over the river, Colonel Taylor laid on a fire-plan for 23 September: 'If we could not carry it across, we would throw it across.' But not only were the airborne cut off, but the DCLI group also. Indeed, to Trooper J. W. Conway, of Lieutenant Young's troop, the situation then appeared bleak: 'We had the choice of either being taken prisoners or fighting to the last man.' Major General Stanislaw Sosabowski of the 1st Polish Independent Parachute Brigade Group had already used Conway's wireless set to broadcast a message to XXX Corps: 'All we can do now is trust in God. We have no food or ammunition. God bless you all.'

Even more serious was the fact that Nijmegen had now been cut off by strong counter-attacks from both sides of the 'corridor' near Uden and Veghel. Instead of being available for operations in the Betuwe, the Grenadier and Coldstream Guards had to be sent hurriedly in the opposite direction – back towards Eindhoven – to reopen the road. Fighting continued there for four days and during this period very little got through. XXX Corps also began to run short of food as well as ammunition. While the Germans in Arnhem were feasting on British rations, XXX Corps was in part subsisting on captured German rations. It was time, reluctantly, to decide to withdraw from Arnhem. And because of the wide, fast river with its muddy flood approaches, this would not be easy to carry out.

CHAPTER FOURTEEN

Relief and Evacuation of Arnhem:
23–26 September

On 23 September the situation in the Betuwe was still shaky, the reinforcement of Driel and the advance to Elst proving to be the unpleasant walk that Harzer had arranged. On this day, Brigadier Essame's brigade took Elst, not along the main Arnhem–Nijmegen road, but by driving from the west and penetrating Harzer's 'barrier' of Dutch and German infantry backed by tanks. The job of 43 Division was to ferry Poles across the river and put two of their own battalions across to enlarge the airborne bridgehead on the far bank. The task was far beyond the boating resources of the division; not more than a few hundred Poles got across, and they left the boats on the far side, where they were shelled to pieces in the morning.

The Germans held the high ground at Westerbouwing and north of Arnhem, with perfect coverage over both the bridgehead and the Betuwe; further, the approaches to the river were part of the soggy flood plain and were even more of an obstacle than the fast-flowing water; finally, the Germans were expecting them and had put out forward posts along the polder.

The 200 Poles who got across were more or less cancelled out by the 500 German Navy marines who joined Krafft's force opposite them on this day, although these men were without officers, almost without NCOs, and lacked both greatcoats and blankets. Stiffened with SS, however, they were useful in defence, always the easiest form of warfare.

The position on 24 September was that the Germans had received tank reinforcements — the first of 60 Tigers from

Heavy Tank Battalion 506, which had arrived from Germany. But these great vehicles could not be used in masses in the narrow streets of Oosterbeek, and 45 of the 60 were given to 10 SS Panzer Division to thicken up the firepower of the defensive positions round Elst. Their guns completely outranged those of the British and American tanks.

As far as the airborne perimeter was concerned, the Germans decided to assault it with artillery and mortars, to save the lives of their infantry. They did, however, attempt to cut it off from the Neder Rijn by advancing along the river bank.

The British decision to withdraw from Arnhem appears to have been made on the morning of 24 September by General Horrocks, then at the headquarters of 43 Division. A possible factor in the decision to retreat may have been the fate of the class 40 rafts that were to ferry tanks over to the airborne; they had landed up in Elst and been captured.

In any event, the first stage of withdrawal was to put a battalion from the Wessex Division – 4 Dorsets – over the Neder Rijn to form a firm screen behind which the airborne could retire to the river and be ferried back across it. The assault-crossing of the Neder Rijn by 43 Division was definitely off. The code-word for the evacuation to take place would be 'Berlin'.

The attempt to pass 4 Dorsets over was an almost complete failure. The plan looked all right, provided that the nature of the terrain was not taken into account, plus the fact that the Germans held the 100-foot-high hill of Westerbouwing. Only about 300 men got across, plus a few Poles. The latter were not cooperative and held on to the boats for some hours without making much use of them; possibly they felt that they were fighting soldiers, not mud-bound pack mules *cum* water-rats. The boats were then taken away by the Dorsets, whose own boats were in a bogged truck miles back towards Nijmegen.

Consequently, only two companies were able to make the attempt, and they had to wait three hours before struggling to get the boats and their own weapons and equipment by hand some 600 yards through orchards, over the flood dyke, down the steep, muddy face of the dyke, and over the flood plain to the river, which was now flowing at its fastest speed, to face a 50 per cent loss of boats during the crossing.

Major W. M. C. Whittle, commanding B Company, wrote in the regimental history:

> On the spot the strength of B Company was 2 officers and less than 30 other ranks. Where the trees started there was a steep bank about 100 feet high, and the enemy were well dug in on the top of it. We started the assault and met very heavy opposition; it was only too easy for the Jerries on top to roll grenades down on us, and we eventually gained the top at the expense of 50 per cent of our strength, for when we occupied the trenches at the top we were reduced to about fifteen.

The other parties, similarly scattered, arrived if at all in small groups and were soon surrounded and forced to surrender. Major Whittle's party dug-in and waited for daylight, which brought sniping, machine-gun fire, a polite offer in perfect English to surrender, and an attack from 'a well-meaning couple of Spitfires'. A few Dukws had got across with supplies, but even these were swept wildly downstream by the force of the current.

There were 20 Dukws in all and the officer who brought them up to Driel was Lieutenant Colonel E. C. W. Myers, Commander, Royal Engineers, of 1 Airborne Division, who had crossed the Neder Rijn on 22 September with Lieutenant Colonel Charles Mackenzie in order to contact XXX Corps, a desperate expedient made necessary by the wireless failures. Now, his intention was to get back into the perimeter with the Dukws and their supplies. He chose the ferry site at Heveadorp, under the hill at Westerbouwing, because here and here only did a road lead to the water's edge, carried across the flood plain by a ramp. The opposite bank was in enemy hands, but it was hoped that the Dorsets could clear it. He wrote:

> I was carrying a letter which had just arrived from General

Browning, Commander 1 Airborne Corps. Its contents, which I had memorized, gave instructions to General Urquhart, the GOC 1 Airborne Division, to withdraw the survivors of 1 Airborne Division the following night if this night's attack did not succeed in relieving the situation. We got two Dukws safely into the river. I jumped on the third; it was the last to get across. We reached the North bank, only to discover that the infantry were held up by strong enemy fire right on the banks of the river. I decided that I must get on to my own Divisional Headquarters in view of the importance of the message which I carried; for I knew, from what I had seen already, that the attack would not relieve the situation in the perimeter.

In order to reach the perimeter from the ferry site, Myers bent double and splashed eastward through the shallows of the river until he reached it.

Myers reached HQ at 0630 on 25 September, and his deputy, Lieutenant Colonel J. C. Winchester, records that Urquhart issued the plans for withdrawal about 1100. They were very simple. Two routes to the river bank were to be marked out with tape, so that the men could find their way in the dark. Winchester marked the one route, which led in several places to within 40 yards of the enemy. The men would have to muffle their boots with cloth and make sure no equipment jingled.

The ferrying operation from the southern bank was to be controlled by the Commander Royal Engineers of 43 Division, Lieutenant Colonel M. C. A. Henniker. His plan included a noisy, visual demonstration to the west by a brigade with pontoons and bridging lorries, in order to give the impression that an assault-crossing was intended at that point. Two ferry points were set up, one opposite Oosterbeek and the other downstream near Westerbouwing. Each point was manned by one British and one Canadian Field Company of Engineers, the British equipped with 16 light canvas assault boats, propelled by paddles, the Canadians equipped with 21 wooden storm boats powered by outboard motors.

The former were easier to man-handle towards the water but would not be able to cope with the current when it ran full; while the latter required about a dozen men to carry them, even when the going was fairly firm, but, although slow when heavily laden, had enough power to slant across the current without falling off downstream.

The war diary of 5 Dorsets, who formed a reception area opposite Oosterbeek, summed up the night of 25–26 September: 'The evacuation of the Airborne Forces was carried out according to plan, but torrential rain and shell and mortar fire made it a ghastly operation.'

Major H. L. Tucker, OC 23 Canadian Field Company, wrote in his report that he received his orders from Colonel Henniker at 1000 hours on 25 September, giving time only for a brief reconnaissance of the area. It did not look inviting.

The whole of this part of Holland is low-lying and the roads, which are built up well above the level of the surrounding terrain, are separated from the fields by wide, deep ditches. The roads are narrow, with soft shoulders, and totally unsuitable for heavy military traffic. Entrances to fields are also narrow and difficult to negotiate, even in the daytime when clear visibility may be had.

Eventually, he found a railway yard that offered hard standing space on which to concentrate his heavy vehicles. Two lieutenants reconnoitred the river bank for the best crossing-places and found two, but even so a bridge would have to be built on the approaches. In a few hours the convoy was brought up, the routes to the river taped, and 14 storm boats and 17 motors unloaded. Carrying them forward over the dykes was difficult.

Two floodwalls blocked the path from the off-loading area to the launching sites. The first of these was about 20 feet high with banks sloping to about 45 degrees, the second was about half the height and the slope much less severe. These obstacles became most difficult to negotiate. The heavy rain softened the ground and the churning of men's feet as they struggled over with the storm boats soon created a slippery mess which lent no footing whatsoever. Hand ropes were fixed, but even with these the going was extremely difficult. The first boat was launched at 2130 hours, but it had been badly holed when the men carrying it slipped coming down the floodwall. It would have sunk before it could have completed a crossing. The next boat was launched at 2145 hours and set off with Lieutenant Martin in command. This boat did not return and neither Lieutenant Martin nor any of the crew has been seen or heard from since. Corporal McLachlan captained the third boat and returned bringing the first load of airborne troops; he completed 15 trips before he was relieved by a fresh crew. The fourth boat, in charge of Corporal Smith, made its way safely to the bridgehead, but swamped when a mortar fell close by on the return voyage. Smith and four of his passengers got back. The rain caused the motors to give endless trouble and was responsible for their failing altogether in many cases.

Colonel Henniker was with the assault boats of 260 Field Company of his own Division.

The first assault boats, led by a sapper subaltern, pushed off into the stream at 2115. For a long time nothing happened. I paced the shore like a cat on hot bricks oppressed by most gloomy forebodings. Had they upset the boats and all gone silently to the bottom, weighted down by steel helmets and rifles? Had they rowed straight into the waiting Hun on the far bank? Or had they merely been washed downstream to God knows where? It was a tense interval. But in battles the worst occurs as seldom as the best. Across the dark waters came the sound of dripping oars. Then I saw a boat. It held about a dozen men. I could see airborne pattern helmets. Never was there a more welcome sight. First one boat, then another, then another. About a hundred men came silently ashore with a few wounded. The boats stole back into the night. The bearing and demeanour of these men were first class. Whether reaction set in afterwards and these splendid soldiers later presented a less soldierlike appearance I do not know. Maybe, but they were all right on the night. More and more boats were launched and then I heard the motors of the Canadian storm boats start. No music could have seemed more sweet. Soon there was a steady stream of men filing back along the tapes. By the small hours of the morning the current had quickened and made the rowing of assault boats almost impossible. But the Canadian storm boats continued with unabated zest. If the assault boats got the first hauls, the storm boats certainly got the greater ones.

On the north bank, long queues of paratroopers formed along the tapes marking out the routes to the river, the noise of movement covered by heavy fire from the Wessex Division on the south bank. Major H. F. Brown, an engineer officer wrote:

> We all shaved for the first time during the operation, muffled our boots, stopped all jingles, and started off in a silent swaying crocodile for the river. I led what remained of the 4th Parachute Brigade, 54 souls. We passed very silently within 10 yards of a German mortar position and eventually, guided by glider pilots at main turnings, we reached the river banks where orderly queues of men waited their turn for the boats.

Major Winchester acted as a beachmaster on the northern shore.

> The discipline on the river bank was excellent. There were very few ferry craft and most of the men had to wait a long time under heavy shell and mortar fire. Those who were strong swimmers took to the water, stripped except for their personal weapons, and made room in the boats for non-swimmers and the wounded, of which there were many.

Private John Wilson, of 21 Independent Company, recalled:

> There was a Bofors gun firing tracer across the river to mark the spot. At this point there was an orderly queue across the polder down to the river bank, and when the occasional mortar bomb burst near by, one noticed a unified bending of the knees by this queue. Apart from that, everybody remained more intent upon maintaining his place in the line.

Wilson was unlucky and was captured on the river bank 'while waiting hopefully for some more boats'.

The combined total of those saved in the operation was under 3,000 out of the 10,095 men who had landed at Arnhem.

The German casualties seem to have been of the order of 3,000, or about half the British losses, although it is difficult for anyone to say because of the chaotic state of the hurriedly improvised units that were thrown into the battle. Harzer, looking back after more than twenty years, paid tribute to the 'valour' with which the airborne defended themselves, but wrote:

> It is with personal pride that I regard this German victory, because it was achieved, not by regular units, but by railway workers, Arbeitsdienst and Luftwaffe personnel as well, who had never been trained for infantry work and were actually unsuitable for house-to-house fighting,

CHAPTER FIFTEEN

Model's Counter-offensive on the 'Island': September—October

Up to 25 September, the British had been attacking on the 'Island', in difficult circumstances and with their supply lines cut south of Nijmegen. After only a very brief pause, the Germans went over to the offensive to drive the British out of the Betuwe. But first they had to clear the battlefield of Arnhem and round-up the remaining airborne troops, many of whom proved persistent evaders and escapers.

As the historian of 9 SS Panzer Division records, the paratroops were hated and also respected for one and the same reason – they were good fighters. Which meant heavy casualties for their opponents, and many friends killed. There was no hatred, only pity, for those British units that fought at Arnhem in an obviously incompetent manner, and were therefore not dangerous.

After the battle, more than 200 airborne men remained at large or escaped, hidden by the extremely efficient Dutch 'Underground', which did not unnecessarily provoke the Germans, apart from attacks on railways, but kept all German units under observation. They were aided by both Dutch and German rumours that the 'Island' was to be used as a springboard by the Allies for another attack to outflank the Siegfried Line and drive for the Ruhr. As a result of this, the Germans began to evacuate the civilian population from Arnhem and the Ijssel Line and the consequent movements helped to conceal the fact that a number of the 'refugees' were British soldiers in disguise.

Among them was Major Hibbert, who was still keeping a day-to-day diary, which he eventually left behind him, buried under a flagstone in the church of Otterloo, but recovered eight months later. He recorded the rumours, for instance, that Second Army had crossed the Rhine at Huissen on 30 September, and noted that the 'evaders', far from thinking at first of escape over the river, were rather concerned to organize and arm themselves in order to help with the assault-crossing when it came.

The odd thing about Market Garden and its aftermath, in contrast to 1940, was the lack of complaints about the 'Fifth Column', in spite of the fact that, this time, there really was one. True, it lingered on in British suspicions of odd incidents – a signpost turned the wrong way, suspiciously accurate artillery fire, guides who lost their way and then disappeared when the firing started, a dispatch rider who rode down a column yelling out, 'Retreat – there's a pocket panzer division up the road!' (There was.)

But, on the German side, 'Dutch terrorists' were normally invoked only as a convenient excuse for not doing what was impossible anyway. In Major Krafft's very detailed war diary, his failure to block the river road to Frost's battalion was explained by saying 'The enemy would have got to Arnhem in the shortest possible time and would not only have occupied it, but strongly fortified it with the aid of Dutch terrorists.'

Although some enthusiastic young men did turn up when the airborne first landed, they faded away with the first mortar bombs and Krafft's battalion was bothered only once, on the first day: 'We did have trouble with Dutch terrorists about 2–300 metres from the Battalion's original defence position. They were suitably dealt with!'

Much the most effective action of the Dutch was the railway strike that began on 17 September and helped paralyse German transport, although a number of the strikers were executed. Much more use could have been made of what the Resistance really had to offer – rapid telephone communications and accurate information on the enemy and his movements, but apart from the railway strike, very little appears to have been coordinated by the Allies.

The traffic across the Neder Rijn on the night of 25–26 September had consisted of 3,000 British survivors of 1 Airborne Division, going south. The traffic on the following night, going the same way, consisted of a battalion of some 500 Germans with 20-millimetre guns who were not aware that 43 Recce Regiment had posts established as far west as Randwijk. These were driven in and the position was not restored until the 27th, by counter-attack from the tanks of 8 Armoured Brigade and a battalion of 214 Infantry Brigade, which wiped out the German bridgehead. In the early hours of 29 September, the Germans attacked again, with novel means and in a vital place.

The main remaining bridges on to the Betuwe – Arnhem road bridge and Nijmegen road and rail bridges – were now of crucial importance, in view of the forthcoming German offensive against the large British and American forces being maintained there in what was, in effect, a salient thrust deep into German-held territory. How vulnerable it was is illustrated by the fact that the German positions on the 'Island' came to within 500 yards of Nijmegen road bridge on its eastern side.

Both bridges were under constant shellfire and continual air attack, and on 28 September a particularly determined assault was made at dawn. German jets diving out of the sun near-missed both bridges, 'dislodging one section of the frail railway bridge from its seating and causing slight damage to the more robust road bridge', according to Guards historians. There was no effective counter to the jets, because British jets did not arrive over Nijmegen until the spring of 1945 and these were in any case inferior to their German equivalents.

During this period there were two 'Guardians of the Bridges' at Nijmegen: Colonel Henniker, Commander Royal Engineers of the Wessex Division, who was succeeded by Colonel 'Joe' Vandeleur of the Irish Guards. As soon as the engineers had evacuated the airborne from Arnhem, they were detailed as bridge guards at Nijmegen. In addition, Colonel Henniker was given a machine-gun company, a troop of self-propelled anti-

tank guns, and a troop of towed 17-pounder anti-tank guns.
The latter were sited at the north end of the road bridge, while
the mobile SPs were held in reserve on the south bank between
the two bridges. Colonel Henniker wrote:

> From the bridge German tanks were visible. Much the like-
> liest hazard appeared to be an armoured attack. It would not
> have taken long to destroy it, because of its design. The
> bridge was a bowstring girder composed of a great steel arch
> on each side of the bridge, springing from masonry piers
> which stood in shallow water at either bank. The roadway
> was slung beneath the girder. Had German tanks been able
> to get on to the bridge, it might have been possible for their
> troops to throw a string of explosives over one of the steel
> arches and detonate it with a time switch. Quite a light
> charge placed in this manner would have demolished the
> bridge; and I made my dispositions accordingly. It did occur
> to me that saboteurs in a civilian vehicle might try to use the
> bridge and contrive to abandon a vehicle full of explosives on
> the roadway. Even though the bridge was often under fire, an
> extraordinary amount of civilian traffic flowed over it, and
> our sentries were kept busy checking it through. I asked for
> searchlights, because I saw also a possibility of the Germans
> slipping downstream with a boatload of explosives to attack
> the piers of the bridge. But the searchlights were refused by
> the nearest anti-aircraft artillery commander who pointed
> out that his responsibilities would be immeasurably in-
> creased if he had to illuminate the target he was supposed
> to defend.

Both the latter possibilities – Germans in civilian clothes in
a civilian vehicle and an approach by boat or barge along the
Waal – were of course typical ruses employed in 1940 by
Special Battalion No 100, whose task had then been the capture of the bridge, not its destruction, and they had indeed
planned to approach by water. The battalion had now been en-
larged to form the Brandenburg 'Division' and by the neatest of

ironical coincidences the reverse task – that of destroying the bridges – was given to them in 1944. But as it was 1944, they used the methods of 1944 and not those of 1940, although the principle was the same – the use of a handful of highly trained men at a key point.

They had employed the same methods against the Ben-ouville bridge, near Caen in Normandy, in June of the same year; but through an embarrassing error, the operators blew the wrong bridge – the German-held one! Consequently, the gambit did not become known to the British Army and when used at Nijmegen a few months later, came as a stunning surprise.

It was Colonel Henniker's custom to visit the bridge guards both at last light and first light, the most likely times of an attack. On the morning of 29 September he had returned to his headquarters after 'stand-to', when his adjutant came in and asked if the bridges were intact. 'Having just been down there about ten minutes before, I was surprised by this question, but the Corps Commander had received a report from the Dutch that the bridges had been blown up.' Then the telephone rang and the OC 553 Field Company was on the line to report: 'The railway bridge has been blown up.' Five minutes later the OC 204 Field Company, guarding the road bridge, wirelessed a message: 'Bridge blown up.'

I went down to the bridges and found the men standing to. The railway bridge had a pier missing. The road bridge had a hole 70 feet long in the roadway, between the main bow-string chords of the centre span just where the arch enters the main South bank pier. The stringers, crossbracing and roadway were torn to bits and folded upwards. 'How did that happen?' I asked. Nobody knew.

As the salient was very narrow and bisected by the Waal, what the Germans had done was to put a team of 12 frogmen into the water about five miles upstream of the bridges and let them ride the fast current down to the target. The explosives consisted of cigar-shaped naval mines of near-neutral buoy-ancy that would be floated down the river, guided by the frog-men.

The railway bridge party controlled two such mines, linked by 20 feet of rope, and the object was to straddle one of the bridge piers. The road bridge party had to control four such mines, also linked by rope, and again straddle a pier. Until then, they would stay on the surface; only the final placing of the cylinders required the use of breathing apparatus. Once this was done, they were to ride on down the river with the current until they were swept back into German territory again.

But, as at Caen, they over-estimated the distance they had travelled — an easy mistake, particularly on such a wide river with featureless banks, quite devoid of landmarks — and so emerged too early on to territory being observed by part of 43 Recce Regiment and the 'Free Dutch'. Two of the frogmen were fatally wounded in the shooting that then occurred. Two others escaped.

The railway bridge torpedo-mines had been well placed, each containing 1,220 pounds of hecanite, and this had brought down the centre span. But the road bridge party had chosen the wrong pier to attack; instead of the north pier in some five feet of water, they had chosen the shallower south-ern pier. In order to make the mines 'live', a special float chamber had to be released. The mines then turned vertical and sank, starting up a clock time fuse. There was insufficient water around the south pier and only one of the mines ex-ploded, the others being stranded on the mud at low water, in a horizontal position, and the pier itself was not destroyed, only part of the decking above. This was quickly bridged by XXX Corps Engineers, while Dukws, storm boats, and raft ferries kept the traffic moving.

In his review, the chief engineer of 21 Army Group, Major General Sir J. D. Inglis, reported the frogmen's attack as 'suc-cessful' generally and for the railway bridge 'highly successful' (it was out of action for the rest of the war). He wrote:

This incident led to the provision at Nijmegen of a whole series of different types of booms varying from naval river nets down to balloon cables supported on jerry-cans. The problem soon became a vicious circle. The river nets were extremely difficult to moor in the fast current of the Rhine and would not stand up to large quantities of debris carried down by the floods. It seemed necessary therefore to provide some kind of boom upstream to divert the debris. This boom in turn required protection against floating mines and so on. In the end the solution appeared to be large numbers of light booms made of balloon cables on jerry-cans, so that a series of mines coming down and exploding on the boom would not penetrate the defences before fresh booms could be strung to replace those cut. For the rest, patrol boats, searchlights, and Bren-guns were provided to sink by fire any suspicious looking objects floating down the river. Fortunately for us the temperature of the water fell rapidly after the Nijmegen incident and produced conditions which no swimmer could stand. The possibility of ice conditions greatly complicated the boom problem. The only solution seems to be to remove all booms, except possibly the balloon cable type, as soon as ice conditions intervene.

The winter, now only a few weeks away, was to be an exceptionally hard one, locking Europe in snow and ice for month after month. To the soldiers, mostly men from the towns but now mostly living in the open, the casual phrase of the history books, 'winter campaign', took on an entirely new dimension; their political rulers had no intention of allowing them to go into 'winter quarters', the more civilized custom of former times. Their sufferings were to be shared by the civilian refugees also.

Despite the worsening weather, German infiltration attacks were taking place all along the northern edge of the Betuwe, but the main drive was with armour straight down the road from Elst towards Nijmegen bridge, which began on 2 October, under the fire of about 150 German guns. They hit the Irish Guards, whose historian wrote:

> In their effort to get Nijmegen bridge they brought up everything they had and carefully stage-managed their attack. Squads of 'man-pack' flamethrowers advanced towards the embankment, squirting streams of burning oil. Just behind them came ten tanks, firing steadily to protect them, and behind each tank filed a section of fifteen men. Further back were more infantry in open formation. Our right-hand platoon was burnt and shot out of its trenches; it fell back on No 4 Company and there re-formed. The tanks swung round, destroyed the 17-pdr anti-tank guns and pressed on to encircle the embankment. It looked for a moment as if they were going to have a clear run through to Battalion HQ.

But the attack was checked and by mid-day had clearly failed.

In the Dutch Staff College examinations, the approach to Arnhem from Nijmegen was a set question, and any aspirant who took the direct route via Elst was failed automatically. The Irish Guards had in fact taken that route to relieve the paratroops, and failed; now the Germans had tried it in the opposite direction against the Irish Guards, and they had failed. It rather looked as though the Dutch knew what they were talking about.

A few days later, the Irish Guards were relieved and Colonel 'Joe' Vandeleur became garrison commander of Nijmegen. Colonel Vandeleur wrote:

> The previous Commander had been more concerned about anti-aircraft defence. I persuaded him to give me six 3·7 AA guns, six Bofors LAA guns, and six multiple AA machine guns which were to be used purely for river defence. The top span of the bridge was in view from the Reichswald Forest; and the bridge and the roundabout just south of it came in for a good deal of shelling. A smoke unit kept up a persistent

smoke screen to hide the bridge. Lighting effects upon the scale of Elstree Studios were established along the water-front.

This was in addition to searchlights, tugs in mid-stream, a battalion of medium machine-guns, and Royal Marines with depth-charge throwers. They tried to anticipate the next form of attack – frogmen, midget submarines, E-boats, parachutists, floating mines.

I gave orders that every floating object of any size or type should be immediately engaged by every gun and machine-gun available. This included orange skins. I had at my disposal a light aircraft to reconnoitre up river. It discovered a large raft, rather of the Canadian pattern, being constructed about three miles upstream. The Germans never used it. It would have had a most destructive effect on the boom.

In his history of the Wessex Division, General Essame wrote:

The enemy now displayed a sense of humour usually regarded as foreign to his nature, and entertained himself by floating haystacks and large logs down the stream. In the dark these were taken for more frogmen or even one-man submarines.

But it was no joke. The Germans did attach mines to floating tree-trunks and tried to detonate them under the bridge from one-man submarines launched from Emmerich. The difficulties proved too formidable, however.

These weird forms of warfare on the Rhine and Waal were matched by events along the Neder Rijn to the north, where in mid-October a body of 130 'evaders', mostly escaped airborne men, were being concentrated for a mass crossing of the river. They had to be moved through German territory for distances of between 8 and 15 miles before they could gain the bank of the Neder Rijn. One body of 40 men, commanded by Major Hibbert, rode down to the crossing-point in two lorries supplied by the Dutch and among much German traffic. As they were actually getting out of the trucks, soon after dusk on 22 October, a German bicycle patrol came riding down the road straight into the mob of 40 Englishmen, plus Dutch guides shouting instructions in Dutch–English. The Germans slowed down and rang their bells angrily, for the milling mob to give them right of way, and then rode on.

The entire force, mostly armed and now totalling 147 men, had finally to reach the river across 1,000 yards of open ground between two Germans posts, and then move 800 yards along the bank to the actual crossing-site.

It would have been a hazardous move with a highly trained company [wrote Major A. D. Tatham-Warter of 2 Parachute Battalion]. But with a mixed bag of 120 parachutists, largely RAMC orderlies, 10 British and US pilots, 2 Russians and 15 Dutchmen, all of whom were unfit and many of whom had never seen their leaders in daylight ... our chances of slipping through unobserved were remote. Before we reached the river the party most closely resembled a herd of Buffalo, and I think it was this fact, which probably misled the Boche as to our numbers, added to the fact that the US parachutists on the South bank had been patrolling very vigorously on previous nights, that got us through. Although the Germans were aware of our presence, they were obviously too windy to take us on.

They were all brought back over the river early on 23 October by men of 101 US Airborne Division, which had taken over part of the 'Island' in the middle of Model's counter-offensive three weeks before. So ended the evacuation of the airborne from Arnhem, a month after the battle had ended.

Part III

The Rhine

1945

CHAPTER SIXTEEN

Winter

'All through the winter we made an intensive study of the Meuse and the Rhine,' reported Major General Sir J. D. Inglis.

The three main conclusions were, first, that icing conditions were liable to occur any time between December and the end of March, and that on the Rhine in particular they might prove very severe, so severe that no floating bridges could possibly stand. It was also evident that our plywood pontoons would not stand up to much less severe icing conditions, because even thin ice floating down the river would quickly cut through their thin wooden skins. The second conclusion was that although the winter and spring months would see the end of the floods on the Meuse, severe flood might occur on the Rhine at almost any time in the year, certainly up to the end of June. It did seem, however, that March and April were slightly less subject to flood than other months. From the engineer point of view, therefore, the end of March was the best date for the assault crossing of the Rhine.

The third important conclusion drawn from our study of the Rhine was that, having failed to capture Arnhem and the island lying between the Waal and the Neder Rijn, we had lost control of the Germans' ability to cause very serious flooding of that island. It was clear from this, therefore, that the original plan for entering Germany on the Nijmegen–Arnhem–Zutphen axis was no longer possible, and that we must seek for crossing places upstream from the point at which the Easternmost arm of the Rhine Delta, namely, the Ijssel, begins. The built-up area of the Ruhr was obviously to be avoided, and if the crossing was to be carried out by the 21st Army Group, crossing places must be found between the Ruhr and the Ijssel. This boiled down to Rheinberg, Wesel, Xanten, Rees and Emmerich. Emmerich was ruled out as an assault crossing because it was overlooked from Hoch Elten. True to form, the Rhine gradually rose in January and February and flooded the island between Nijmegen and Arnhem through the breaches made by the enemy in the dykes. He also flooded a considerable area just east of Nijmegen on the south bank of the Rhine.

Meanwhile, the equipment for an army group assault on Europe's major river was being brought up. It consisted of 22,000 tons of assault bridging equipment, including 2,500 pontoons, 650 storm boats, 2,000 assault boats, 60 river tugs, 650 outboard motors, 70 small tugs, 600 propulsion units, 260 miles of steel rope, 80 miles of balloon cable, plus 15,000 tons of material for the semi-permanent bridges that would take the place of the floating bridges once the assault had succeeded and exploitation into the heart of Germany had begun. This was done largely between December 1944 and February 1945 after Antwerp had been opened as a supply port.

In spite of the fact that the Market Garden axis had been repeatedly ruled out by the British, because of the fact that the Germans could flood part of that axis at will, the ghost of that failed offensive lingered in German minds long afterwards.

The German parachutists who relieved the exhausted and badly equipped defenders really were elite troops, probably better even than the Waffen-SS, and their entry on to the 'Island' was a measure of German uneasiness. They were being redeployed to help defend the north bank of the German Rhine against the British Second Army assault that was due to follow the clearing of the south* bank of the Rhine by First Canadian Army during the Reichswald offensive that began on 8 February.

* Or the east bank and west bank, respectively, for the course of the Rhine begins to curve south beyond Emmerich.

The deliberate flooding of the 'Island' by the Germans, which the British had foreseen, began early in December, by which time the levels of the Waal and Neder Rijn were rising anyway. At one time there had been three divisions on the 'Island' – Guards Armoured, 43rd Wessex, and 101 US Airborne. These had now been withdrawn and their place taken by two ordinary infantry divisions, the 51st Highland and the 49th West Riding; the former had served in the Western Desert, the latter more appropriately in Iceland (their divisional sign was the polar bear). Later, the 51st were drawn off by the Ardennes offensive, and the Polar Bear Division were left in undisputed possession of the title 'Nijmegen Home Guard'.

For three days, 2 South Wales Borderers had been holding Elst when, on 3 December at dusk,

> a shattering explosion was heard. Reports came in a few hours later that the water was rising in all the dykes at an alarming rate followed shortly afterwards by a report from our forward company, that the canal on their front had broken its bank and that water was pouring across the fields. It became evident that the enemy had blown the 'bund' and the 'island' was threatened with becoming submerged. The forward company had to be withdrawn – at least one section swimming out of their post . . .

The Germans followed up with a small-scale attack, which was beaten off. But their main, dangerous effort was made at Haalderen, held by 7 Duke of Wellington's Regiment for the last three days.

At 0300 hours the first report came in of Spandau fire and shelling; then of a strong attack developing. It was in fact being carried out by II Battalion of Fallschirmjäger Regiment 16 whose leading elements penetrated deeply into the British position, covered by the stormy night and relying on the floods to have disorganized the British, for if the British held on, the leading German company was vulnerable. Nevertheless, a break-through led directly to Bemmel and Nijmegen bridge.

The British CO ordered all his companies to hold where they were, then began to arrange for the artillery and mortar fire necessary to smash up the German reinforcements and any assault forces about to go in.

There was indescribable confusion in the village – Spandaus, Brens, rifles, Stens and grenades being freely used in between houses and across the street. Boche cries in good English of 'Stop that firing' were frequently heard and ignored. One voice shouted out in perfect English, 'Stop that bloody Bren. We've got a wounded man here.' But as the British had not moved, daylight found the leading German company wedged into the middle of the DWR, under fire from three sides. 110 of them surrendered, in a hopeless position, and they had lost more than 50 dead. Losses to their reserve companies were not known. Some of the prisoners stated that Nijmegen bridge had been the ultimate objective, which an engineer unit was to have destroyed. The DWR's casualties were officially listed as: '10 killed, 19 wounded, and 2 missing (believed drowned).'

The 'Island' was now really an island, because the area to the west, from the Waal to the Neder Rijn on the line Andelst–Zetten–Randwijk was four to six feet deep under water, and only the houses and farms stood up out of the floods. All patrols were boating exercises, with the boats liable to run aground unexpectedly on uncharted obstructions, such as the tops of wire fences or the stone parapets of submerged bridges; and when the enemy was met, he was either in a house or boatborne, too.

But soon the winter froze much of the landscape under snow and ice, and the latter made silent movement difficult when moving across the eerie waste of old battlefields.

On 16 December, Eisenhower paid the penalty for his 'broad front' offensive, and in a drive reminiscent of 1940 the Germans drove through the Ardennes, treating the Americans as they had the French, and using paratroops and 'Trojan Horse' units. This was awkward for Montgomery's 21 Army Group, because it disrupted movements already taking place that were intended to clear the Rhineland as a preliminary to crossing the Rhine. I noted in my diary:

Our divisions have been caught on the hop, in the middle of being transferred northwards from Second Army to First Canadian Army for the attack into the Reichswald, and are now being switched back to the south again, towards the Ardennes, leaving behind them the vast stocks of munitions which were being accumulated around Nijmegen for the offensive.

The Canadians were not worried in the long term, for I noted on 22 December:

Rundstedt's offensive would seem to have as its aim the cutting off of 21 Army Group from the American Army Group (Bradley's), and in particular the isolation of Brussels and Antwerp by a drive to the coast. This appears to be rather an ambitious scheme.

What the Canadians were worried about mainly was the fate of their own headquarters, which at that time had under its command not merely all the Canadian divisions but virtually every British division as well, except for the 'funnies' of 79 Armoured Division, and was busy turning them round from their own offensive to go and help the Americans stem the German offensive. If Canadian Army HQ was knocked out by paratroops or 'Trojan Horse' units, there would be utter confusion at a time when control was critical.

Junkers 52 transport aircraft had been reported on airfields east of Nijmegen, and it was believed that General Student had three parachute divisions in reserve; and that an armoured force was ready to cross the Maas,* where we had only thin

* This was the information available at the time. According to Colonel

screening forces and little in reserve, as everything had been
diverted to help the Americans.

This apparently ominous picture began to build up on 23
December, when a teleprint warning was issued:

> There is a possibility that the HQ area might be attacked
> by small bodies of paratroops and of fighting patrols which
> have infiltrated SOUTH from the RMAAS [.] Also that small
> bodies of desperadoes and assassins might move into the
> area their object being to cause confusion and a diversion
> from their attack further SOUTH[.]

This latter was apparently a reference to Otto Skorzeny's
commandos and the Brandenburg Division in general, the suc-
cessors to Special Battalion No 100.

After some false alarms, on 26 December the news was:

> Airborne troops dropped in battalion strength just outside
> Tilburg and Breda last night, but, so far as is known, none
> penetrated to the centre of Tilburg. The night before, how-
> ever, 5 German paratroops were picked up in the centre – 3
> dressed as clergy, 2 in British uniform.

A young Dutch journalist whom I met a few days later had
been picked up on the night of the 26th, while going home late
after preparing copy for the paper. He was taken by Canadians
into a guardroom for questioning, before being released.

C. P. Stacey's official history, 'The Canadian Army 1939–1945', the
position was even more alarming. 'Colonel-General Kurt Student, the
experienced and formidable commander of the German Army Group "H",
has described the preparations he had made: the three infantry divisions,
two parachute divisions and 150 armoured vehicles that were to attack
across the Maas; the parachute battalion, led by an officer who had
taken part in the rescue of Mussolini, which was to drop among our
artillery positions; the minor naval units that were to assail our shipping
in the Scheldt. The objective was to be Antwerp. But the great scheme
depended on the progress of the Ardennes offensive, and that was
shortly stopped dead.'

In the guardroom [he said], were eight German parachutists – two in regulation parachutists' uniform, the rest in
British uniforms or civilian clothes. The two in German uniform were wreathed in smiles and telling the others of the
sticky end awaiting them, while *they* were now safely out of
the war.

From this, he concluded that the disguised men were real
Nazis, the other two just ordinary Wehrmacht. Weapons were
Schmeissers and dynamite.

So far only sabotage troops had been dropped, and most of
these had been seen off by Canadians whose offices were out
along the Bredaweg near the drop zones; in bright moonlight,
the attackers had an unenviable task in trying to penetrate the
town.

The headquarters, numbering about 2,000 men, was scattered all over Tilburg in unmarked offices, thus presenting a
virtually impossible target to sabotage paratroops of the
'Trojan Horse'. If a full-scale airborne attack developed, each
building was to be held individually, by its occupants, for a
week. The reasons for anxiety lay not in the 'assassins and
desperadoes' but, as I noted in my diary on 1 January, in the
fact that 'Not all the German reserves had been committed in
the Ardennes offensive', and that Antwerp was wide open.

Canadian Army appreciations of the enemy, including this
one, had almost throughout taken the correct slightly pessimistic line, in strong contrast to the invariable optimism of the
British and the even more euphoric Americans, who until now
had thought the German Army liable to instant collapse.
Consequently, the effect of the 'Trojan Horse' paratroops on
the Canadians was negligible, whereas on the American front a
'Fifth Column' panic of positively 1940 proportions, and just as
unrealistic, developed. It was even rumoured that a plot existed
to assassinate Eisenhower at his HQ back in Paris.*

* Well described in *The Battle of the Ardennes*, by Robert E. Merriam
(Souvenir Press, 1958). The author was an historian on the staff of
US Ninth Army and saw these events at first hand.

The second wave of attack consisted of 20 Beavers that were to fire torpedoes into the resulting chaos; these torpedoes were fitted with hooks, so that they would catch in the nets suspended from the booms and so destroy them. The third wave of attack consisted of four Beavers, each towing a tree-trunk from which was suspended three tons of explosives. Photo-electric cells had been built-in to the tree-trunks, which were timed for release at dawn; when the shadow of the bridge fell across the cells, this would trigger the firing mechanism.

Although the British defences were not regarded by the Royal Engineers as being impregnable, they were sufficiently in depth to foil the elaborate three stage German attack. The last attempt on the bridge failed in the thunder of gunfire and the roar of exploding mines. The bridgehead over the Rhine, gained at such cost in 1944, was only a backwater of the war now.

As far as 21 Army Group was concerned, the effect of th\
Ardennes offensive was to delay the battle for the Rhineland b\
approximately one month. Once Allied armies were on the wes\
bank of the Rhine, Germany was definitely finished, her main\
traffic artery dominated and the Ruhr itself in the front line,\
the Saar overrun. The actual crossing of the Rhine would be a\
formality. The British—Canadian drive had to go in from the
Nijmegen area, parallel to the Rhine instead of towards it, because that was the pattern of existing roads. Consequently,
although Nijmegen was the road and rail head for the offensive,
the great Waal bridge played no part in it.

The build-up was restarted in mid-January, with trucks
going through Tilburg at the rate of 800 an hour, and it was
probably these movements towards Nijmegen that caused the
Germans to suspect an attack towards Arnhem on the old
Market Garden axis. As we have seen, in January they reinforced the 'Island' with refitted and up-to-strength parachute
regiments from General Student's command, in the mistaken
belief that the British would drive north instead of east.

Very probably, it was the Germans' fear that a new drive to
Arnhem was intended that spurred them to make one last attempt to destroy the great Waal bridge at Nijmegen. This they
carried out on the night of 12–13 January 1945. The history of
the West Riding Division noted: 'On 13th January the Division
fought a naval "engagement" against German torpedoes lashed
to logs, and against two midget submarines!'

In all, 24 midget submarines set out from Emmerich for the
attack. Unlike the one-man torpedoes, they were true sub-
mersibles, miniature submarines 25 feet long controlled by a
single man who had to wear breathing gear and with an armament of either two torpedoes or two mines carried externally.
Designed in February 1944 and used against the invasion fleet
off Normandy, the Germans called them Beavers.

The first wave of attack on 13 January consisted of 240
mines put into the Rhine and allowed to drift downstream with
the current towards the booms guarding Nijmegen bridges; it
was hoped they would break open at least some of the booms.

CHAPTER SEVENTEEN

Reichswald and Remagen:
February—March

The object of Montgomery's 1945 Reichswald offensive, spear-headed by XXX Corps, was to leave a springboard on the east bank of the Rhine in preparation for a 21 Army Group crossing of the river north of the Ruhr, in time to take advantage of the best predicted period — that is, when the flood plain had dried out and the danger of fresh floods was least. That period was the last week of March. This stretch of the Rhine, when crossed, gave access to the good tank country of the North German plain, where the best use might be made of superior Allied mobility, and where good roads and railways led to the German North Sea ports, the Baltic, and Berlin.

A glance at a relief map shows the geographical advantages of this route, which curves round to the north of both the densely built-up area of the Ruhr and the frequently moun-tainous stretches of the river to the south. The political advan-tages, at this stage of the war, were equally obvious. The question now was, not who was going to win the war, but who was to win the peace; and a successful drive on the northern route would block off the Russians from Denmark, which they might otherwise be tempted to occupy, and could also lead to the capture of Berlin.

21 Army Group had already made immense preparations for the crossing of the Rhine on the sector that would give these advantages, but the difficulty of the crossing depended on a German decision: whether they would choose to fight and be defeated west of the Rhine, or fight and be defeated east of the

Rhine. Hitler decided that there was no point in 'moving the catastrophe' from the west bank to the east bank; and Albert Speer, his war production chief, estimated that once the Allies gained the west bank in the region of the Ruhr, the resulting dislocation of Germany's main coal and steel centre, together with its river transport lines, would mean an economic collapse within four to eight weeks. Hitler decided to buy time by fighting on the west bank, in the hope that the dissensions, both military and political, that were now apparent on the Allied side, would fatally split his enemies.

The northern end of the Siegfried Line, which had been extended to the Reichswald, was held by the German 84 Infantry Division, backed by about 100 guns. First Canadian Army attacked it on a six-mile front with four divisions – 2nd Canadian, 15th Scottish, 53rd Welsh, and 51st Highland.

It was 2nd Canadian that smashed through the German border village of Wyler on the main Nijmegen–Kranenburg–Kleve road. 3rd Canadian Division, with amphibious vehicles, was to attack later, on the northern flood plain by the banks of the Rhine; the Germans flooded this area deeper still by blowing holes in the winter dykes. The tanks of Guards Armoured and the infantry of 43rd Wessex were in reserve. Supporting the attacking infantry were three independent armoured brigades, and the specialized tanks of 79 Armoured Division.

Surprise was achieved, because although the build-up in the Nijmegen area was too obvious to conceal, the direction of attack was unexpected, and the Germans, as we have seen, feared another drive from Nijmegen to Arnhem across the half-flooded 'Island'. As soon as they realized the true objective, they would of course reinforce the Reichswald instead; and in order to catch these reserve divisions in motion, Ninth US Army was to enter the battle from the south, from its positions along the River Roer. It had not yet advanced across the Roer because the high dams controlling the water level of this river were in German hands, and the Germans could flood the assault area at will. This posed some awkward decisions for the

American command, which was committed to attack on 10 February, two days after the British and Canadian assault had begun and while the Germans were still moving up their reserves to the threatened point.

On 10 February, the XXX Corps attack was going well into the Reichswald and hopes were high in some quarters. The German decision, however, was to blow the Roer dams, producing a temporarily impassable obstacle in front of Simpson's men but failing to catch them in the middle of an inadvisable assault. That was the last card gone; once the 'ace' was down, it could not be played again. The floods would subside and there would be no great physical obstacle to the American attack. But until the Roer floods did subside, XXX Corps would have to carry the brunt of the battle alone.

One by one, the Germans were committing almost the last of their good-quality divisions, many from the parachute army. Nevertheless, the British and Canadians fought their way forward through the maze of prepared defences, taking Kleve in the process.

Indicative of the statistics of survival during the advance was a café incident in Tilburg at about this time. A group of Scottish soldiers, none of them more than twenty years old, straight from the noise and shock of the Reichswald battle, were sitting quietly until the proprietress's baby began to cry — and cry — and cry. Their nerves were so on edge that one youngster jumped to his feet and shouted out that if the baby didn't stop its screaming he would bash its head in against the wall. The unfortunate mother went white, realizing that he was quite capable of doing it, and rushed the infant out to a back room.

Simpson's Ninth US Army attacked over the Roer on 23 February, against comparatively light opposition; on 10 March the battle ended with the fall of the Rhine town of Xanten to the Guards Armoured Division, after a desperate struggle. As the weary prisoners marched past, Colonel 'Joe' Vandeleur ordered his staff to stand to attention and himself saluted them. The bitter last stand of the German rearguards enabled their commanders to evacuate a sizable part of their force, in defiance of Hitler's orders.

Two thunderous explosions on the morning of 10 March signalled the fate of the bridge at Wesel, and an officer of the Irish Guards wrote:

> I'm afraid we wasted our time in Tilburg last February studying means of capturing the bridge intact by an armoured dash. They say the German armour is going south, so most of it will be facing the Americans for a change and not us, when we start on the other side.

The abrupt change was the result of an American initiative on 7 March.

Naturally, at this time every commander carried at the back of his mind a picture of a Rhine bridge, beautiful and unblown. So, too, did Hitler. He had ordered that anyone who failed to blow a bridge in time was to be shot. But he had complicated an always difficult decision by adding that anyone who blew a Rhine bridge too early was also to be shot. 'Too late' is easy to recognize; 'too early' is disputable. And fears of blowing too early may indeed lead to being unable to blow the bridge at all. If a state of chaos can be achieved, the decision becomes even more difficult and the attacker may well be able to 'bounce' the bridge. This, initially, had been the intention of Horrocks, commanding XXX Corps; but the thawing of the previously hard-frozen ground at the very start of the Reichswald attack had prevented a swift drive by Guards Armoured.

In the first week of March Simpson's Ninth US Army, on Horrocks' right, made a number of apparent attempts to 'bounce' major bridges over the Rhine. Two of these attempts were made near Düsseldorf, one at least employing a 'Trojan Horse' element of American tanks disguised to look like German tanks, with German-speaking Americans riding on them. One bridge was at Obercassel and the other at Uerdingen. Both attempts failed, and they may have been intended to fail. The matter is still partly 'classified', but it seems probable that they were merely part of a large-scale deception plan.

Bridges at Düsseldorf were worthless, because on the other bank there were 80 miles of densely built-up area – the Ruhr – stretching eastward as far as Hagen and Dortmund. Stalingrad was just such an industrial complex bisected by a major river; and a crossing at this point would have meant a super-Stalingrad. These probes, which resulted in the blowing of the bridges, were made during the night of 2–3 March; and on the night of 4–5 March another part of Simpson's army was ordered to storm the Rhine at Rheinberg, but met strong resistance. Rheinberg made more sense, as it was near Wesel, which carried main roads clear of the Ruhr complex, but was still very much a secondary choice.

On 5 March, the Americans also captured Cologne, but with no real hope of getting the Hohenzollern road bridge, which in any event gave access only to the Ruhr from a different direction, with a choice to the south of the mountainous, wooded terrain of the Westerwald and Siegerland. It is very beautiful country, but would be no one's first choice for mobile warfare.

By the 8th, 'hurry up' calls were going out, particularly for artillery, in the area of Lieutenant General Courtney Hodges' First US Army, part of Bradley's 12th Army Group. But some of the movements in the area of Bradley's Army Group, which had Patton's Third US Army on its right, in the Moselle area, had begun suspiciously early.

William C. Hendrix, of Bartlesville, Oklahoma, was then a corporal with the 467th Anti-Aircraft Artillery (Automatic Weapons) Battalion, operating in a ground support role in the First US Army. Their half-tracks carried either a 37-millimetre cannon and two ·50-calibre machine-guns, or four ·50s, all in turrets. In early March they had been supporting the advance of the US 69th Infantry Division about 40 miles south of Remagen.

On 5 March we were relieved of this assignment [recalled

Hendrix], and told that we were to support troops who were to attempt a Rhine River crossing. We were not told where this crossing was to be attempted.

As they eventually arrived at Remagen, Hendrix assumed that this was the objective all along, but it seems more probable that it was one of two favourable areas – near Bonn and near Koblenz – where Bradley wanted to attempt an encirclement of the Ruhr, a move that would be complementary to that of his rival Montgomery to the north, provided it did not draw off too much force from the main thrust. As many of the 'deception' plans of the period were designed more to deceive other Allied generals than the Germans, official records are not always to be taken at face value.

In the afternoon of 6 March we began to encounter great quantities of amphibious equipment and US Navy personnel [recalled Hendrix]. I asked one of the sailors, 'What the hell are you guys doing so far from the ocean?' He replied, 'We're going to take you across the Rhine!' I then asked if our engineers had surrendered or gone home, and he countered by asking if I had ever seen the Rhine River. I told him that I had not. He then informed me that the river was very wide and deep and that the crossing would necessitate an am-phibious operation. I began to realize that this operation was going to be difficult. We reached our staging area later that afternoon and began to wait for further orders. About 5 PM on 7 March I heard a great cheer go up in the main part of the staging area and saw a great deal of activity. A few minutes later one of our officers, Lt Wallace Gibbs, came rushing up to us in a Jeep and yelled for us to load up. He said, 'We have a bridge across the Rhine and by damn we're going to keep it there'. Approximately one hour later we were at the Remagen bridge. Someone had raised a large sign on the steel structure between the stone supports which read, CROSS THE RHINE WITH DRY FEET – COURTESY OF 9TH ARMORED DIVISION. The printing was not too well done but this was undoubtedly the most welcome sign I had ever seen.

Remagen was equidistant between the two chosen stretches for crossing — Bonn north towards Cologne and Andernach south towards Koblenz. However, the main road route on the opposite side, the Cologne–Wiesbaden–Frankfurt autobahn, was some distance inland from the river, and ran south not quite parallel to the Rhine. And the Ludendorff bridge at Remagen was a railway bridge only.

The route was a difficult one for an army, which moves in a mass of huge and unwieldy vehicles, including mobile workshops, tank-transporters, and towed guns among its necessary impedimenta. When the Americans first sighted the bridge on 7 March, the Germans were still moving back across it, and their impedimenta included horses and cows. The first reaction was not to the bridge but to the spectacle of the Rhine itself, winding broad between high cliffs topped by ruined castles and spires, and with the steep face of a 600-foot-high volcanic rock, the Erpeler Ley, facing them on the other side of the great gorge.

There should have been anti-aircraft guns emplaced on the flat top of that near-vertical basalt cliff, but most had been moved to Koblenz, where an American crossing seemed more likely, and only now were new guns being moved up. Indeed, the Germans had only just completed the four-day task of laying planks across the railway lines on the bridge, so that it could carry the road traffic of their retreating army.

The American's second reaction was to realize what a target the mass of men, vehicles, and animals made as they moved slowly across the bridge, and to think of bringing down mortar fire on them. But Lieutenant Karl Timmerman, commanding the company of mechanized infantry of 9th Armored Division that first saw the bridge, decided that the target merited artillery and tank guns as well, so he held fire. His colonel came up, but could not obtain permission to use artillery, so he ordered the tanks to go forward with their supporting infantry to sweep the bridge with fire and interfere with any attempted demolition.

The 9th Armored was commanded by Major General John Leonard and divided into two large battle groups of mixed tanks and armoured infantry, known as Combat Commands A and B, similar in composition to Groups 'Hot' and 'Cold' of Guards Armoured Division. It was elements of CCB, commanded by Brigadier General William Hoge, that had first sighted the bridge in the early afternoon and seen in it only a moving traffic target. But it was Hoge himself who saw the chance of capturing the bridge and urged his units on through the town of Remagen towards the bridge approaches.

There was an understandable reluctance to get on that bridge, because it looked like a trap, and even if it was not, the effect would be exactly the same if the Americans got on it, or even across it, and then the Germans blew it up. Indeed, as the leading infantry broke cover under the fire of their tanks, just after 1430 hours a considerable explosion shook the earth on the west bank. It was not a demolition charge, but a delaying charge, which blew a 30-foot crater in the approach road. Some of the charge and wires on the bridge itself were now visible, as were the German engineers working frantically to complete their preparations. The crater made a quick dash by tanks impossible; now only infantry could cross on foot, slowly, under fire from the bridge towers as well as from the far bank, and the bridge was over a thousand feet long.

Timmerman, whose caution had prevented an enthusiastically premature mortaring of the bridge, was now to lead the attack on it. Hoge, whose drive had got his units on to the approaches quickly, ready to attack under fire protection, now received an order from III US Corps. That day's operation, to take Sinzig and Remagen, was cancelled; instead, he was to drive south along the river towards the good crossing-place at Koblenz, now being threatened by an unofficial advance of Patton's Third US Army.

If Hoge let the attack on the bridge go in, he would be disobeying orders. If the Germans blew the bridge under his leading troops, he might lose a battalion for nothing, and contrary to orders; and would almost certainly lose his command and ruin his career. Only a success can justify disobedience, and the chances of success were not high. The Germans themselves were now firing on their own bridge, and it seemed likely to go up in the air at any moment. On the other hand, the prize was a great one, and might both shorten the war and save many American lives later. Hoge ordered the attack to go on. But as Timmerman was urging his company to get up and go forward, there was another explosion and, masked by smoke, the bridge seemed to sway and rise in the air.

On the German side of the river, the doubts and decisions were just as agonizing. The German forces facing Bradley's 12th US Army Group were in fact on both sides of the river, but those still on the west bank were concentrated at widely separated points covering the most likely crossing areas – Bonn and Koblenz. Between them was a 60-mile gap leading to Remagen that was almost uncovered because the German Army Group commander, Field-Marshal Model, considered that the defects of the Remagen route made it an unlikely objective for the Americans.

The German Army commander defending the Remagen sector, General Gustav von Zangen, disagreed with his superior. The defences of the bridge were weak, and although Model forbade him to reinforce it, he also disobeyed orders; instead of trying to hold firm on an impossibly long line west of the river, von Zangen instructed his forces to retreat to the Rhine in a direction that would place them, on the west bank, between the Americans and Remagen bridge. This might delay the Americans long enough to strengthen the bridge defences.

All Brigadier General Hoge stood to lose was his rank, his command, and his career. General Von Zangen stood to lose his life as well, if his decision proved to be the wrong one; or if Hitler, now a nervous and physical wreck, thought it was. But the German command structure was now chaotic and first one general and then another was given direct responsibility for the defence of the bridge, and various liaison officers, unknown to each other, arrived at the bridge to confuse the junior officers on the spot. It was death to allow a bridge to fall intact into enemy hands; but it also meant a very probably fatal court-martial to blow it too soon.

Hauptmann Willi Bratge commanded the 36-man security company guarding the bridge, while Hauptmann Karl Friesenhahn led the 120 engineers whose task was to destroy it, if necessary. Bratge's force also included 500 Volkssturm (Home Guards), 180 Hitler Jugend (schoolboys), 120 Russians, and about 220 flak gunners and rocket-men. By 7 March, the Volkssturm were fading rapidly, and only six remained; the artillerymen were also disappearing unaccountably, and the 36 men he could really rely on were all convalescent soldiers fit only for 'light duties'.

Model's headquarters was still telling him that he needed no more, because the Americans were driving for Bonn. There was no threat to Remagen. They refused to believe Bratge's appreciation, that the American tank-gun fire he was hearing was from a strong armoured force bound for the bridge; they passed it off as from a light force protecting the flank of the American drive towards Bonn and the good crossing-place there, north of the Drachenfels, the Dragon Mountain of the Siegfried legend. The 'third man' on the German side this day was Major Hans Scheller, who arrived as liaison officer from LXVII Army Corps, with orders to supervise the defence or demolition of the Ludendorff bridge, whichever seemed appropriate.

It was Friesenhahn who had blocked the bridge approach on the west bank by blowing a 30-foot crater. He had waited until the very last minute, because a retreating German battery was due to cross, and when the Americans arrived first, he reluctantly fired the charge. He was blown unconscious by a shell from an American tank as he ran back across the bridge to the eastern bank, but eventually reached it with the two other survivors of the demolition party. He reported to Bratge, who was standing at the entrance to the railway tunnel on the east bank.

Bratge wanted the bridge itself blown immediately, but Major Scheller had forbidden it; not only was Scheller superior in rank, but he was some way inside the tunnel at that moment. So Bratge had to go a quarter of a mile over the railway tracks, forcing his way through a crowd of civilian refugees, to find the major; and when found, the major was still doubtful, because of Hitler's order that no bridge was to be blown prematurely. At length he consented, and Bratge had to struggle back to the entrance to give the order to Friesenhahn.

There were some 60 separate charges on the bridge, wired to a detonating device actuated by a key. Everyone dropped flat as the engineer officer turned the key – and nothing happened. The American tank guns were raking the bridge and probably one of their shells had cut the main circuit. Now it was impossible to blow the bridge scientifically. However, there was a small 300-kilogram emergency charge that could be set off merely by lighting a simple fuse, and an engineer sergeant ran the gauntlet of American machine-gun fire for 80 yards in order to set it burning. As he ran back, the charge exploded.

But the bridge still stood. The Germans were shocked. So too were the Americans. When they thought the bridge had gone, the feeling among the assault infantry was not dismay, but relief. Lieutenant Timmerman had some difficulty leading them out on to the bridge; they thought it was a suicide mission, and he knew it was. However, after some hesitation and at first in ones and twos, they got up and followed him. Once on to the structure, the fast water of the Rhine was 80 feet below them; the chance of surviving a demolition blast and a fall of 80 feet into the river in full equipment was negligible. While the rumour in Nijmegen had been that the Americans had already captured the north end of the bridge, the rumour in Remagen was that a German prisoner had stated that the bridge would be blown at 1600 hours precisely. Neither rumour was strictly true, but might have had the effect of speeding the operation for capture.

In any case, once on the bridge the American infantry were

very anxious to get off it. Behind them came a group of engineers, who began dealing with the demolitions. The tanks and
tank-destroyers (self-propelled guns) covered them and engaged targets that were holding them up, mainly machine-gun
posts in the bridge towers and a barge lying in the river. The
right-hand tower was still resisting when the leading Americans rushed it. There were only seven men inside, all of
whom surrendered.

One hundred yards from the east bank of the Rhine, the
railway tracks entered a tunnel in the hillside, and Lieutenant
Timmerman ordered a patrol to go inside, cautiously. They
took several prisoners near the entrance where, logically, the
defenders would be; and did not realize that, further in, the
tunnel was filled with Germans. Most of these were civilians
who had retreated from the American shells that had been
aimed at the tunnel mouth until a few minutes before; and they
were now trying to disarm the German soldiers and convince
the officers that they ought to surrender. Major Scheller had
disappeared, and only Bratge and Friesenhahn were left. Bratge
asked if anyone wanted to fight, and as no volunteers were
forthcoming, he decided to give up.

There were still German defenders on the heights of the
Erpeler Ley, however, and Timmerman's men had to storm this
before the bridge could be considered in any way secure. He
was reinforced by two more companies of the 27th Armored
Infantry Battalion, but they had little more than small arms,
and the situation seemed so precarious that some of the men
began to slip away and drift back across the bridge to the west
bank of the Rhine. Meanwhile, the American engineers were
completing the 'delousing' of the bridge and were filling in the
30-foot crater on the west bank approach, so that tanks could
cross to support the vulnerable infantry. They were also busy
patching up the holes in the bridge flooring blown by the two
emergency demolition charges.

It was dark when the first platoon of Pershing tanks began to
cross; and in spite of white tape laid to guide them, they could
not see it, nor could they see each other. Bumping together like

monstrous Dodgem Cars, the tank column crossed and drove
off fast to find their infantry. The infantry they found were all
German, and although some wanted to surrender, others
opened fire.

Next to cross were the self-propelled guns of 656th Tank
Destroyer Battalion. The leading platoon was commanded by
Forst Lowery. While it was still daylight, Lowery recalled,

> One of my destroyers sank a German naval vessel. At least
> the commander, who was rowed ashore in his dinghy by
> sailors, was dressed in his full uniform, complete with epau-
> lets, and carried his sword across his knees before sur-
> rendering it to me. Very formal note. The vessel itself looked
> like an ordinary Rhine river boat.

The tank-destroyers came across the bridge at a faster pace
than had the Pershings, presumably because of the critical
nature of the situation, and the lead destroyer slipped a track
into one of the hastily repaired holes made by the demolitions;
it hung there, part of it over the river 80 feet below, part of it
blocking the hurriedly planked roadway. The whole platoon
came to a halt, and there they remained for the rest of the
night, in the middle of Remagen bridge, while engineers
worked at the problem of how to extract the heavy and cumbersome vehicle.

Up to now, only a few of the troops who had got across had
slipped back to the west bank. But now that the bridge was
blocked to vehicles, rumour swept the troops holding on to
their precarious positions on the Erpeler Ley, with only small
arms to pit against 20-millimetre cannons. The principal
rumour was that all troops had been ordered to withdraw, and
it originated with an officer. One third of them 'withdrew',
although it was more of a panic flight than an orderly retreat,
leaving the American bridgehead weaker still.

They were still stumbling back to safety when the first reinforcing battalion arrived. Its colonel, Lewis Maness, had been
told that he would have no trouble, there was nothing across

on the other side but 'demoralization'. But by dawn the engineers had extracted the tank-destroyer and covered the hole
into which it had fallen. Vehicles and men began to cross in a
steady stream.

The reactions at various levels of the American command
were interesting. Brigadier General Hoge was apprehensive,
because he had disobeyed orders to attempt the capture of the
bridge; but his divisional commander, Major General Leonard,
backed him and convinced III US Corps: they in turn had little
trouble with the commander of First US Army, Lieutenant General Hodges, who enthusiastically telephoned Bradley, the
army group commander.

'Hot dog, this will bust him wide open!' was Bradley's reaction. He authorized Hodges to put in the 99th Infantry Division, as well as the 78th and 9th Infantry Divisions, which had
already been ordered to exploit the opening gained by the 9th
Armored Division. But Bradley did not immediately inform
Eisenhower, because Remagen meant a diversion of effort into
unfavourable terrain and Bradley already had plans for a crossing by Patton far to the south, which was also not a part of the
agreed Allied plan, for the main effort to be in the north
towards Berlin. He probably had a bad conscience.

However, typically, Eisenhower blew hot when he first heard
the news, and then, later, grew cold and forbade any large
build-up across the Rhine at Remagen. The supreme commander then telephoned Montgomery, anticipating obstruc-
tion, but Montgomery was extremely pleased. 'It will be an
unpleasant threat to the enemy and will undoubtedly draw
enemy strength on to it and away from the business in the
north.'

In fact, all Montgomery was worried about was that Eisenhower would try to close up to the Rhine all along its
length, which meant cracking open new sections of the Siegfried Line, a slow and bloody business, before launching a crossing on the good northern route where the Siegfried Line had
already been overwhelmed at great cost by 21 Army Group.
Eisenhower probably had a guilty conscience, too, because this

was in fact his intention, Allied agreements notwithstanding.

Montgomery's prediction proved accurate, and the defenders of the Remagen bridgehead helped the northern thrust (and also Patton's unofficial southern advance) by drawing to themselves a frenzied German effort to wipe it out, using much of their reserves and including perhaps the weirdest assortment of weapons ever to be collected together in so small a space.

Forst Lowery recalled:

> After crossing, my platoon took up positions along the river in the Erpel, area, firing on whatever threatened the bridge – boats, swimmers, floating objects, and a weird variety of aircraft which came over one at a time trying to bomb the bridge. We saw what must have been the death throes of the Luftwaffe. They must have collected enough fuel for one plane and then sent it out. Everything from the plywood jets which made their first appearance about this time through an old Ju 88.

> The dismal March weather and the use of smoke generators obviously helped in preventing enemy air attacks from destroying it [wrote Lieutenant Colonel William H. Anthony, who was then with the 809th Field Artillery Battalion]. Although the near-misses and pounding that Remagen took sure must have helped weaken it. During that period Remagen was a real hot spot, and with the anti-aircraft batteries surrounding the place there was the greatest ring of conical firing one could ever hope to see.

On 17 March the bridge finally collapsed. Armand Duplantier of the 372nd Field Artillery was not impressed by the news. 'The bridge had been hit so many times by shells and bombs that it could stand up no longer,' he noted. 'But it made little difference, because the front was some 28 to 30 miles wide along the Rhine, and there were about 4 or 5 auxiliary bridges across.'

The loss of the bridge would have cost Bratge his life, had he not been taken prisoner; Major Scheller was shot, as were a number of people who had had nothing to do with it, including an engineer major who, after the Americans had captured the bridge, led a daring attack to blow it up, but failed. And, as Lieutenant Colonel Anthony put it, 'It's a cinch that finding that Rhine River bridge must have upset some preconceived plans, because, considering the terrain alone, it couldn't have been a picked spot for a river crossing.'

Some of the American airborne commanders wanted 'to get in on the show', but were refused by Eisenhower. This was to be symptomatic of the Rhine crossings as a whole. On the American side – and the Americans now had in Europe forces three times the size of the combined British and Canadian armies – the last stage in the downfall of the Third Reich was to be treated, not in mere mundane military terms, not in vital political terms, but as some stage show, with the actresses carefully examining their make-up and arguing about the relative prominence of their names outside the theatre, all with an anxious eye to the 'first night' reviews next day. And in these terms it has been treated ever since, with the rival actresses' personal ambitions spoken of as if they were expressions of the purest American patriotism.

However, from what happened subsequent to widespread crossings of the whole river, it is clear that the rival American prima donnas were being 'conned'. There *was* a real political objective behind all the dressing-room tantrums, but it was at the level of SHAEF and the President of the United States; and it was to be achieved. Russian dominance of half Europe, including not merely half of Germany, but of many smaller states, such as Czechoslovakia, was to be ensured by the actions of future-President Eisenhower.

CHAPTER EIGHTEEN

Oppenheim: 22–23 March

On 7 March I noted in my diary: 'Cologne is ours. Patton, farther south, instead of maintaining the defensive role as per instructions, has leapt forward 30 miles, and is still going.' The spearhead of his advance was Major General Hugh Gaffey's 4th Armored Division, which had made the breakout from St Lo in Normandy and later relieved Bastogne.

What happened was that with the connivance of Bradley, Patton had made a deep penetration and then cut in behind the Siegfried Line defences of the Saar, then under painful frontal attack by US Seventh Army in accordance with Eisenhower's desire 'to close the length of his entire line to the Rhine'. Eisenhower's stated reason was to avoid the possibility of a German counter-offensive; his real reason may only be conjectured.

Bradley's stated reason for encouraging Patton's drive was to avoid the possibility of his army group's being given a static role on the west bank of the Rhine, while Montgomery made for the Baltic and Berlin; and this may well be true.* His afterthoughts, that the British plans were 'shrewd' and that he and other American generals were political innocents at that time, able to think only in terms of the current military situation and unable to grasp the fact that every military decision now taken affected the political and economic shape of Europe for at least the next twenty-five years, is a little hard to believe. Possibly the full truth still cannot be told.

In large organizations, civilian or military, the managing director has to 'project' himself and/or the company 'image',

* See *A Soldier's Story*, by Omar N. Bradley (Eyre and Spottiswoode), pp. 515–17.

and both Montgomery and Patton were sufficiently up-to-date to realize that methods suitable for a battalion commander or the proprietor of a small garage in the matter of employer—employee relationships simply would not do where organizations with a payroll of hundreds of thousands were concerned. They were alike also in their ruthlessness towards subordinates, although Montgomery bowler-hatted at the top only, while Patton spread himself far and wide.

Typical of his method was a story I heard from Americans just after the war, concerning an occasion when Patton suspected that his armoured spearheads were not getting their replacement tanks because the crews of the tank-transporters were 'whooping it up with the local damery'. Some, my informants admitted, were doing exactly that; but most were simply held up by blown bridges. However, Patton did an aerial reconnaissance of his own area, saw tank-transporters laid up under trees in every direction, and ordered the 'busting' of every sergeant commanding a tank-transporter that day. This was gross injustice, because if a tank-transporter is held up for any reason, good or bad, it makes such a target that it is common prudence to take it off the road and under cover.

However, the principle of 'no excuses accepted' is one valid method of driving men on; and in addition Patton was extremely quick to find and exploit enemy weak spots where these existed. In the final drive to the Rhine, what Patton scented was not just a weak spot but the imminent collapse of most organized opposition and thus a good chance of 'taking the river on the run' and thereby wiping Montgomery's eye. In British parlance, he intended to 'bounce' a crossing.

Although one would never suspect it from reading most American authors on the subject of the Rhine crossing, the concept — far from being a Bradley—Patton patent — is as old as warfare, and no one owns the rights to the idea. Actually carrying it out is a different matter, however, and as we have seen, Horrocks' attempt to 'bounce' the Rhine bridge at Wesel with Guards Armoured Division foundered in the floods and fierce opposition. How Patton's army fared is best seen through the eyes of junior witnesses.

Max Gissen, now of Weston, Connecticut, was then an infantry first lieutenant.

We, the 26th Infantry Division (from Massachusetts) [he wrote], approached the Rhine after breaking through the Siegfried Line in the Saar. What happened there, the intensity of the fighting, the casualties taken, were all of much more importance to us than anything that happened at the Rhine or after. We broke through at Serrig, Beurig, Merzig, not far from Trier and we drove along a line that roughly paralleled the Saar River, capturing places like Reimsbach, pushing on through Dottweiler, Furth, Landstuhl, etc. We had jumped off on 13 March and the initial progress was slow. The Siegfried was said to be roughest at that point and I can easily believe it. Once it cracked, though, about the third day of the attack, prisoners began coming in in larger numbers. In one place we took six 88s intact and 190 prisoners. This was near Thalexweiler and at dusk of the 19th we were approaching Furth. The 20th was a crazy day. What had been a stubborn retreat became a real rout. The Air Force had a field day, the infantry no longer walked but mounted everything on wheels and pushed on as much as 25 miles a day, leaving behind pockets of Germans to be mopped up or taken prisoner without resistance. Some, of course, fought on and raised the devil with the few rear-echelon troops. But after the Bulge, and before the dreary, muddy, inch-by-inch crawl through Lorraine, the few days before we reached the Rhine seemed a lark. I came into Kaiserslautern at night with only two men and couldn't find any enemy troops at all. Only Polish and Russian forced laborers, cadavers wandering aimlessly about and suddenly become creatures to be feared by the terrified civilians.

During the entire preparation for the crossing, I was the liaison officer between the 104th Infantry and 26th Division headquarters. During this brief period I reported to GI, II, III,

THE RHINE
NIJMEGEN to STRASBOURG
25th. MARCH 1945

Forest Area
Built up Area

Westerwald

Taunus

ARNSBERG
SIEGEN
LI

Sauerland

LUDENSCHEID
ALTENKIRCHEN

HAMM

MUNSTER

DORTMUND
HAGEN

The Roman

BOCHUM
WUPPERTAL
REMAGEN

RECKLINGHAUSEN
REMSCHEID
SIEGBURG
U.S. 1s
(H

GLADBECK
ESSEN
DUISBURG
DUSSELDORF
BONN
COLOGNE

WESEL

FLOOD

PLAIN
XANTEN
(DEMPSEY)
2ND.
BR. ARMY

KREFELD
U.S. 9TH. ARMY
(SIMPSON)
DUREN

German

EMMERICH
1ST. CDN. ARMY
(CRERAR)
CLEVE

R. MAAS
R. ROER

AACHEN

ARNHEM
NIJMEGEN

Netherlands

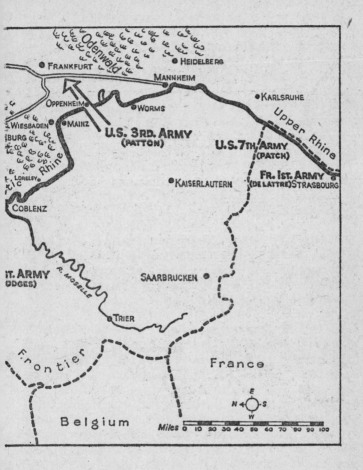

Odenwald

●FRANKFURT   ●HEIDELBERG

MANNHEIM

OPPENHEIM●   ●WORMS   ●KARLSRUHE

WIESBADEN●   ●MAINZ   Upper Rhine

IBURG   **U.S. 3RD. ARMY**
                  (PATTON)   **U.S. 7TH. ARMY**
                                            (PATCH)

LORELEY●   Rhine   ●KAISERLAUTERN   **FR. IST. ARMY**
t'c   **(DE LATTRE)** STRASBOURG

●COBLENZ

IT. ARMY
(ODGES)   R. MOSELLE   SAARBRUCKEN ●

                  ●TRIER

F r o n t i e r   F r a n c e

B e l g i u m   Miles 0 10 20 30 40 50 60 70 80 90 100

                        N ← E / S
                            W

and IIII, and to the division chief-of-staff and the division commander. I have no doubt that from the standpoint of Corps, Army and Eisenhower, all was going according to plan, but to me there seemed to be one hell of a lot of confusion. On the way from the Siegfried Line, the supply-road situation had become badly snarled because our Seventh Army had come up to our right flank and, in country where the roads were inadequate at best, the competition for even a dirt track was fierce. The men, however, were relaxed. No one dreamed that we would cross with the suddenness that we did. The natives in the Oppenheim area around which we sprawled were surly. But many of the young people, especially the girls, did not seem to be crushed by the presence of conquerors and many liaisons were quickly formed even when one discounted the routine boasting.

He added: .

With Patton, it was always attack, attack and (no barbs across the sea here) he never waited around to 'tidy up' as Montgomery did. He was a driving commander, quick to make the most of the slightest opening allowed by the enemy and twitching to force one if it wasn't there.

The final decisions were taken at a conference on 19 March when, with Eisenhower's approval, Bradley authorized two Rhine offensives – the first to be made out of the Remagen bridgehead by Hodges' First Army, the second to be a crossing near Mainz by Patton's Third Army; both armies would then link up in a 12th Army Group drive that would rival, or excel, that of Montgomery's 21st Army Group in the north. Once 12th Army Group was committed, it would no longer be possible to detach divisions from it to aid the northern thrust, if that should be required.

Militarily, it made sense only in terms of US Army, and particularly US Third Army, prestige. Politically, it made sense only if the ultimate objective was to free Czechoslovakia before

OPPENHEIM 213

the Russians arrived. But Eisenhower must have had strict orders from his political masters to ensure, at all costs, that it was the Russians and not the Americans who occupied Czechoslovakia. And although he would never rein in Patton in the over-riding interests of Anglo-American offensives else- where, he was to find no difficulty in stopping or diverting any number of US armies when Russian interests were threat- ened.

But Patton, apparently, did not realize this. He saw the Rhine only as a glorious opportunity to score off Montgomery and steal some of the limelight from Hodges, whose Remagen coup had temporarily snatched the headlines for First Army. As Montgomery's crossing was planned for the night of 23–24 March, it was necessary (from the propaganda point of view) for Patton to cross not later than the night of 22–23 March. On the 19th he therefore ordered forward from Lorraine, the men who never got any headlines at all – the engineers and their bridging convoys.

Concentration on the deeds of the fighting troops obscures the fact that the actual crossing of a major river by the initial assault units is a mere fraction of the real effort involved. First to sustain a major blitzkrieg by army groups, then the pro- longed occupation of an immense area of conquered territory, which was the prospect in view, requires rather more than a handful of rubber boats or even a few pontoon bridges. Ar- rangements had to be made, not merely to bridge the major river but all rivers to be encountered beyond, and also, within a short space of time, to erect semi-permanent high-level road and rail bridges that would be immune to floods and bad weather.

The problems in the Mainz area were not of the magnitude encountered on Montgomery's front opposite Wesel, and Patton had prudently collected sufficient bridging material some time previously, although as its origins were dubious, he was less inclined than Montgomery's publicity machine to stress the vast amounts of material involved. Having ordered up his bridging train, he then began 'to tramp around and shout' at his commanders, in order to get them to cross the Rhine a day or two earlier than was administratively convenient.

In particular, he pushed the XII Corps commander, Major General Manton S. Eddy, to get across at Oppenheim, near Mainz, on the 22nd, whereas the 23rd would have suited Eddy better. So Eddy passed on the bad news to Major General S. Leroy Irwin, commanding the 5th Infantry Division. The news was bad only in the sense of the timing. Oppenheim was topographically an easier proposition than two other areas, both along the 'Romantic Rhine' downstream from Mainz in the Koblenz area, which Patton had also selected previously as crossing-points in case the Mainz area proved to be more heavily defended than appeared probable.

In fact, there was nothing the Germans could do at Mainz. The 50 miles from Mainz to Mannheim was held in theory by the German Seventh Army, but this 'army' consisted of one actual corps HQ, another corps HQ in process of formation, no regular divisions, but only a hotch-potch of depot and line-of-communication troops incorporated in the disorganized remnants of four former divisions. Their armoured reinforcements consisted of five SP guns. Had Patton waited another day, two more would have become available, making a total of seven. Even these were there only by chance, part of a unit re-fitting and earmarked for use at Remagen, in Hodges' area.

Late in the evening of 22 March, six battalions of the 5th Division began to cross the Rhine in assault boats at two places near Oppenheim, were opposed by what was probably a platoon, and by dawn had formed a small bridgehead at a cost of 28 men killed and wounded. Next, it was the turn of the engineers to build temporary bridges and rafts, and then the infantry of the 26th Division and the tanks of 4th Armored began to cross, a procedure that took several days. Contrary to expectations, not a shot was fired and casualties were fewer than those of a similar exercise in pre-war manoeuvres.

At the morning 12th Army Group briefing on 23 March, a Third Army representative had stated: 'Without benefit of aerial bombing, ground smoke, artillery preparation, and air-

borne assistance, the Third Army at 2200 hours, Thursday
evening, 22 March, crossed the Rhine River.'

That is, 23 hours before Montgomery was due to cross, with
such assistance.

Shortly after, Bradley himself announced that the US Army
could cross the Rhine almost at will, almost anywhere, without
air bombardment, and sometimes even without artillery. His
subsequent criticism reveals the motive: 'Had Monty crashed
the river on the run as Patton had done, he might have averted
the momentous effort required in that heavily publicized crossing.'

Bradley's boast proved to be not quite correct. The 'Romantic Rhine' was better defended and offered an imposing
physical obstacle, the Rhine gorge, where the river has cut
deeply into the rock so that the sides are high and steep. The
Lorelei feature, for instance, is a mass of rocks rising 430 feet
above the river level, with its base 76 feet below the river
surface. The width of the Rhine at this point is only 650 feet,
but nevertheless one is forced to admire the assault troops who
placed the American flag on top of the rock.

Two assaults were made near Rhens on the night of 24–25
March, and both failed, the few men who succeeded in crossing
being withdrawn. An assault at Boppard succeeded, as did opposed crossings made at St Goar and Oberwesel on the 25th.
Nevertheless, one can only conjecture why they were ever carried out, because the narrow twisting valleys that lead down
into the gorge were unsuitable for the deployment or even the
passage of the mass of heavy vehicles that is a modern army.

However, American generals were notoriously less careful of
the lives of their men than the British generals, who, as junior
officers in the First World War, had received an unforgettable
lesson in appalling waste.

On 26 March the US Seventh Army, part of the 6th Army
Group, crossed at Worms, between Mainz and Mannheim, but
took heavy casualties from shell and mortar fire; they were not
able to assault until some 10,000 rounds of counter-battery fire
had been shot away in the space of little over half an hour. The

last crossings of the Rhine were made by the French First Army near Speyer and Strasbourg. The preparations were pitifully inadequate and the losses heavy, but the objective, which was political and not military, was gained. This was to establish a French 'presence' over the Rhine inside Germany, as a bargaining counter for the post-war period.

Important though this was for France, it was a minor matter compared to forestalling the Soviet on the Baltic at the gateway to Scandinavia, the ultimate objective of 21st Army Group's stage-managed crossing and the only one with a vital political aim as the prize. It was also the most critical as regards the time factor. Eisenhower was unique in his insistence on 'broad front' policies of advance. The Russians were not sweeping into Europe on a broad front, with all the armies keeping step; instead, they were making their main drive for the politically most vital objectives – Berlin and the gateways to the Baltic. Their line bulged out here towards the west, leaving Czechoslovakia and Austria uncleared to the southeast, hundreds of miles in the rear of the Red Armies driving for Berlin and the Elbe. Montgomery's real target was not the German Army, now a secondary matter, but the attainment of a geographical line that would deny to the Russians any further foothold in Europe.

CHAPTER NINETEEN

Rheinberg to Rees: 23–24 March

The 2nd Lincolns took Winnekendonk, the last village but one on the road to Xanten and the Rhine. That village and those few hours cost the battalion 87 officers and men — a tenth of their numbers, had they been at full strength. In this manner the British had had to fight every foot of the way to the Rhine.

And the Canadians also. The war diary of the Highland Light Infantry of Canada for 6 March, the day of the attack on Xanten, noted:

'Weather — dull. Visibility — limited. Morale — poor — coys have taken heavy punishment and are all far below strength. Officer and NCO casualties were heavy.'

The result of the bitter fighting on the British and Canadian front was that shattered towns and torn-up roads, half-cleared minefields and blown bridges stretched from the German border in the Reichswald to the banks of the Rhine. But, as we have seen, the vicissitudes of that battle had allowed the Ninth US Army, also part of Montgomery's 21st Army Group, an almost uninterrupted run to the river near Rheinberg.

Indeed, the Americans had so little opposition in front of them, and the physical obstacles to a crossing seemed to them so small, that they thought an immediate assault over the Rhine on the heels of the fleeing Germans would have succeeded. This did not suit Montgomery, who specialized in 'set-piece' battles such as Alamein and the D-Day landings; and the Americans were told to wait.

In Montgomery's view, the area would allow only one division to be used, three weeks in advance of the planned date for the assault — 31 March, soon after brought forward to 24 March — and the unpredictable results might upset the carefully orchestrated battle he had been planning since December. There was in fact no hurry, because the Rhine itself at this point dictated the dates of attack by its flood record, and the 21 Army Group scheme was geared to that.

If an American division had got across and then had its bridges destroyed by one of the periodic floods, or otherwise got into trouble before the entire army group was ready to cross, a calamitous rescue operation would have had to be mounted. In the circumstances, with the war definitely won, it was hardly worth risking, militarily, quite apart from the risk of unnecessary casualties.

Although Montgomery has been criticized for it, the 21 Army Group crossing had to be a 'set-piece' assault, for three reasons: the topographical nature of the Rhine at that point; the type of battle that had preceded the approach to the Rhine by the British and Canadian armies; the quality and quantity of the opposition that the Germans were capable of offering to a crossing at that point.

The forces available to Montgomery also favoured the 'set-pieces'. These included the specialized landing craft, amphibious vehicles, and amphibious (DD) tanks accumulated as a result of the D-Day landings; the great superiority, both in quality and quantity, of the British, Canadian, and American artillery over the German artillery; and the availability of a two-division airborne corps. Immense power could be harnessed to ensure rapid and certain success, provided a waiting period of two to three weeks was allowed in which to bring it forward and deploy it.

And, as will become apparent, an early and ill-organized assault at this point would almost certainly have failed; even if it had succeeded, thousands of men would have been killed and maimed who otherwise might have survived. The fact that a delay would enable the Germans also to bring up reinforcements mattered little, because Montgomery's resources were greater. On balance, a delay favoured the 21st Army Group most decidedly.*

Therefore, there was a pause, during which the whole front of the 21st Army Group was screened by smoke in order to aid the deception plan. That the attack was coming on the sector Rheinberg to Emmerich – from just north of the Ruhr to just south of Nijmegen – could not be concealed; and that Wesel, the best road and rail communications centre, must be the most vital objective was as obvious as the fact that London is the capital of England. All that could be achieved was to pretend that the frontage of the attack was longer than it in fact was, and so spread the German defenders unnecessarily thin.

Emmerich was threatened when in fact assault at Emmerich was ruled out by Montgomery on account of the pimple-shaped hill nearby on which the medieval village of Hochelten stands. In the basically flat flood plain of the Rhine delta, this feature commanded the whole of the Emmerich area back to the Reichswald. This deception was successful, and the German armoured reserves were stationed here. Montgomery had achieved one of his standard gambits – to put the enemy 'off balance', while remaining himself 'balanced'.

It was also necessary to prevent German patrol activity across the Rhine, which might reveal the deception. The British measures were successful and the 2nd Lincolns, for instance, captured a complete patrol of 11 men from 7 Fallschirm Division.

This German parachute army, together with the two armoured formations that were its reserve, represented almost the last best the Germans had. Why it opposed 21 Army Group and not Bradley and Patton may best be left to conjecture.

* This would be quite obvious, and it would be unnecessary to stress it, but for the fact that all the more superficial American writers on the subject have, willy-nilly, assumed that the Rhine itself was uniform along its entire length (which is like saying that the geology and scenery of the North American continent is uniform) and that because few German troops opposed Patton, there can have been few German troops opposite Montgomery.

Patriotism did alter some of the details of Montgomery's plan. Originally, the assault was to have been made entirely by the British Second Army, with the Canadian First and the American Ninth crossing later in the pursuit role, the former into Holland. But the American commanders definitely objected, and it seems possible that someone in the Canadian Army may have asked for representation. Whoever it was, it was certainly not the troops concerned. However, this time there were no dark suspicions of Montgomery's motives, or any belief that the British were trying to hog the 'glory' of the assault, or any hypersensitive suspicions that omission equalled aspersion.

The Canadian Army was at least as good as the British Army and in some respects, notably the assault, probably better. It was left out because that pimple at Hochelten overlooked its sector. Therefore, the plan was very slightly amended to allow General Crerar to raid Emmerich if he thought fit, or even cross independently if he thought fit; and if he did not think fit – and of course he did not – then allowance was made for the Canadian Army to cross via the British bridges, turn left to take Emmerich and Hochelten from the far bank, and then build their own bridges at Emmerich. This was what actually happened.

To give Canada representation in the actual historic crossing, a Canadian Scottish brigade was attached to the British assault formation, the 51st (Highland) Division. A Canadian parachute battalion was due to drop with the British 6th Airborne Division in any case, which was to go in side-by-side with the 17th US Airborne Division, so there were no squabbles there. However, as Simpson's Ninth Army HQ did not like being left out of the assault, the front was reshuffled to allow them to attack at Rheinberg; but because Rheinberg did not count but Wesel, being the main communications centre, did, this was to be transferred to the Americans as soon as the British had secured an adequate bridgehead, for the passage of the bulk of the American forces.

In short, the whole army group line shuffled to the left, with the Americans taking over part of the British sector in stages, and the Canadians extending the line left to Emmerich in theory only for the first stage, because this was the deception area, but in fact for the second stage.

The 'star' of the Rhine crossing was in fact the river itself. British and Canadian engineers had been studying the topography, hydrology, and history of their section of the Rhine – Ruhr–Nijmegen – since early October 1944. Firstly, with the winter in view, and then with the spring campaign in mind.

The history of the Rhine in the delta area was complicated and disputed. The river had changed its course a number of times, not merely in geological time but in historical time. One of these changes had occurred about AD 150 and another about AD 1275, although archaeological evidence since discovered points to a somewhat earlier date, of around 1200. In most cases a loop of the river had been cut off and abandoned, the Rhine tending to straighten somewhat. These old loops of the Rhine, of varying ages, were now marshes or winding lakes occurring on both sides of the river, on the approaches to the near bank and also on the approaches to the far bank. Large-scale maps show them clearly, but not the maps one can normally include in books of this or similar format; and therefore it has tended not to be realized that to talk of a 'Rhine crossing' in this area meant in fact crossing, or better still going round, many older Rhines, which made the approaches to the present Rhine bad or impossible going to vehicles of any sort, let alone the extremely heavy impedimenta of a modern army.

It is possible that this erratic behaviour of the river in the low-lying delta area (a former seabed) was due to later but slighter changes in sea-level, as the dates tie up with coastal inundations elsewhere. This is hardly surprising, because the Rhine is fed at source by mountain snow melts, a basic cause of alterations in sea-level, and in its lower, flatter reaches would inevitably be affected by the results of a rising or falling sea-level, but more especially by the former.

And, of course, in the long term what the river was doing was carrying down sediment from its upper reaches to deposit them in its lower reaches, thus helping to create the flat lands of Holland and the neighbouring areas of Germany. Here, the Rhine is not very deep, averaging only about 10 to 15 feet according to statistics, but it is wide – normally about 1,000 feet (at Cologne 360 metres, at Düsseldorf 310 metres, at Emmerich 400 metres).

Its peculiarity is that in times of flood, that simple average of 1,000 feet in width suddenly increases to as much as three miles in width. Similarly, the current speed varies from a mere two to a full five and one-half knots. The latter figure can best be appreciated by thinking of a solid wall of water moving at a speed twice that of a man walking briskly. The force exerted by only two knots of moving water roughly equals that of the wind force of a hurricane. The river at full speed may be roughly considered as applying to bridges, pontoon or other-wise, and to rafts and to boats, a force three times more powerful than a hurricane. Any army attempting to cross when the river reached its peak speed or width was bound to be foiled; and if a sudden flood occurred when the crossing was actually underway, with everything depending on the anchors of the frail pontoon bridges, then catastrophe was in sight. In short, although in normal conditions the Rhine was only a medium-difficult obstacle, from the purely physical point of view, it was as potentially treacherous as a known hurricane area in the hurricane season.

The crossing of the Rhine by a handful of men in a few rubber boats would be no great feat; but modern armies are like juggernauts, and therefore it was with the approaches to the Rhine that the engineers were principally concerned. It is difficult to construct a bridge to which no approach roads lead, and pointless to construct a bridge where there are no good exits on the other side. Therefore, the crossing of the Rhine, anywhere, was not so much the problem of assault, as of the construction of adequately robust roads and bridges and the regulation of traffic.

The peculiarity of the 21st Army Group sector of assault was that there were considerable physical obstacles, not to the assault itself, but to the traffic on the approaches. For those interested in the techniques of river-crossing, it will be well to quote the engineer appreciation of the problems of spring assault.

On each side of the river are low lying areas forming the flood plain. Natural flooding is contained within a flood bed by a system of dykes. The surface of the flood bed is pasture land with a clay surface on sand and gravel. It is intersected by innumerable ditches and by abandoned meanders of the river. Some of the latter have stretches of stagnant water and others consist of peat bog. These form obstacles to cross-country movement. At abnormally high river levels the entire flood bed is under water. Flooding occurs after either heavy rainfall has swollen the Rhine and its tributaries, or a period of frost and heavy snow. In the latter case the flood reaches its peak approximately three weeks after the thaw has set in. The dyke system consists of the following: (a) Low Banks enclosing open polders;(b) Summer Dykes about one foot above summer high water level (these run along the edge of the normal river course and have easily sloping faces); (c) Winter Dykes about 6 to 10 feet high which are normally sufficient to contain the winter floods; (d) Main Dykes, about 10 to 16 feet high with sides sloping at approximately 30 degrees, which are designed to control the fullest extent of flooding (they are continuous on each side of the river in the area between the Ruhr and Nijmegen). Breaches of these main dykes could result in very extensive flooding of the flood plain.

This was the appreciation on which Montgomery's careful plans were based. It proved to be defective in one respect only.

The winter 1944 to 1945 had been true to form. There had been two major floods, which reached their peak level on

30 November and 17 February. Luckily, the thaw came sufficiently early to allow the floods to subside before Operation PLUNDER (the ground side of the Rhine crossing) was launched. The weather during March was good, with the result that the flood plain and winter flood bed dried out quickly. Excellent air cover and maps were available for planning, and the merits of possible assault crossing sites were readily assessed. First Canadian Army and Ninth United States Army cleared up to the West bank of the Rhine from Neuss to Nijmegen by 11 March, and it was decided that the assault across the river would take place on 24 March. A postponement of up to five days would be accepted if weather delayed the airborne operation. The only serious deficiency in engineer intelligence had been the lack of an accurate cross-section of the river bed. Some, over fifty years old, had been obtained, but proved to be inaccurate. The deepest part of the river was, in fact, ten feet deeper than expected. This was immaterial in the assault crossing, but subsequently necessitated the use of spliced and extra long piles in the construction of the semi-permanent bridges.

A secondary decision by Montgomery, based on a SHAEF estimate of supply tonnages of 540 tons per day per division, was to order the construction, in order to cross the Rhine, of eight more bridges over the Maas. In short, in order to bridge the Rhine, further bridging operations had to take place over a major river in the rear of the crossing-sites; and, further, since there were many small rivers ahead on the northern route on the other side of the Rhine, provision had to be made to bridge these also.

Indeed, the British built more bridges between the Rhine and the Baltic than they did between Normandy and the Rhine. They were mostly small, but they consumed bridging material, and that material had to be available in the rear and then brought forward at the right time.

*   *   *

In one respect it is true that the 21 Army Group planners had over-estimated the size of the German forces that would oppose a Rhine crossing, because these estimates were made in January 1945, before it was clear that the Germans would stage their biggest effort on the west bank of the Rhine, in the Reichswald, and before the capture of Remagen bridge by the Americans, which was to divert further reinforcements from the dwindling German reserves.

Both the Reichswald and Remagen contributed substantially. In January, it had been estimated that, apart from the German field army, some 58,000 German troops would be available to man static defences along the Rhine. On 15 March this estimate was written down to only 30,000 men, apart from the field army.

When the time for the crossing came, the German field army opposing 21 Army Group consisted of 13 divisions, mostly good ones: between Cologne and Essen – four infantry divisions; between Essen and Emmerich – four parachute divisions and three infantry divisions; and in reserve north-east of Emmerich – one panzer and one panzer grenadier division. It was estimated that the Germans on this section of the Rhine deployed 720 field guns, and that some 114 heavy and 712 light anti-aircraft guns were available, mostly in and around the Ruhr, and these, being dual-purpose, could be moved up for use in a ground role, as many of them in fact were.

The Ninth US Army was to make its assault at Rheinberg, largely for prestige purposes and the pleasing of home editors, although this was now dignified by the role of 'protection of the right flank of Second Army'. But as soon as the British had secured a sufficiently deep bridgehead at Wesel, all American bridging was to be concentrated there, and this would then become the main axis for Ninth Army. The British Second Army was to assault Wesel, Xanten, and Rees, and build bridges at Xanten and Rees.

The First Canadian Army were to pretend to be about to cross at Emmerich, hold securely the immensely long river-lines of the Rhine, Waal, and Maas down to the sea, and when

Emmerich had fallen to assault from the bridgehead on the far bank, to centre their bridging operations on Emmerich, preparatory to swinging left into Holland for an assault-crossing of the Ijssel and the capture of Arnhem, after which they would bridge the Neder Rijn at Arnhem for an advance to the Zuyder Zee (i.e. the objectives of the ill-fated Market Garden operation of September 1944, although the axis of advance would be that of the successful German attack of 10 May 1940).

The Second Army was ultimately directed towards the Baltic and Berlin, the Ninth Army was to seal off the Ruhr, and the really vital early objectives were Wesel and Bocholt. These would be the keys to open the route to the Baltic.

It would be anything but an unopposed crossing. For example, Horrocks' XXX Corps, which shared the initial assault in Second Army with XII Corps, consisted at this time of three British infantry divisions, one Canadian infantry division, and the Guards Armoured Division. They would be opposed by 8 Parachute Division, parts of 6 and 7 Parachute Divisions, supported by the German armoured reserve – 15 Panzer Grenadier Division and 116 Panzer Division.

In an assault river-crossing, as indeed in most attacks, the accepted best technique is to attack in column, and not on a 'broad front'. The initial assault would be carried out by a single division, and the success of the operation in part depended on bridging the river quickly and so being able to pour across the rest of the 'column', which, pencil-like, would drive clean through the enemy before he could concentrate sufficient force to stop them.

The chances of success in this instance would have been negligible, had it been merely division against division, for the problems were not dissimilar to those involved in the D-Day landings; and the same solutions were used. The basic idea was to harass and confuse the enemy so that he could not concentrate sufficient force in time to stop the establishment of a secure bridgehead. The methods boiled down to air power, artillery, and airborne divisions.

In Phase I, the air forces isolated the Ruhr; in Phase II they isolated the battle area; in Phase III they bombed the battle area for the three days prior to the crossing; and in Phase IV they attacked German airfields and flak positions on the day of the crossing, kept the area clear of enemy fighters and bombers, blew Wesel to pieces with 277 heavy bombers, and supplied the invaluable Typhoons for close support.

The artillery programme, which was to begin at 1700 hours on 23 March, was to be fired by 600 American and 1,300 British and Canadian guns. The first part of the programme was counter-battery, with special emphasis on knocking out the German flak batteries for the benefit of the airborne troops; followed by a drenching fire on the German infantry positions.

The leading units of the assault divisions would cross at 2100 hours and halfway through the following morning, when the German flak should have been quietened somewhat and the Germans would be bringing up their reserves and making various counter-moves, the two airborne divisions comprising XVIII US Airborne Corps would drop on to the enemy's rear areas, within range of British artillery support, and make his disorganization total.

This novelty in the use of airborne divisions clearly owed a great deal to the awful lessons of Arnhem. The Luftwaffe appreciation of Arnhem had indeed forecast in almost exact detail the nature of the next Allied airborne attack:

> Objectives for airborne troops must not be as far from the front lines as Arnhem was; instead of spreading a landing over three days it should preferably be completed in one day, with forces concentrated as much as possible; another such full-scale assault is to be expected, the lessons of Arnhem being utilized to produce more concentrated landings.

What the Germans did not expect was that the airborne landings, instead of being synchronized with the assault of the ground forces, would take place half a day later. That was playing safe with a vengeance; but it would also come as a surprise and at a time and place most awkward for the Germans as well as being the most expedient time as far as the German flak position was concerned. Even so, this daylight drop was to make Arnhem look like a Sunday picnic. The trouble was, of course, the immediate availability of flak guns from the formidable defences of the Ruhr, tuned to concert pitch after five years of fighting RAF Bomber Command.

But guns were a Montgomery speciality, and this time, including the light pieces which added a 'pepperpot' to the bombardment, he had about 4,000; heavier guns being radar-directed.

On 23 March at zero hour, 'The noise was so terrific that conversation in Battalion Headquarters became almost impossible,' complained the historian of the Lincolns. 'Our targets were pre-selected and the guns lost the paint from their barrels,' recollected R. G. Saunders, then with 103 Regiment RA Mobile Radar Site. 'Well behind us were big guns, in front an SP was having a go. An hour later I was off duty and couldn't go to my hole to sleep, the noise was too much.'

All the previous day, motor transport convoys had been passing through Nijmegen nose-to-tail. The actual crossing was to be literally like D-Day, carried out mainly by armoured and armed amphibious craft, not frail storm boats or rubber dinghies with paddles.

All day on 23 March, there had been gunfire, mixed with the noise of bomber and Typhoon formations; and this was reciprocated shortly after sunset by numbers of German reconnaissance aircraft dropping flares over Nijmegen and the main routes out of it, MAPLE LEAF and RUBY. But the noise of tank convoys roaring along the roads to the Rhineland sometimes drowned the sound of the German aircraft engines. At any one instant, hundreds of tracer shells from the Bofors guns were streaking up the night sky, so that when Montgomery's bombardment began, the thunder of continuous gunfire ran along the Rhine for almost 50 miles, from Nijmegen to the Ruhr.

In the American assault sector, eight miles long, 1,500

bombers attacked German airfields, and American guns fired 65,000 shells in 60 minutes. On 24 March, at 0200, the US 30th Division was to put three battalions across as the first waves of its three regiments; at 0300, the US 79th Division was to put two of its three regiments across. The total casualties in the initial assault waves of these two divisions amounted to 31 killed and wounded.

Apart from 1 Commando Brigade, which was to assault Wesel at 2200 hours on 23 March after the night bombers had dropped more than a thousand tons of bombs on the town, the British assault was a Scottish affair. XXX Corps nominated two brigades of 51 (Highland) Division to assault on the left at 2100 hours on 23 March, while XII Corps ordered 15 (Scottish) Division to attack on the right at 0200 hours on 24 March. Attached to the 51st as follow-up was the Canadian 9th (Highland) Brigade.

The two assault brigades of the Highland Division were 153 and 154 and they were ferried across in Buffaloes of 30 Armoured Brigade. These were tracked, armoured, armed amphibious vehicles. Their ferry service began at 2100 hours on 23 March, 23 hours after Patton had crossed far to the south, and in 154 Brigade their first customers were the 1st and 7th battalions of the Black Watch, followed by the 7th Argyll and Sutherland Highlanders. The 1st Battalion of the Highland Light Infantry of Canada, attached to 154 Brigade in order to secure Canadian representation in the river-crossing, went over at 0400 hours on 24 March.

Losses were light, just as they had been in Normandy on D-Day, except on one American beach where the assault was made by men instead of machines. A properly conducted beach assault or river-crossing should in fact result in only slight casualties; the losses occur when the real battle begins. That is, when the enemy has identified the areas of penetration and has brought up his reserves to meet them.

Just like a coastal assault, a river-crossing is essentially a struggle to build up a bridgehead faster than the enemy can bring in troops to corral it off or wipe it out; and the losses therefore normally occur later, inside the bridgehead during the build-up phase. How severe this struggle would be, in the case of the Rhine, depended on the success of the air, artillery, and airborne strikes on the German rear areas; and on such a long front, this was bound to be variable.

Although the quality of the static troops was poor – many were elderly Home Guards of the Volkssturm – the German field army was a good one, and the parachute regiments were particularly good; they fought heroically, and, of course, skilfully, not always the same thing. Parties held on in the ruins of Wesel and Rees for longer than had been expected, considering the preliminary punishment they had taken, and caused delay to the bridging and rafting operations that should have taken place at these points. While at most points the defenders had either been obliterated or rendered hopelessly 'bomb happy' and incapable of serious resistance, on the left of the American sector and on the left of the British sector, aided by favourable open ground, some German units remained intact and in the last defence of their homeland put up a fight that, for once, may truly be described as 'fanatical'.

CHAPTER TWENTY

Air Drop over the Rhine: 24 March

Distressingly, just as an army advance is basically a traffic problem and a river-crossing basically a bridging and rafting problem, so even the dramatic arrival of soldiers from the sky is mainly an air marshalling and organization problem. The airborne side of the Rhine crossing, Operation Varsity, was, wrote General Gavin, 'the most complex simultaneous airborne-troop carrier lift of the war'. This is best realized by considering first the end product – the delivery to the German-held areas just in the rear of the Rhine of 17,222 soldiers, 614 jeeps, 286 guns and mortars, and hundreds of tons of fuel, food, and ammunition in the space of some two hours.

One-half of the combined procession, the American, was two hours and eighteen minutes long; that is, it took that space of time for the massed formations of troop transports and gliders to pass a single given point. A general who, by using his brains, could shorten this time by, say, 15 minutes had made a critical contribution to victory. And ever since Arnhem – five days to deliver one division – the decision had been made to make the landings both as rapid and as concentrated as possible, and close enough to the ground troops to be within gun range of the medium artillery.

Overall planning was the responsibility of General Brereton's First Allied Airborne Army, and the assault force was designated XVIII US Airborne Corps, commanded by the American Major General Matthew B. Ridgway, with the British Major General R. N. Gale as his deputy. This formation was placed under the command of the British Second Army for the operation. It consisted of the comparatively inexperienced 17th US Airborne

Division, commanded by Major General William Miley, and the experienced 6th British Airborne Division, commanded by Major General E. L. Bols. The parachute troops flew in American transports of IX Troop Carrier Command, while the air-landing troops flew in British gliders towed by British aircraft of 38 and 46 groups, RAF.

The American division when airborne consisted of 913 transports and tugs and 906 Hadrian gliders; the British division of 683 transports and tugs and 444 Hamilcar and Horsa gliders – a total of 1,596 aircraft and 1,350 gliders, of which the British component would start from 11 airfields in England, the American component from 15 airfields in France, to merge together in a single operation, side by side, just over the Rhine. A supply mission was to be flown within two hours by 120 American Liberators. In addition, the battlefield and neighbouring German airfields were to be attacked by more than 3,000 bombers, while more than 5,000 fighters would protect the armada and attack ground targets. That is, some 11,000 aircraft and gliders, mostly in mass formations, would be travelling to and from the target in a matter of a few hours.

It was the last great airborne operation of the war, and one of the most costly. Fourteen Liberators and 53 transports never came back, while 440 transports were badly damaged. Glider losses were much heavier. About 100 British glider pilots were killed, of whom 60 were RAF men who had hoped to fly fighters or bombers and were not very enthusiastic about the 'match-boxes'. Unlike the Americans, who did not use their glider pilots in combat, the British had hitherto insisted on the pilots being army personnel – trained soldiers – expected to fight on the ground, but Arnhem had taken a very heavy toll and the RAF men filled the gaps.

The gliders presented an especially difficult marshalling problem in the air, and this was the last time they were ever to be used on operations. The marshalling was difficult anyway, because the two airborne divisions started from 26 different airfields in two different countries, and the armada, in Gavin's words, 'contained at least five elements of different characteristics and speed'. Timing was rendered even more critical by the stubborn fact that a tug aircraft towing a glider had one fixed speed, variable only by a few miles per hour either way. It could not slow down, nor could it speed up.

For the planners, further variables arose from the fact that the American transports were of two different types, the old C-47s and the newer and faster C-46s; and that there were three types of glider, including the monster Hamilcar, which could only be towed by a Halifax bomber, and many types of tug aircraft, all of them under-powered for the job, with a towing speed of about 140 miles per hour.

The glider got airborne at about 70 miles per hour, so that on take-off it rose above the tug, struggling for altitude at a speed that meant a certain stall if one engine cut out, and inexperienced glider pilots would occasionally fly wing-tip to wing-tip with the tug or, worse, try to help the tug by increasing the glider's altitude, which pulled up the tail of the tug at the moment when the tugpilot was trying to get his nose up. Pilots who had survived enemy fire to earn decorations died in this manner at the hands of helpful glider pilots. The British bombers used as tugs had most of their armament removed to save weight, and the value of what remained was problematical, if German fighters got in among them. On the Rhine crossing, none did.

While the world's first assault by glider-borne troops at Eben Emael on 10 May 1940 had involved a stealthy long-distance motorless flight at dawn by 11 small gliders carrying seven or eight men each, the world's last glider attack was carried out by 1,350 gliders, some large enough to hold howitzers and tanks, arriving in full daylight in the middle of the morning in the middle of a battle. The concepts were totally different, because while the German experiment had involved landing key personnel – specially trained engineers – to demolish key parts of a key fortification, the Rhine landings on 24 March 1945 constituted a mass assault by storm troops. The rapier and the bludgeon, in other words.

But, given that 1945 was not 1940, and that the enemy,

instead of being an unsuspecting neutral, was thoroughly expert in the techniques of airborne landings, and that there was no key point that would cause the fall of all the rest, this probably was the best solution of how to use existing airborne resources. As Gavin wrote,

> The enemy situation was more favourable than it had been for some time. Their units were taking special precautions against an airborne assault. Gunners had to sleep at their posts at all times. Selected and specially organized anti-airborne forces were covering all likely drop and landing areas.

The target, broadly speaking, was the German gun area on the hills and in the woods behind Wesel, which was the key point of the river-crossing. As with the ground troops, the Americans would be on the right and the British would be on the left. All landed correctly, except for one American regiment. The techniques, both for paratroops and gliders, were different from those of Arnhem and other previous operations where time had been lost by concentrating at a rendezvous after landing and before moving off for objectives, some of them many miles away. Now, the units would land in concentrated tactical groups on or very near their objectives and go straight for them without further ado.

Most men's memories were of burning planes, sometimes their own, and burning gliders, and gliders falling like shot birds, and tug aircraft diving straight into the ground. The 513th US Parachute Infantry Regiment had flown from Amiens in 72 of the new C-46s, some two dozen of which were shot down.

Major General Ridgway summed up the whole operation:

> The impact of the airborne divisions at one blow shattered hostile defence and permitted the prompt link up with ground troops . . . permitting Allied armour to debouch into the North German plain at full strength and momentum.

This was true, generally, but the airborne assault was con-

centrated ahead of the *Schwerpunkt* on the drive over the
Rhine–Wesel. At other points, it had little or no effect, and this
was particularly true of the extreme left flank, where the 51st
Highland Division met unbroken units of the German field
army, of much higher quality than the static troops and elderly
Volkssturm, badly shaken by the tremendous bombardment
and the sight of an armada of paratroops and gliders descend-
ing on them. The main defence had clearly been put up by the
veteran flak gunners of the Luftwaffe, veterans of the Ruhr, and
the Allied air forces' attempt to knock out the 20-millimetre
flak positions had been largely unsuccessful.

CHAPTER TWENTY-ONE

Erlekom to Emmerich:
24 March–3 April

On the day of the Rhine crossing, 24 March 1945, the head-quarters of First Canadian Army was south-east of Nijmegen in the hilly wooded area captured by Gavin's Americans the previous September, some three miles from the nearest German-held sector of the Rhine and just downstream of the junction where the broad German Rhine becomes the wide Dutch Waal and the narrower Neder Rijn branches off north-west by Pannerden to join the Ijssel at Arnhem. That is, within easy walking distance of the war, for the first time. And at this time, we had very little to do and were given one day off in seven.

This was a result of Montgomery's policy of battle-planning. HQ First Canadian Army had planned and controlled the battle of the Rhineland while HQ Second Army, with no divisions to command, was planning and preparing for the Rhine crossing. Now, HQ Second Army was controlling the current battle, while the Canadians were planning for the conquest of north-eastern Holland and the third Battle of Arnhem, while at the same time absorbing into their ranks 1 Canadian Corps, being transferred from Italy, so that for the first time First Canadian Army really would be all-Canadian, or nearly so.

The policy of putting an army headquarters within easy artillery range of the enemy was new, and I believe the idea may have been that no one would suspect the offer of such a tempting and vulnerable target, although the Allies were better at knocking them out than were the Germans – in Normandy the HQ of Panzer Group West had been obliterated at a critical moment, and two days before the Rhine was crossed, the HQ of the German First Parachute Army was attacked by fighter-bombers and the army commander, General Alfred Schlemm, severely wounded. HQ Second Army had once been dislocated by bombing, but up to now the only attempt on HQ First Canadian had been the abortive drops by parachute saboteurs back at Tilburg.

My diary recorded briefly the British break-out from the Rhine bridgehead, 28 March:

7 Armd Div went into the bridgehead last night, and just went clean through the Germans and out of sight. No one knows where they are now.

29 March:

7 Armd Div and G's Armd Div, who followed them over, are on the loose and out of sight, God knows where. The Recce vehicles of 7 Armd Div were coming up to Munster, when the main body of the Div was crossing, that's the sort of war it is. But the Parachutists still fight fiercely in the north.

It was a repetition of the break-out from Normandy, but this time with the British spearhead driving for the Baltic, the American 9th diverted (by Eisenhower) to cut off the Ruhr, and the Canadians in their left-flank, hard-fighting role nearest to the coast. But before the break-out could begin, the engineer work had to be done. On 26 March, 'Waterloo' bridge (class 9) and 'Lambeth' bridge (class 15) were completed; at 2400 hours on 26–27 March, 'London' bridge (class 40); on 28 March, 'Blackfriars' bridge (class 40); and on 29 March, 'Westminster' bridge (class 40). Engineer casualties were 155 killed and wounded.

But the Germans still held most of Holland. The Canadian drive westward along the far bank of the Rhine, from Speldrop and Bienen, was intended to cut them off; but it could not gain momentum until the Canadian engineers had built their bridges at Emmerich; and before that could be done, Emmerich must fall. This was to be almost the last battle of the German Rhine, apart from the French crossings far to the south.

The Battle of Emmerich took place inside a box about a dozen square miles in extent. The bottom line of the box was the Kranenburg–Kleve–Kalcar road, some five or six miles distant from the Rhine and running roughly parallel to it. This road was plumed with dust from the vehicles rolling towards Xanten and Rees, and shaken by the salvoes of the heavy and medium guns drawn up in the fields on the Rhine side of that road.

The road from Kleve to Emmerich runs north-east through Kellen and Warheyen to the near bank of the Rhine, with Emmerich on the far bank. There was no bridge, but there had been a number of ferry sites; and some of the piers were to be utilized for the bridges that the Canadian engineers were about to construct. The first two, 'Melville' and 'Contractor', were to be 1,348 feet and 1,757 feet long respectively.

Construction of Melville bridge was to start simultaneously from both banks of the Rhine, the moment the far bank was clear. The equipment necessary for the far bank, which included bulldozers, was to be ferried across. Three rafts for this purpose had been constructed during the night, and then hidden round an upstream bend of the river. 32 Field Company were responsible for the far bank, 33 Field Company for the near bank, while 34 Field Company was to construct and bring into position the floating bays of the bridge.

The signal to indicate 'Go ahead with your bridging' was a large blue sign marked with the number '32', which would be erected in Emmerich by an engineer officer accompanying the leading brigade of the 3rd Canadian Division into the town. This signal was made at about mid-day on 31 March.

The bridge into Emmerich was to be built during the night and would be completed by the next day. This seemed to me enormously impressive, particularly when I recollected that Portsmouth City Corporation had taken ten years to build a

100-yard bridge across a ditch by the airport. Canada went even higher in my estimation.

I did not understand all the technical difficulties – the effect of the high wind on the floating pontoons, for instance – but the width of the river, the speed of the current, the mass of material that had to be moved, and the work that had to be done on the approaches was clearly immense. What I had witnessed were parts of the first stages of the building of Melville bridge, a 1,348-foot-long class-40 floating Bailey named after Brigadier J. E. Melville, a former chief engineer of the Canadian Army. It was opened to traffic at 2100 hours on 1 April for a total building time of 33 hours, nine hours ahead of schedule.

FINN route led to the rafting site, and MAGGS route was named after Major Percy J. Maggs, OC of 32 Field Company, RCE, responsible for the far bank. Maggs had been up all night on 30–31 March, building and then concealing from view two class-40 rafts and one close-support raft. He returned to his billet at 0630 on 31 March and before he could get any sleep a Don R arrived with orders from the CRE to cross the river and recce the far bank. 'We arrived back at noon just as the signal came through to commence bridging,' he wrote. The naval craft I had seen were in fact helping to get his equipment over.

The Class 40 rafts were powered by four 8 hp Petter engines driving props through flexible shafting. Since the Rhine current was about 5 knots it was felt that this might prove inadequate, so an LCV(P), manned by Royal Navy Personnel, was lashed into each raft and we soon set off with the first load, which was a bulldozer. Mine sweeping on the far bank got under way, the bulldozer was put on shore and it proceeded to build a ramp to get the bridging lorries up on to the bank. Once this was completed the two rafts began shuttling the stores across the river and in due time construction got under way.

Eighteen bridging lorries had to be ferried over and unloaded, without help from pioneers, and the area checked for mines — 30 Riegel mines were found under the roadway and removed. Buildings were pulled down for use as rubble, but this hardly made any difference to Emmerich. As Colonel Capstick, then a lieutenant, commented: 'The whole city was a shambles. The rails at the railway station seemed to be tied in big knots.'

The work on the near bank was easier, because there was no rafting to do before bridging could begin; but putting in the floating pontoons in a fast current and a high wind was difficult. They had to be manoeuvred into place by power boats and infantry landing craft, and then anchored.

> For anchors we used a Bailey panel with 3 big anchors wired securely to each one [wrote Capstick]. This would make about a 900-lb anchor. 300 feet of rope was tied to each anchor. And I remember figuring it out that we used 18 miles of rope for all the anchorage in the Class 40 bridge. From the morning of 30 March until 1400 hours on 1 April — 55 hours — we slept only for a couple of hours in the morning of 31 March.

Further upstream, other Canadian engineers were preparing a class-70 and also laying anti-mine cables. One of them, George I. L. Reid, recalled,

> The Germans sent bombs down the river and we had to pay cables across to pick the bombs off before they hit our bridge. The fast rising and lowering of the river was a hazard to us, also the river rose as much as two feet overnight. There was also a terrific undercurrent which made it very hazardous for the boys working.

34 Field Company, building the floating pontoons for the class-40, experienced the same trouble. Sapper E. H. Isley wrote,

> We started to build the Bailey pontoon bridge about 5 o'clock the first night. We had quite a few pontoons built when the tide came in about midnight; they were all dam-

aged but one. There were about 35 men holding on to it and we had pikes drove in the ground, but we thought it was going to get away from us. I thought the whole bridge was going to go out.

But it did not, and Melville bridge was completed nine hours earlier than planned.

Traffic at this stage was one way only: UP. That is, if you got over the Rhine you didn't get back until a return DOWN bridge had been built. So for the engineers there was no respite. After completing Melville late in the evening of 1 April, Maggs recalled:

Some time was spent in clearing up, mooring the rafts and getting back to HQ. I crawled into a sleeping bag just in time to be roused by a Don R with a message for me to report to the CRE. We were informed that another bridge, only a class 15 instead of a class 40, was required to serve as a return bridge, so we started organizing for this second effort. By 0800 on 2 April the men were back on the job but they were tired after a long spell with little sleep and there had not been time for the detailed planning which went into the first bridge. The weather worsened and in the wind and rain an LCVP pushed a floating bay too quickly and it sank. The wind continued to rise and was blowing directly upstream. The floating bays as they come into bridge drop their upstream anchors and pay out until they are on correct line. But this time wind pressure rose above the drag of the current and as the bridge was built it formed a great arc upstream. So it was necessary to get out quickly and lay the downstream anchors and the bridge was slowly warped into line. This Class 15 bridge was 1,757 feet long between bank seats and was finally opened to traffic at 1800 hours on 3 April. I slept well that night, having been 4½ days without sleep.

Lieutenant W. W. Gemmel, who had been on the Arnhem

rescue operation with 20 Field Company, was now with 30 Field Company, which had helped build the even longer Blackfriars bridge upstream at Rees for British traffic. This 1,865-foot-long class-40 bridge was built in 40 hours. British engineers had previously built the class-15 Lambeth bridge just upstream. 'This was an assault bridge and we heard that they had heavy casualties,' wrote Gemmel.

There would have been heavy casualties at Emmerich, but for the continuous counter-battery fire in general and in particular the barrage that drenched the heights of Hochelten during the assault that coincided with the start of the bridging operation on 31 May. Technically, Emmerich was the reverse of Oppenheim. There, the near bank consisted of a terraced escarpment 100 feet high, which overlooked and dominated the far bank, and which the Americans lined with tanks. But at Emmerich, the entire plain back to Kleve was overlooked and dominated by the Hochelten feature on the far bank. Hence, the need for a smokescreen early on and considerable artillery support. But the work of the engineers, here as elsewhere, was without glamour.

As Major Maggs explained:

The normal deck of a Bailey bridge consists of 2-inch thick planks laid loose across the steel stringers and held down at the ends by timbers called ribbands which were bolted down. However, when a bridge was likely to be in use for some while and especially when it was to carry tank traffic a second layer of 2-inch plank, cut so it could be laid in herring bone style, was nailed on to the regular planks. This was called a skin deck. It meant driving quite a few nails to skin deck a bridge like the Melville, and one of the Sappers at Emmerich looked up from his work and said, '*They sure got us pepped up about this crossing of the Rhine, but I never thought I'd cross the ruddy thing on my hands and knees.*'

CHAPTER TWENTY-TWO

'Fortress Holland': 2–13 April

Four weeks short of five years from the day the Germans launched Operation Yellow, on 10 May 1940, the situation was almost exactly the same – but with the roles of defender and attacker reversed. The irony was unconsciously stressed by the German command, which in the first week of April re-designated the area held by their Twenty-fifth Army as 'Festung Holland' – Fortress Holland. Once again, the Netherlands were to be defended on river lines – the Ijssel and the Grebbe. Unfortunately for the defenders, these defences had been reconstructed since 1940 to face the other way – westwards, against an Allied seaborne invasion.

The forces available to Generaloberst Johannes Blaskowitz probably did not amount to more than 120,000 men. This was not the German Army of 1940, and their quality was variable – they included Volksgrenadier divisions and Dutch SS. The commanders and staffs, on the other hand, were far better than in 1940; immensely experienced and skilful after nearly six years of war, during which Germany had conquered almost the whole of Europe, from Norway in the north to the African desert in the south, from the borders of Spain to the mountains of the Caucasus.

They were faced by an almost entirely volunteer army, General H. D. G. Crerar's First Canadian Army, composed now of II Canadian Corps, which under Lieutenant General G. G. Simonds had landed in Normandy on 6 June 1944, and 1 Canadian Corps, which under Lieutenant General C. Foulkes had just been moved to Holland from Italy where it had been fighting since the summer of 1943. In their view, the change from the mountains and strongly built stone houses of Italy to the flat lands of Holland was a military improvement from the attacker's point of view; and the facilities, both in the latest weapons and in hitherto-unknown luxuries at the front, were far superior.

Of the British divisions that up to now had always formed part of the Canadian Army, only the 'Polar Bears' of the 49th West Riding Infantry Division now remained under command; although the 79th Armoured Division still farmed out its specialized assault vehicles to all three armies – American, British, and Canadian – forming Montgomery's 21st Army Group. There were also a few Belgian and Netherlands Resistance men organized in light infantry battalions, and, of course, the Polish Armoured Division.

Only the political command bore no relation to that of 1940. Instead of a single source of political power – a somewhat nervous Adolf Hitler, apprehensive about his southern front and anxious to finish off matters rapidly in the north – there were innumerable pressures on the military command, ranging from the foolish to the downright devious. The move of 1 Canadian Corps from Italy, although it has never been admitted, was clearly aimed at giving more strength to Montgomery (and specifically British objectives in Europe for the post-war period), thus making him less vulnerable to American pro-Russian manoeuvres ordered by Eisenhower but clearly instigated by Roosevelt and his advisers.*

The main pressures on Montgomery at this time cancelled each other out. On the one hand, the Dutch government-in-exile, which had left Holland very swiftly in May 1940, in April 1945, was anxious to get back just as quickly. They produced 'harrowing stories of misery and starvation' coming, quite truthfully, from the Netherlands as a reason for a company by the Canadian Army into western Holland and a speedy liberation of such 1940 objectives as Rotterdam and The Hague.

* In some circles in the United States, it was said, the principal threats to the USA were regarded as being Roosevelt, Stalin, and Hitler – in that order.

But, as Colonel C. P. Stacey, the official Canadian historian, wrote:

> It was questionable if it would be a kindness to the folk of western Holland to turn their country into a battleground ... and the Germans were likely to flood still more land as a measure of defence or spite.*

Indeed, 'liberation' had become a bitter joke among all Allied soldiers. While the verb 'to liberate' meant simply to 'loot', the word 'liberated' used as an adjective to describe a city, town, or village implied a totally devastated former population centre through which roads had to be cleared with bulldozers and the stench of death hung sweet and sickening on the air.

By now, very few European and Russian towns and cities remained that were not in this unenviable state. What Rotterdam had endured in 1940 would be a bagatelle compared to what was now in store, not merely for that city, but for The Hague, Leiden, Haarlem, and Amsterdam, among other places, according to a Canadian order issued on 12 April, as a result of pressure from the Netherlands government-in-exile. This was cancelled at the last minute, as a result of orders filtering down from the top that were themselves the result of an American decision of 4 April.

On that day, the vital northern thrust by the 21st Army Group to secure the North German ports and reach the Baltic before the Red Army was endangered by the transfer of Simpson's Ninth US Army to Bradley's army group with a new role that would ensure non-interference with Stalin's ambitions, thus weakening Montgomery's drive. Consequently, he had insufficient forces remaining with which to carry out his main objective, the political denial of Denmark and the route to Scandinavia, to the Soviet, as well as the militarily non-essential clearing of western Holland, the political aims of

* *The Canadian Army 1939–1945* by Colonel C. P. Stacey (Ottawa, 1948); see also *The Victory Campaign*, Chapter XXI, by the same author.

which were known only to the Netherlands government-in-exile and formed no part of British policy.

The political considerations were simple in comparison with the military problems. Many plans were put forward and studied by the soldiers, but foundered on engineer objections, based on the nature of the Rhine delta and the fluctuations, natural or induced, by which the river might or could be made to frustrate them.

The last suggestion for a completion of Market Garden in 1944 came from Montgomery in early November. This was to be in two stages: first, the clearing of the 'Island' between the Waal and the Neder Rijn; then, an assault over the Neder Rijn near Arnhem aimed at the high ground around Apeldoorn, and including a bridgehead over the Ijssel. The German action in partially flooding the 'Island' effectively blocked this idea in its initial stage, as the base of operations then became even more subject to the winter weather pattern of flooding and icing.

The next suggestion put forward by Lieutenant General G. G. Simonds (II Corps) and worked out by Lieutenant General C. Foulkes (I Corps) had an identical first stage; but in the second stage, instead of driving for Apeldoorn, the Canadians would immediately turn eastward into Germany and drive along the far bank of the German Rhine towards Emmerich. This was in February, long before Remagen. But Foulkes's appreciation showed that both weather and the enemy, including enemy-controlled flooding of the Ijssel, made success unlikely.

When the Rhine crossings became imminent, and it was clear that Emmerich would be captured before Arnhem, two alternative plans were considered. The first plan was basically Market Garden, except that the Neder Rijn would be crossed at Oosterbeek, west of Arnhem, thus avoiding a built-up area in the early stages, but nevertheless risking disaster from the German-held high ground at Westerbouwing that overlooked the bridging site. (A suggested amendment was to cross at Renkum, five miles west of Oosterbeek.)

The alternative plan, to be employed if the state of the ground combined with enemy resistance made the first unlikely to succeed, was virtually a duplicate of Operation Yellow. It is unlikely that the Canadians had studied the German operations of 10 May 1940, but in spite of many minor planning fluctuations, which it would be tedious to recall, this was to be what actually happened. Basically, this depended on the capacity of the Rhine bridges at Emmerich, so the two battles were immediately connected.

Further, the fruits of success at Arnhem would be, not the premature clearing of the western Netherlands, but the opening of an additional supply route, from Nijmegen railhead via Arnhem and Zutphen, which would in its turn assist the great drive to the north from the Rhine bridgehead towards the Baltic. This would make full use of the existing road bridge at Nijmegen, although the Neder Rijn would have to be bridged, as Arnhem road bridge had been damaged in October 1944 by air attacks and in February 1945 had finally been 'blown' by the Germans.

But as Lieutenant E. F. Burkart of the 49th Division wrote:

At the risk of being thought frivolous, I would remind readers that this was a battle that very nearly did not come off . . . Higher Authority seemed quite unable to decide how to attack Arnhem.

Doubtless the planners were recalling the Roer dams and the effect the consequent flooding had had both on the British–Canadian offensive through the Reichswald and the timing of the American attack.

Stage one of the third Battle of Arnhem began on 2 April 1945 (code-name 'Destroyer'), stage two on 11 April (code-name 'Cannonshot'), and stage three on 12 April (code-name 'Anger' or 'Quick Anger'), followed by the drive to the Zuyder Zee (code-name 'Cleanser'). The last was a latterday Market Garden, the others were virtually a second Operation Yellow.

'Destroyer' was the clearing of the 'Island' between Nijmegen and Arnhem; 'Cannonshot' was a drive out of Germany into Holland across the Ijssel far to the north of Arnhem,

directed at the high ground of Apeldoorn on an axis that drove
into the Netherlands between Zutphen in the south and the
Deventer to the north; and 'Quick Anger' was an assault on
Arnhem across the Ijssel to the east, from Westervoort, on the
same axis and in the same place and with the identical initial
objectives of 10 May 1940, down to and including the capture
of Fort Westervoort.

'Cleanser' would be the break-out from the bridgehead in
the Arnhem area secured by the 49th West Riding Division by
the 5th Canadian Armoured Division, with its axis directed to
the Zuyder Zee, 30 miles to the north – with, in effect, the 49th
Division taking on the role of 1st Airborne and the 5th Canadian Armoured taking on the task of Guards Armoured. But
now, in 1945, this drive to the Ijsselmeer would link with other
Canadian forces driving out of Germany into Holland towards
Apeldoorn, a plan that was a mixture of Market Garden and
Operation Yellow.

The parallel with the latter was most striking, in that the
Canadians would be attacking Holland out of Germany, from
bases that were mainly in the Reichswald. Now they held Nijmegen, but then the Germans had held most of Nijmegen by
0445 on the morning of 10 May, less than an hour after they
had attacked out of the Reichswald and roared down the road
from Wyler. There was therefore only an hour or so's
difference, apart from the fact that, this time, the attackers
had previously taken the bridges at Nijmegen.

As far as the 'Island' was concerned, the Canadians started
by occupying the southern half of it; but then the Germans had
taken the eastern part of it, from Pannerden and Doornenburg
to Angeren and Huissen by late afternoon or early evening on
10 May, with the Dutch falling back.

On the Ijssel front, east of Arnhem, the Germans had left
Germany at 0355 hours, following the road that nearly paral-
lels the railway line leading to the Ijssel bridges, and had
reached Westervoort by 0440, where blown bridges prevented
their armoured trains from crossing. Nevertheless, they had
put Fort Westervoort out of action, crossed the Ijssel, and were

in the western outskirts of Arnhem by 1100 hours, heading for Oosterbeek and, eventually, the Grebbe Line, where they were halted.

This parallel was to be precisely re-enacted in 1945, but more slowly and with immense fire power and masses of armoured vehicles. The Germans had simultaneously attacked well to the north of Arnhem, another gambit that was to be repeated. As numbers of Dutch SS troops were to fight with the Germans in 1945, so even some of the defenders were still Dutch; and, it must be admitted, they fought well, even desperately.

The line-up in 1940 had been two regiments of the German 207 Infantry Division, storm troops from the SS Standarte 'Der Führer', an armoured train, a passenger train, and detachments of Special Battalion No 100. They were opposed by a weak force consisting of 22 Frontier Battalion and III Battalion of the 35th Regiment of Infantry.

In 1945, the attack along the equivalent axis from Westervoort was to be carried out by the 49th (West Riding) Infantry Division, attacking initially on a narrow one-battalion front; supported by the Sherman tanks of 11 Canadian Armoured Regiment (Ontario Regiment) from 5 Canadian Armoured Division; with specialized aid from the 79th Armoured Division, which provided a squadron of Flails from 1 Lothians & Border Yeomanry, a squadron of Crocodiles from 1 Fife & Forfar Yeomanry, the Buffaloes of 11 Royal Tanks, and the Avres of 617 Assault Squadron, Royal Engineers.

The Flails (or 'Crabs') were gun-Shermans fitted with a rotary chain on booms for exploding mines; the Crocodiles were gun-Churchills with a flame-gun in addition; the Avres were gunless Churchills fitted instead with a large mortar. The last two were appropriate for dealing with concrete defences, such as pillboxes, at close range. They had materially helped the cracking of the Siegfried Line pivot in the Reichswald.

Gun support was fairly lavish. It included the 49th divisional artillery, the 5th Canadian Armoured divisional artillery, 1 Army Group Royal Canadian Artillery, 11 Field Regiment, RCA, and 1 Rocket Battery, RCA. The latter would engage Fort West-ervoort initially. RAF Spitfires and Typhoons would ground-strafe before the attack, and some of the assault troops would be brought up river from Nijmegen in landing craft belonging to Force 'U' of the Royal Navy.

The days were past when 20 cyclists in faked uniforms and wearing cardboard helmets could open the attack with a ruse; and prepared defences were no longer to be cracked by a covey of motor-cycle combinations aided by a couple of tanks backed by armoured trains and troop trains. With rivers on two sides and hills on the other two, Arnhem was a geographically diffi-cult nut to crack. But that it was going to be cracked, there was little doubt.

As Colonel Stacey remarks, the composition of the de-fending forces 'remained something of a mystery to our Intelli-gence before the attack'. At the time, we were told that it was 34 SS Division 'Netherland', the Dutch SS, but it seems to have included many miscellaneous units of which the largest was the 858th Grenadier Regiment of the 346th Infantry Division.

No gun-state is available, but they certainly had a fair supply of artillery and also rocket batteries, the so-called Nebel-werfer, nicknamed 'Moaning Minnie' by the staid British and 'Screaming Meemie' by the more uninhibited Canadians and Americans. Although called mortars, they were really multi-barrel rocket projectors on wheels, fired electrically from a distance. Six barrels to one piece was a popular arrangement, and the calibres were large – 150, 210, and 300 millimetres. The projectiles needed only a very thin casing and had maxi-mum blast effect, whereas a shell, which has to withstand the shock of discharge from a rifled barrel, has a thick casing and proportionately less explosive content; although accuracy and range are much greater. The unanimous choice of female no-menclature for something so noisy and so deadly to the male may be of interest to psychologists.

The German military historian, Paul Carell, has complained that 'the achievements of this splendid branch of the army have not so far had the acknowledgement and publicity they deserve'. That omission will be rectified.

'Destroyer', the clearing of the 'Island', was carried out on 2–3 April, with the Germans simply falling back to the Neder Rijn and retreating across it to the far bank. This attack was carefully timed to coincide with the advance of 3 Canadian Division out of Emmerich, and was carried out by the West Riding Division with Canadian support in infantry, tanks, and guns.

The plan still was to cross the Neder Rijn in the Driel area, but embarrassing events occurred. The smokescreen laid down to conceal the preparations was ineffective and on one occasion left a number of senior inspecting officers in clear view of the Germans on the hills beyond the far bank of the river.

Therefore, on 7 April, the plan was altered for the last time, and General Foulkes decided to move the 49th Division to the east, across the Neder Rijn near Doornenburg, and thence to Westervoort. This was yet another striking parallel, for this had been the German crossing-place on to the 'Island' on 10 May 1940, when they had captured the fort at Doornenburg after an assault-crossing.

No assault-crossing was necessary here, as both banks of the Neder Rijn were held at this point by the Canadians, and after a rafting operation had proved unsuccessful because of the steep banks of the river, 294 Field Company, Royal engineers, built the class-9 folding boat bridge called 'Gremlin' near Doornenburg. 'Practically the whole of the 49th Division passed over the bridge in two days, nearly wearing a hole in it in the process', wrote their historian.

The dykes of both the Neder Rijn at Driel and the Ijssel at Westervoort presented an impassable obstacle to vehicles. 756 Field Company, Royal Engineers, had already prepared the bund at Driel in three places, by boring down 35 feet and filling the holes with explosives. About 400 tons of soil needed to be removed in this manner before vehicles could approach the river. These charges were blown anyway, just prior to the real assault, as a diversion. The same unit had to prepare the bund at Westervoort for blowing in three places, but this was not to prove a success, partly because of damage to the cordtex and electrical leads caused by Typhoons, British shelling, Canadian shelling, and German shelling, but also because of the sticky nature of the bund clay.

The engineers were to move into Arnhem close behind the assault with a bulldozer, a half-track, and a three-ton winch lorry, as well as carrying out miscellaneous tasks that included both mine-clearing and barricade demolition as well as attaching green lights to the groynes as a guide for a pre-fabricated pontoon bridge that would be floated up the Ijssel to Westervoort. A class-40 bridge was necessary to take the armoured vehicles that would follow the assault infantry. Everything was very carefully prepared and timed, and nearly everything went wrong.

The 56th Infantry Brigade (2 Glosters, 2 South Wales Borders, 2 Essex) were to carry out the assault and gain an initial bridgehead in the area of Fort Westervoort, the silk factory near the 'Spit', and the 'Spit' itself – the name given to the apex of land where the Ijssel meets the Neder Rijn; then they were to clear the southern sector of Arnhem. 146 Infantry Brigade (4 Lincolns, Hallams Y & L, 1/4 KOYLI) were to pass through the assault brigade and enlarge their bridgehead. 147 Infantry Brigade (7 DWR, 11 RSF, 1 Leicesters) were to secure the high ground west of Arnhem and then exploit west and north-west.

Arnhem lies in a half-circling bowl of wooded hills that overlook the low dykeland, bordered by the Ijssel and Neder Rijn, to the south-east; and the battle would not be over until the attacks had taken not merely the streets but the heights as well. It was basically an artillery and infantry task; there was no chance of deploying armour until the battle was won, and a few tanks were there merely to support the infantry at this stage. The bulk of the armour was held back for the break-out later, to the north.

On Thursday, 12 April, I wrote in my diary: 'The guns on the Island before Nijmegen begin to beat away at nightfall. 49 Div, for so long the "Home Guard" of Nijmegen, are going in to take Arnhem.'

Lieutenant E. F. Burkart, then intelligence officer of 2 Glosters, wrote a narrative that was published in the regimental magazine three years later.

During the day of 12 April, Typhoon attacks were made by the RAF on various targets connected with the operation, including the area of the fort, which was shot-up with rockets. At 8.40 PM – H hour minus two – the timed artillery programme began, reaching a crescendo during the last hour. The artillery support itself was provided on a reasonably heavy scale – not as great as during some previous operations – but two especial features were the use of 'mattresses' and the 'pepper-pot'. The 'Mattress' was a land-based version of the multiple rockets fired from naval craft during the Normandy invasion, and one 'mattress' had a very much greater effect than a normal shoot by a regiment of artillery. The 'pepper-pot' was the use of all spare weapons under divisional command – in this case including heavy mortars, machine guns, A/tank, tank, and AA artillery – in a harassing role on the back areas of Arnhem. The purpose was to frustrate any movement or concentration of reinforcements, ammunition or supplies and was aimed at likely targets, rather than confirmed centres of enemy defence. In this way too it was possible to bluff the enemy as to the direction of the attack, without at the same time sparing any of the targets essential to its prosecution.

Arnhem had been heavily fortified by the Germans after the airborne battle, but these defences mostly faced the Neder Rijn, where indeed both the British and the Canadians in turn had originally planned to attack.

An integral part of the assault plan was the blowing of a gap in the bund by the sappers [Burkart's narrative continued]. This was necessary to allow the Buffaloes of A and C

Companies to take to the water directly opposite their objectives, only being exposed to hostile fire at the latest possible moment. Charges were laid during the day, yet while the long procession of Buffaloes was moving from its assembly area close alongside the line of the Emmerich–Arnhem railway, news was received by the CO that in fact the earlier confidence of the sappers had been misplaced, and that the charges had failed to do their part satisfactorily, due it was thought to wires being cut in the earlier Typhoon attack. Thus it was that at 10.40 PM – H hour – under a cold and clear night sky, lit by the artificial moonlight of searchlights, the carefully laid plans went wrong. It is to the credit of the careful briefing and determined responsibility of platoon commanders that the assault was made at all. Shortly after the first intimation of A and C companies' check, it was learned at Bn HQ that B Company were having trouble with the engines of their assault boats. In fact the simultaneous assault by four companies proved to be an assault by D Company, followed some half hour later by B Company. Then A and C Companies made the crossing, ferried in only three Buffaloes, which had been manhandled over the bund, after emptying their loads to reduce weight over the muddy incline.

But pushing on fast through the minefields, all four companies were on their objectives by 0300 hours on 13 April. They had Fort Westervoort, the 'Spit', and the outlying part of the silk factory area. Some hours later, Captain R. V. Cartwright, who was exploring the inner cells of the fort, discovered 60 armed Germans hiding there; they surrendered. Meanwhile, first South Wales Borderers, then 2 Essex, had passed through the limited bridgehead gained by the Glosters.

There would have been no tanks at all, but for a piece of good luck to offset the bad. The initial timing of the assault had gone wrong in two places – the Glosters were late in getting their full strength across, whereas the pontoon bridge that was to carry the tanks had started off ahead of schedule and appeared likely to arrive opposite the German machine-gun positions on the far bank before the infantry. In fact, the Glosters got there first, with about one minute to spare, and by 0930 on 13 April a class-40 bridge spanned the Ijssel at Westervoort.

The tanks, specialized armour, and 146 Infantry Brigade began to cross. That is, 10 hours and 40 minutes after the assault. The Germans had taken 11 hours and 20 minutes to get their assault bridge across at the same place in 1940, and their first wave of rubber assault boats had been broken up and driven back by the Dutch. In 1945, the armoured amphibious Buffaloes had carried 260 loads across the Ijssel for the loss of two vehicles and a dozen crewmen killed or wounded.

The leading battalion of 146 Infantry Brigade was 4 Lincolns, and they suffered more heavily than the assault battalion, the Glosters, particularly in the clearing of the 'factory' near the two railway embankments just outside the town, which lies well back from the Ijssel, with many factories on its south-eastern outskirts. This delay meant that the battle for the built-up area of Arnhem did not begin until early evening, and less than half the West Riding Division was engaged throughout the greater part of the 13th. The OC of the Glosters had reasonably expected to lose about 100 men, but in fact had only 32 killed and wounded, in spite of the plan going awry through no fault of his.

The Lincolns, however, lost 55 men killed, wounded, and missing that day, and there has been some criticism of the battalion plan. The basic problem was the flood plain of the Ijssel – a large expanse of open, water-logged ground, virtually devoid of cover, which lay between Fort Westervoort and the built-up area of Arnhem proper. The complex of fortified railway embankments (carrying the Emmerich–Arnhem line plus a branch line to the goods station), backed by the fortified outskirts of the built-up area, backed by artillery and mortars on the high ground beyond that, was likely to take heavy toll of any attacker who came on in a hurry.

The author of a private newsletter, *4 Lincoln Activities for the Month of April 1945*, wrote:

We had about a two-mile march to the position where the Coys were to start passing through the leading Bde. The Country was very flat and open and one felt very naked from the high ground and church spires of Arnhem. The Bn formed up under cover of a large railway embankment and at 1200 hours started to move forward with D Company in the lead. The plan was for this Coy to pass straight up the Bn axis to seize an important cross roads about 800 yards from the start line. C Coy was to follow and mop up behind them. The start line was a railway embankment, a hundred yards beyond which was another railway embankment. The axis passed under these two railways. Beyond the second railway was a very large factory. There were signs of enemy on the second embankment and the road underneath it was blocked. D Company was therefore forced to push on without their tanks. At first all went well.

D Company was commanded by Captain R. V. Francis, with Captain J. R. Ainger as second-in-command. The latter, now Major Ainger, MC, recalled:

The original plan drawn up by the new CO Lincolns was talked out by the very experienced Company Commanders as being far too risky as it meant ploughing through boggy ground, very open, before reaching the cover of the railway. It was eventually decided to go left along the road to the bridge immediately in front of the factory with D Company leading. Anybody would have realized that the bridge would be blocked and covered by machine-guns. We attempted to clamber over the barricade before being driven back and had to wait for the 'odd' tanks (of 79 Armoured Division) to break up the barricade before we could move forward. Consequently we lost some very good men who had fought with us all the way from Normandy and had even been in Norway. I remember being pretty sour about the whole plan of attack, and the scheme proved as bad as anticipated. When eventually the barricade was cleared a factory

manned by mixed unknown troops who fought to the last
had to be cleared. There were long lines of shelving running
up and down the factory and the opposition went from one
to another making life very difficult. The factory was eventually cleared due to some excellent leadership by Francis. I
was so disgusted at losing so many good men at such a late
stage of the war, that I concentrated on my own job rather
more than usual and kept away from the rough stuff in
the factory.

Now, after the specialized tanks had destroyed the barricade
under the railway bridge, the first troops of fighting Shermans
from C Squadron, 11 Canadian Armoured Regiment, came up.
The first troop was led by Lieutenant (now Lieutenant Colonel)
F. S. 'Steve' Wotton, the second by Lieutenant (now Captain)
H. W. Macdonald, who won his Military Cross this day. Wotton
recalled:

C Squadron took the right hand road through the factory
area and did its initial attack over a railway embankment
with the British infantry clearing a large factory which I
understand was in the cellulose business and was, in peacetime, a competitor to a British firm which employed the
Company Commander who I was working closely with. I can
recall some interesting comments by the Company Commander prior to the battle that we should ensure a very
thorough covering fire for his men as they cleared the
factory.

Very soon, two companies of the Lincolns were struggling to
clear the factory, which had been turned into a fortress, so it is
not clear who made that grim joke.

Immediately the covering fire had ceased, Francis led D
Company out of its toehold in the factory to begin clearing the
whole building. 'This was no easy task as the factory was a
labyrinth of passages, stores and sheds, while the roofs were
alive with snipers,' wrote the author of the newsletter. 'The

enemy fought back very hard, for the most part at very close range indeed.' C Company had to join D Company by advancing to the factory while being raked by German fire both from the factory and from the railway embankment.

The two Coys Comds then divided up the factory between them and set about the final expulsion of the enemy. This was a hard and costly business. In places the enemy resistance was fanatical. One enemy officer received five bursts of bren through him before he was finally stopped, another wounded Bosche tried to throw a grenade at anyone trying to approach him. By the evening, however, the factory was clear, although the enemy was still managing to hold out on the outskirts of it. A quick check up in the failing light revealed 32 enemy dead.

The Lincolns had lost only five killed, but had 50 wounded, in 'some of the hardest fighting the Bn had met during the campaigns'.

Meanwhile, the Canadian tanks and the rest of the Lincolns were trying to by-pass the factory and get forward into the town. The Canadian war diary noted:

Lt Wotton managed to force his way North of the factory but was unable to strike East because of an anti-tank gun covering the corner. Lt Macdonald was then ordered forward. By-passing Wotton's troop, he made a lightning move across the corner to knock out the gun, thus opening the way for the advance. Employing by-pass and block tactics, Macdonald's troops had soon cleared well to the east of the factory, where he was obliged to hold firm, while the infantry mopped up the factory area. The situation was now immensely relieved, and by 1600 hours the remainder of C Squadron had crossed into the town.

Macdonald was by far the most experienced of the two leading troop commanders and he was not impressed by the battle.

We were kept mucking about at first. Example of how *not* to win a war — two to three miles of armoured fighting vehicles, many of types I'd not seen before, all on one road. There was so much stuff there, that all you had to do was line it up and let it go. The Germans couldn't have stopped it. Why attack Arnhem at all? Go over the Ijssel elsewhere and cut it off. Artillery are hopeless in streets, all blood and guts, like Stalingrad. And in streets, only the leading one or two tanks can operate. You can't deploy the rest.

Macdonald's troop of four Shermans now had two with the normal 75-millimetre guns, two with the long 17-pounders.

These 17-pounders were held back from Italy [he explained], because after Normandy, we were second-class citizens. It was a beautiful weapon, you could thread needles with it at 3,000 yards. We used to practise-shoot at barrels marked with white crosses at that range. So the first job I had to do at Arnhem was to knock off some spires, where OPs were thought to be. I was told: go along the dyke and clear those spires with a 17-pounder. Afterwards, about 2 PM, the battle had been going on since dawn, but hadn't got very far. The Brigadier was dissatisfied. So he married us with an infantry company. The company commander, a major, was a real soldier.* One in a thousand. One of the best I've ever served with. I was with every Div in the British Eighth Army and some in the US Fifth Army, and I knew only two like him. Working his men through the streets, then on during the night, and didn't have many casualties. The Germans didn't stand a chance against guys like him.

* Major J. O. Flint, DSO, MC, commanding B Company, 4 Lincolns. Such personal identifications are difficult, but Mr Macdonald, who travels widely for his firm, Canadian Forest Products Oversea Limited, gave me an interview during a visit to London, and from his hotel we were able to ring Major Flint, with whom I had also been corresponding, and they very soon confirmed the identifications, principally because one of Flint's platoon commanders had just been killed when the tanks came up.

It was this combination of two experienced infantry and tank commanders that late that afternoon finally broke the German 'crust' and took the attack right into the town and beyond.

By 1945, we were the professionals and the Germans were the amateurs [commented Macdonald]. They were using boys of 16, and so on. They were not what they had been, and they knew the war was over, too. The Germans here were not as good as in Italy, where we fought the Paras — they were pretty rough people. We didn't take 200 prisoners in the whole campaign. In Arnhem, the crust was broken on the first day, to the centre of the town.

The South Wales Borderers had been pinned down in houses on the outskirts all day, and even when tanks were brought up and another infantry battalion joined them, they were unable to advance. Then, suddenly, recalled D. B. Hollins,

Towards evening, which was again a bright sunny one, enemy opposition collapsed, and we were ordered to climb on all the available vehicles, when we swept through the town, meeting only light sniper opposition. The tanks simply blew all opposition away. We rested comfortably that night in deserted shops, clearing the rest of the town the following day.

We were Army Troops [said Macdonald of 11 Canadian Armoured Regiment]. Our job was to crack the crust — then the Armoured Divs would go through. Ours were usually set-piece affairs, seven to ten days of training with the infantry beforehand. But I'd never seen these guys [4 Lincolns] before, I just had ten minutes with Flint. We met in a house in a built-up area, with a slight incline. One of his platoon commanders, Lt H. V. Burns, had just been killed. He told me where the start line was, and the avenue of advance. I told him: I'll be in the lead tank; the other tanks will be behind me; I want flank protection from your leading platoon; no infantry to get in front of me. This was going to be the tough part, going through the built-up area.

Macdonald led in a Sherman with a 75-millimetre gun, followed by a sergeant in another 75-millimetre tank. They had five-man crews with both a turret and bow machine-gun. The two Shermans with 17-pounder guns had room only for a four-man crew and had no bow machine-gun, so they brought up the rear. Only the first two tanks could fire. The machine-guns of Macdonald's lead tank would fire continuously, going down the streets, the bow gunner raking the lower rooms left of the road, the turret gunner taking the lower rooms right of the road. The machine-guns of the sergeant's tank immediately behind would do the same, but taking the upper rooms of the houses. Unlike Italy, where house walls were often of stone a foot and a half thick, machine-gun bullets would probably penetrate.

Macdonald's main concern was being picked off by snipers in the top levels of the houses. Even in daylight, a tank is virtually blind, and in order to control the battle Macdonald had to be able to see over the top of the turret. He had the turret flap up behind him, so was protected from the rear; he had infantry sections walking along the sides of the road level with the three tanks behind him, so that they protected him from the sides; and even so, he was careful not to keep his head up, but to pop up and down for rapid checks on the situation. So they rolled forward through the streets of Arnhem, machine-guns spraying continuously, with no regard for the rifling, which was ruined.

There was a very slight delay on the 75-millimetre fuses, and Macdonald used this to occasionally slam a high-explosive shell at the road surface and burst it in the air ahead of him. The German defenders were in deep dug-outs between the house-fronts and the pavements. When Macdonald saw one, he stopped, switched the 75-millimetre gun until the muzzle was practically in the dug-out, and then his gunner pulled the trigger.

Whenever I came to a street corner, I stopped the tank, got out, and told the infantry section commander: 'I'm going to blast the corner house. Then, when I wave my hand, two infantrymen go lickety-spit into it. OK?' Next morning, when the machine-guns had cooled down, there was no rifling left, and the bullets were coming out sideways.

But the technique took the tanks and the Lincolns through to their objectives that night. At midnight, they halted the advance. Macdonald told Flint: 'We got to gas up (takes two hours), then go on again at 5 AM. Can you guard the Shermans, and let us sack up?' Aware of the vulnerability of tanks at night, Flint had patrols out all night, plus a close guard on the armoured vehicles.

CHAPTER TWENTY-THREE

Arnhem to the Grebbe:
13 April–4 May

The Hallamshire Battalion of the York and Lancaster Regiment was to pass through the Lincolns, and from the eastern part of the built-up area launch an attack on the wooded heights beyond the town, from which heavy fire had been coming all day. But as Major General M. G. K. Halford wrote in a contemporary account,

The Lincolns met much stiffer opposition than expected and their anticipated rate of advance was much slowed down. The result was that the Hallamshires' attack, which was planned for daylight, was only able to start at 1930 hours. The plan was for one company to attack at a time, each leap-frogging through another company in turn. Each company attack was preceded by a short, concentrated artillery programme and a 'matress'. This latter was a massive concentration of about 400 rockets firing into a limited area on the objective. It was believed that nothing could remain alive at the receiving end of this weight of high explosive. On the slopes of the high ground which was the Battalion's objective there was a thick wood, beyond this some barracks, and beyond them again a road junction. Starting its advance at 1930 hours, B Company under Major Grey reached its objective halfway through the wood with little difficulty. C Company under Major Lonsdale-Cooper then passed through, but took a long time getting up the hill through the thick wood in the dark. Nevertheless, by 2200 hours it had captured the barracks, its objective. D Company under Major Mackillop then made a night advance through the woods to the west of C Company and reached their objective at 23 hours, without meeting any major opposition. Both these advances were carried out with some skill as the woods were thick and it was a dark night. During the day seventy-four prisoners were taken. At this time the commanding officer decided to wait until first light before continuing operations.

Next morning, opposition had stiffened, but the objective, plus 43 more prisoners, was taken.

The 147th Infantry Brigade, coming into the bridgehead last, met generally much lighter resistance; but to understand what some of them saw in the town, it is necessary to consult Dutch sources. Paradoxically, the inhabitants of Arnhem have virtually no knowledge of what happened there during the third and most destructive battle of all. As the archivist of Arnhem, Mr K. Schaap, kindly explained to me:

You may know that, at the end of September 1944, immediately after the British airborne assault had failed, the inhabitants had been evacuated by the Germans; consequently, at the time of your arrival, the town had been almost completely deserted but for German troops and Nazi civilian 'rescue squads' (i.e., looting organizations) for about 7 months. This accounts for the substantial gaps in our present knowledge as to what really happened. From Allied air photos, taken at irregular intervals between September 1944 and April 1945, and from reports and diaries of Dutch civilians who, most of them illegally and at great risk, had visited the town a rough notion can be formed of the damage already done at the moment of this last battle. (There is not much to tell, I am afraid, about what happened in May 1940; Dutch resistance in and around Arnhem had been but little, and only a few buildings had sustained slight damage.) We are able to draw the following conclusions: (a) During the

September action considerable damage had been done to houses and buildings in the actual battle zones (near the road bridge and in the Oosterbeek 'perimeter'), along the western approaches to Arnhem, and in some parts of the town centre which had been deliberately set on fire by the Germans, allegedly to wipe out the last British resistance. Summing up, the damage had been severe but limited to relatively small areas. (b) Due to several heavy air raids and, especially from December onwards, to artillery fire from the Nijmegen area, destruction took place on a much wider scale. Moreover, the Germans, who now had the town practically all to themselves, plundered and raised fires at random. In early February, the Germans blew up what was left of the road bridge. (c) The Allied advance on Arnhem, in April, was preceded by a heavy artillery barrage which went on for several days and resulted in considerable additional damage; as there was no fire-brigade left, and the Germans did not care at all by now, fires spread freely and rapidly, causing much destruction that could have been prevented. From the military point of view it may be doubted whether such a heavy artillery supporting programme (including rockets) was really necessary under the circumstances, as the German forces in the area were only small and weak; no doubt the Allies were understandably intent on limiting their risks as much as possible, but on this particular occasion it took the form of senseless waste.

One of the targets was the Arnhem zoo, and the author of an article in *The Yorkshire Pud*, the magazine of 7th Battalion, the Duke of Wellington's Regiment, noted that C Company became 'involuntary custodians' of the animals, 'but the day before our arrival an elephant had succumbed to shell shock as result of the heavy bombardment of the immediate area of the Zoo'.

Private Reg Dunkley, who had been fourteen years old when the war started, was with A Company of 7 DWR.

We were to take the high ground behind Arnhem. Just

street clearing for our platoon, flushing out trouble when we found it. It was all high ground (for Holland!), a suburban area, undamaged. Not even windows broken. Walk into a room of a house you had to clear, and you'd find cutlery still in the drawers, everything untouched. There was no sign of looting in the houses we investigated, they were just like this room here, with carpets, curtains, furniture. It was ghostly, being in an empty town. You felt that you had no right to be there and that someone was watching you, in case you did something you shouldn't. You were looking over your shoulder all the time. The other lads felt it, too. But the only sign of looting we saw was in the street where the road curved gently left. On the left-hand side was a farm cart, with clucking coming from it. We were doing it, four men to each side of the street, so I lay down with my Bren, taking up a covering position. But it was all right, there were no Germans there, only the hens which were in a sack on the cart, in which was also a litter of German equipment and weapons, and a big wooden box, locked, full of paper money, brand-new, done up in elastic as if from a bank.

At one point we came to a round house in a lake, an ornamental lake with lilies. Someone in the leading files saw movement behind the windows of the house and loosed off a few shots. A white flag was waved from a window, and we went forward over a causeway across the ornamental lake to the house. Inside were some German medics, who surrendered. It didn't strike you very much at the time, but it's surprising how you can be involved in a little battle on a platoon sector. It was quiet with us, but away on our right there was what sounded like mortars and loads of MG-fire down in a little hollow which we couldn't see.

The final advance was made uphill towards a wood, with D Company leading, A Company following behind. It was actually a 'tongue' of woodland – trees with small saplings and high shrubbery in between – some 200 to 300 yards beyond a road that ran at right angles across the line of advance of the DWR.

In the verges of the road were many convenient round holes (presumably those dug by the Germans as funkholes for the occupants of vehicles under air attack); and A Company went to ground in these holes for the night. But there was no sleep for anyone. D Company in front were counter-attacked all night by what were believed to be Dutch SS troops ('Landsturm Nederland'), and there was a 100 per cent stand-to.

Next day, D Company attacked in their turn, supported by Canadian tanks; and the enemy countered with his own tanks — three little French Renault vehicles, armed only with two-centimetre cannon, which were quickly knocked out.

The following morning there was a call for a section to recce the wood in front from which the German counter-attacks had been coming all night [Dunkley told me]. This was our section of A Company. We were the oldest serving members — we had been with the Battalion since France — while the rest were mostly reinforcements, and this was why we were chosen.

So off we went, seven of us in line abreast, mostly armed with automatics. Two Brens (I had one), three Stens I think, and two with rifles. Object, to pinpoint any German positions dug-in in the wood. We had gone about 150 yards into the wood — out of sight of our people, from whom we were hidden by lots of shrubbery — and probably the Germans had an OP in a tree; anyway, the stonk opened just like that. It was not tank fire. Nor was it 88s. A distinct whistle of shells. No word of command was given to retreat — but, and this is funny — we just turned through 180 degrees and ran like the dickens. The sergeant in charge (Sergeant Roden) was hit and killed by the same shell, which fell very close to both of us. I heard it coming for perhaps three or four seconds, then it burst, fairly close, I suspect, for I can recall, when I was back in hospital, picking out tiny bits of shrapnel.

I knew I was wounded. There was a singing and ringing in my ears. I knew my right kneecap had gone. You know, at the dentist's, you can feel the grating of the instrument on the bone – so I could feel my kneecap grating; and it wouldn't go where I wanted it to. I couldn't speak, and I thought I'd bought it, because they were still shelling. I saw one of our chaps, only the length of our small garden away from me, bending down. I shouted to him, but I could make no sound. So I scrabbed myself along to a sapling (this was where the kneecap wouldn't obey), and propped my back against it, so that I was partly upright and visible to anyone walking near by. My one regret, as I lay there, was that I might have been hit in a bigger operation than this.

How long it took for the stretcher bearers to come, I don't know. Not long, perhaps ten minutes. I didn't know that the Sergeant had been clunked behind me, until I heard the stretcher bearers say: 'Let's get Dunkley away first, the sergeant's obviously gone for a chop.' We were the only two hit out of the seven. I felt no pain, I was numb or senseless, but when the stretcher bearers put me on the stretcher, I lost consciousness.

I came to in the RAP (now in a farmhouse captured by D Company). I assume I had been doped, but I can remember the MO saying: 'Would you like another cup of tea?' I tried to speak, but couldn't, so he said: 'Don't strain, nod.' So I nodded. The tea was very sweet. Morphine? At the RAP they just cut off your clothes and bandage you. The ambulance seemed to be there already, revving up, and I was off in no time. Flown back from Nijmegen in a Dakota, landing perhaps at Blackbushe? Anyway, I was in one of the two hospitals at Basingstoke. I lost my right leg, above the knee.

Now, I get a 90 per cent disability pension. About three or four years ago, I suddenly suffered two epileptic fits. There was no history of epilepsy in my family. My wife was terrified, the first time. I just went mad in bed. The second time was not so bad, because then we knew what it was. I had seen the doctor and had an X-ray. You see these depressions above my left eye? They found I had two bits of shrapnel in the brain there, which had been dormant for

more than twenty years. They didn't take them out, because
they said the damage is caused by the shrapnel going in, and
then the damage is done – there's no point. But you'll have
to take tablets for the rest of your life, they said. I take three
a day.

Another battalion of 147 Brigade, I Leicesters, also found
little resistance left in the town, and their advance was har-
assed mainly by German shellfire.

It wasn't pleasant [wrote Bob Day, a twenty-one-year-old
private in the carrier platoon]. But this was nothing compared with the hell which was let loose on our company
when we were advancing beyond Arnhem – and this came
from our own fire. As you know, other ranks and indeed
junior officers, have little idea about the general strategy of a
battle at the time in question. But we all understood that
one of the officers in our battalion became over-confident,
following our advance through the town, and, against orders,
decided that our company should press on through a wood
on the high ground just out of Arnhem. We eventually came
to a halt in the wood, presumably to consolidate our position, and about half a dozen of us were in a dell. The Bren
gunner and I were side by side against a bank of the dell,
pointing the gun at a house which, we thought, probably
contained a German sniper or two. Suddenly, there was a
dreadful shrieking sound followed by a tremendous bang.

I immediately lay down flat as these sounds were repeated
over and over again in rapid succession for what seemed
liked hours, although, in fact, it was probably only a minute.
Great jagged bits of metal were flying all over the place and
it was far worse than any mortar fire I had encountered (I
had been wounded by a German mortar bomb at Salerno).
When, mercifully, the firing ceased, I looked up in a daze,
scarcely believing I was alive. Then I heard screams coming
from the other side of the dell, and I could see a young
officer with one of his arms nearly torn off. The poor chap

was obviously delirious and several of my section did what
they could to comfort him before he was taken away on a
stretcher. I turned to have a word with the Bren gunner and
saw that he was still leaning against the bank, with his head
bent forward. He appeared to be asleep, so I nudged him. But
he was dead. There was a tiny hole in his back and he must
have been killed instantly by a piece of shrapnel or splinter
from the British rockets which had rained on us so furiously.
I cannot remember his name, but he was a quiet, pleasant
fellow who had told me only a day or so previously that his
wife had had a baby. Others were wounded in that rocket
barrage.

This was the actual effect of a 'mattress', deadly enough, but
falling short of the complete devastation one would expect on
seeing the rockets fired.

On 14 April, the battle was taking place round Arnhem,
rather than in the town, and the thrusts were being made in a
number of different directions. In the morning, for instance,
Macdonald's troop of Shermans was again married up with the
Lincolns for a drive over the flatland south-east of Arnhem,
between the town and the Ijssel, which here curves away
north-east; while in the afternoon he was driving north-west.
The morning attack was 'just a day out with a brigade of infantry', because it took the German defenders of the Ijssel Line in
the rear and in country where the Canadian tanks could
deploy.

The distinction between Canadian armoured and infantry
divisions was somewhat arbitrary.

The Canadian Army was designed to be the Most Armoured
Army in the world [pointed out Macdonald]. All the armoured divs had infantry, of course, and the Infantry divs
had one tank brigade each (to begin with), so the difference
was merely of how many tanks they had. If you lost a tank
you indented for a replacement, and it was there the same
day or night, in a matter of hours. We were always up to

snuff. Usually, we had a regiment of SP guns given to us, broken up one battery per squadron. They were Priests, a tank chassis making a stable base for a gun. This gave a feeling of power, because you could call them up if you were in trouble.

In the morning drive, there was no trouble. There was an embanked road, not then completed, leading out across the flood plain towards the Ijssel between Arnhem and Velp. Leading to the embankment was a wood-covered approach with the last 600 yards open ground. As Macdonald's troop of four Shermans rolled out of the trees, with British infantry mounted on the backs of the tanks, Macdonald could see the German positions.

They'd dug in on the wrong side, facing us. We charged, the four of us, lickety-spit, all guns blazing. When we got there, the Germans were in a state of severe shock, with many wounded. They couldn't control themselves; they rolled down the embankment, faces grey-green in colour, and it took ten minutes for them to regain the use of their faculties. They all just fell into the bag. We took a map off them – it showed their brigade HQ – and we radioed the position back. We took their money off them, then sat down and played cards. In the middle of the game, a machine-gun opened up. Four tanks were facing it, but they were all empty. A sergeant jumped into one with his crew, and went over and dispatched the machine-gunner. Later, we were faced with a house near Velp. We put six rounds into [it], plus MG, then I raised my hand and dropped it, for the infantry to go in fast. They took thirty prisoners, many wounded.

This was the nadir of the German Army. Macdonald and his accompanying infantry took more prisoners that day than he had seen in the whole of the Italian campaign. It was not merely a matter of inferior equipment, but of junior leadership. The best men were dead or wounded. This is always the result of prolonged heavy fighting. As Macdonald pointed out, the people who count are the commanders at company and battalion level. If too many of these become casualties, the division becomes weaker, even though the high command, with increasing experience, gets better.

> In Italy, to begin with, the British Eighth Army pulled the whole show [he said]. The line inclined forward where the Eighth were. Then, after actions where, for instance, all four company commanders in a battalion became casualties, the British divisions became weaker, and the American Fifth Army pulled the Eighth.

Having destroyed the defenders of the Ijssel Line, the force was switched back to the western outskirts of Arnhem, the same day. Here the Germans had many flak guns firing in a ground role at the British infantry trying to clear beyond the built-up area of the town.

> The built-up area was cleared [said Macdonald]. It just stops dead, and open country begins. Flak guns were firing over the open area at British troops to the south-east. The flak guns were exposed, so I asked for artillery. I was not believed, or perhaps they were used to infantry OPs, not tank OPs. The 88-mm flak gun will knock out a tank in seconds, if you show. In a built-up area you are not worried about anti-tank guns, but you are worried when they are in open ground with a full field of fire. This flak, they may have been 88s, I don't know, were just pumping out shells across our front. Our defence overproof sheets were wonderful, they had all the German positions on, even machine-guns. They showed everything. So we wheeled out a 17-pounder tank and fired four rounds. That stopped them, they knew their goose was cooked.

Had the Germans had tanks, it might have been a different matter. The German tanks had thick armour and big guns, and were good in the defensive role; whereas flak guns were virtually immobile and unarmoured. A combination of the two had proved deadly in the past, but guns alone were a poor defence.

Now the way was open to bridge the Neder Rijn and make the long-delayed armoured drive right through to the Zuyder Zee. Canadian engineers put two Bailey pontoon bridges across the river a few hundred yards to the west of the massive ruins of the road bridge, and the rest of 5 Canadian Armoured Division rolled across. Their drive to the north began on 15 April right into the flank of the Germans defending the Ijssel Line against attack from the east around Apeldoorn, and on 18 April the Canadian tanks had reached the Ijsselmeer. Thus the final phase of the ill-fated Market Garden operation was carried out successfully seven months after the airborne landing, and the time taken to do it casts doubt on the practicality of the 1944 time-table.

Even in 1945, with the German Army so weakened as to be unable to strike back, it was not all easy going. Macdonald, for instance, had been roaring along, with the infantry packed on the back of his tank using it as a mobile shooting gallery, when a bazooka shot blew them to shreds all over the armour plate.

We were going a fair clip, and had seen German infantry get up and run [he said]. But one had the guts to stay behind with his bazooka near a railway embankment. He hit the infantry on top of my tank, not the tank itself. Holy catfish.

The projectile, designed to disembowel an armoured vehicle, had a devastating effect on unprotected human flesh.

This drive helped open up the road to Hamburg, but Montgomery's insistence on the importance of the northern drive left too few troops to attempt the capture of western Holland; and therefore there was a semi-official truce on the Grebbe Line, and after the 49th Division had cleared the bank of the

Neder Rijn to that point, all serious fighting ended in Holland, two weeks before the war itself came to an end with total German surrender. Quite apart from avoiding much suffering and loss to the Dutch population, this tacit cessation of hostilities saved many soldiers' lives. The Hallams held this position at the end and described it in the war diary:

> The position was the original Grebbe Line, constructed by the Germans when they anticipated an attack on West Holland from the west. The ground was low lying and wet, and the position consisted of vast defence works raised up above the ground. In front of them lay a vast glacis, formed by the fens bordering the River Grebbe. Beyond the river lay a high feature from which the enemy could dominate the whole position. No movement was possible in daylight, and the position could have been most uncomfortable. Fortunately the truce to admit the taking of food into Holland was now being observed by the enemy, and there was no interference from them. The enemy consisted of 34 SS Div (Landsturm Nederland) and the remnants of 346 Div. No patrolling or harassing fire was permitted. There was nothing to report.

On the night of 4 May 1945, on learning that unconditional surrender of all enemy forces facing 21 Army Group would take place next day at 0800, 'victory was celebrated forthwith'. A double issue of rum was distributed, all the Véry lights were fired up into the darkness to create a celebratory fireworks effect, and rifles and revolvers were fired into the air. Thus the 1945 drive past Arnhem ended at the same place and in the same month as had the German drive to the Dutch-held Grebbe Line in 1940. Ironically, half the defenders were still Dutch. There was a difference only of five years, less ten days, between the Dutch surrender and the German surrender of Holland.

CHAPTER TWENTY-FOUR

Epilogue: April–May

The final stages of the campaign from the Rhine may be marked by a few decisive dates. The fourth of April was the day that Simpson's US Ninth Army was returned to Bradley's 12th Army Group, diverted by Eisenhower from the main drive to the north in order to complete an encirclement of the Ruhr in combination with a break-out from the Remagen bridgehead. An encirclement in such strength of the largely immobile German forces was quite unnecessary, and the object must have been political. As a result of this diminution of strength, it was formally decided by Montgomery and Crerar on 12 April that only two divisions – the British 49th and the Canadian 1st – could now be allotted to western Holland, where they were opposed by some 120,000 men of the German Twenty-fifth Army. This was the day before the third Battle of Arnhem began.

A few days later, about mid-April, with Arnhem fallen and the break-out to the Zuyder Zee begun (which would cut off the German Twenty-fifth Army from Germany) contact was made with Dr Artur Seyss-Inquart, Hitler's Reichskommissar in the Netherlands, and the first wary discussions for a semi-official armistice commenced. On 22 April, these had progressed far enough for Montgomery to forbid any further move westward of his forces, in return for which Seyss-Inquart had agreed not to carry out any demolitions in or flooding of Dutch territory, and to allow in food supplies for the starving population.

On 28 April, an unofficial truce came into operation. The wariness was largely a result of a desire not to arouse Russian suspicions that they were being excluded from a 'deal' with the enemy; and there could have been American suspicions as well.

In the case of western Holland, there was every reason to halt the troops and cease fighting, on purely humanitarian grounds; and there were no valid arguments, military or political, for continuing.

In the case of Czechoslovakia, it was otherwise. Bradley's forces waited for nearly two weeks, until 25 April, for the Russians to 'liberate' that unfortunate country. And just to make sure that the Americans would not be able to forestall the Red Army in Central Europe, SHAEF concocted a story of a mythical Nazi 'national redoubt' based in the mountains of southern Germany and Austria. On 22 April, the enthusiastic Patton, like a bull with the red flag waved in front of him, went charging off in that direction; and there was then no further chance of any unhappy thwarting of Marshal Stalin's ambitions for Europe.

The incautious Bradley, while claiming to have been 'naïve' at the time as regards the critical political issues now being decided, admitted in his autobiography that 'Because Czechoslovakia had already been earmarked for liberation by the Red army, we were not to advance beyond Pilsen, a few miles inside the border.'* That there was a mutual USA–USSR agreement that Russia would dominate Central Europe after the war, and that this agreement is still in force, was made quite clear by official Washington reactions to the second Red Army 'liberation' of Czechoslovakia in 1969.

On the other hand, the drive by Montgomery's 21 Army Group to deny Denmark and the North Sea to the Red Army was successful; and he put sufficient pressure on Eisenhower to obtain, not the return of Simpson's army, but at least the loan of the XVIII US Airborne Corps, three divisions strong. The British 6th Airborne Division went all the way from the Rhine to the Baltic, and when the first Russian tanks rolled into Wismar, near the old Hanse port of Lübeck, they were startled to find the town already in possession of British and Canadian paratroops. Strategically, the Russians were not merely barred from Denmark, but locked inside the Baltic, with no easy access

---

*A Soldier's Story, by Omar N. Bradley (Eyre and Spottiswoode edition, page 549).

to the North Sea for their warships in time of war.

On the American front, however, all was thrown away; by no fault of the troops, Austria, Czechoslovakia, and large parts of Germany fell under the control of one of the most notorious mass-murderers in history and a regime every bit as contemptuous of human life and freedom as Hitler's.

There was no military reason why this should have been – the forces of the western Allies were stronger then than those of the Russians, and although some parts of the agreement to divide up Germany and Austria after the war into zones of occupation had been signed, the Russian treatment of their pledges on Poland was sufficient to show what their real intentions were, and excuse enough to occupy and hold the greater part of Central Europe.

Instead, it was allowed to become an outpost of Russian empire, as a result of a war supposedly fought for liberty and the rights of small nations. The number of deaths during the Second World War cannot be computed accurately, and estimates range from a 'low' of 25 million to a 'high' of 50 million. For this travesty of a future, they had died.

Sources

The basic source is the direct evidence of some 200 participants in these events, half of whom were specially contacted for this book. The narratives of the remainder are among unpublished documents or are to be found in the pages of specialist works published in limited editions. A high proportion of this evidence is contemporary, written either during the war or very shortly after, although afterthoughts are not without value, particularly in those few cases where tempers were lost at the time. I must express my gratitude to the witnesses who helped me directly, to the authors, editors and publishers whose work I have been able to draw upon, and to the very many individuals and organizations who helped to supply documentation and to put me in touch with witnesses. In the latter category I owe a particular debt to the following:

Lt Col C. Grootes, Netherlands Embassy, London.
Lt Col S. J. van Ojen, jr, Chief of Historical Section, HQ Royal Netherlands Army, The Hague.
Prof Dr L. de Jong, Rijksinstituut voor Oorlogsdocumente, Amsterdam.
A. F. Uijen, Head of the Municipal Information Department, Gemeente Nijmegen.
K. Schaap, Archivist, Gemeentearchief Arnhem.
W/Cdr A. R. Boeree, RAF.
Der Verkehrsdirektor, Stadt Duisburg.
The Parachute Regimental Association, Aldershot.
The Institution of Royal Engineers, Chatham.
RHQ First Grenadier Regiment of Foot Guards, London.
RHQ The Household Cavalry, London.
Director, RAC Tank Museum, Wareham, Dorset.
The Dorset Regiment Association, Dorchester.
HQ Royal Anglian Regiment, Lincoln.
Light Infantry Office (Yorkshire), Pontefract.
Hallamshire Bn, Y & L, Sheffield.
Ross A. Godwin, Highland Fusiliers of Canada, Galt, Ontario.

CO, The Ontario Regiment, Oshawa, Ontario.
Directorate of History, Department of National Defence, Ottawa.
Office of the Chief of Military History, Department of the Army, Washington.
Goldsmith's Librarian, University of London.
David Irving, Esq.

I am particularly grateful to the many participants who contributed to the research for this book. In campaign chronological order (with present ranks, where appropriate) they are:

Oberstlt Diedrich Bruns, Grenadier Regt 16, 22 Infanterie-Division.
A. Meijer, OC Artillery Bty, Rhenen.
Sgt M. van Dijk, 8e Grensbetaljon, Groep Betuwe.
Ph. van Heerde, Nijmegen (1940).
V. M. van Dongeren, Rotterdam (1940) and Arnhem (1944).
W. Brugmans, Rotterdam (1940) and Nijmegen (1944).
Herman J. Koppenhout, Utrecht (1944).
Maj Gen Sir Allan Adair, Bt KCVO, CB, DSO, MC, Cmdr Guards Armoured Div.
General Sir Charles Jones, GCB, CBE, MC, CRE, Guards Armoured Div.
Brig. J. O. E. Vandeleur, DSO, OC Irish Guards, Guards Armoured Div.
Col R. S. Langton, MVO, MC, Irish Guards, Guards Armoured Div.
Lord Carrington, MC, Grenadier Guards, Guards Armoured Div.
Col A. N. Breitmeyer, Grenadier Guards, Guards Armoured Div.
Lt Col P. G. A. Prescott, MC, Grenadier Guards, Guards Armoured Div.
Major T. Garnett, MBE, Grenadier Guards, Guards Armoured Div.
Capt J. W. Neville, Grenadier Guards, Guards Armoured Div.
Sgt P. T. Robinson, DCM, Grenadier Guards, Guards Armoured Div.
Brig A. G. C. Jones, MC, 14 Fd Sqn, RE, Guards Armoured Div.
Major Roden Orde, Household Cavalry, Guards Armoured Div.
Capt A. V. Young, MC, Household Cavalry, Guards Armoured Div.
Cpl Eric Meade-King, Household Cavalry, Guards Armoured Div.
Tpr J. W. Conway, Household Cavalry, Guards Armoured Div.
Maj Gen H. Essame, CBE, DSO, MC, Cmdr 214 Inf Bde, 43 (W) Inf Div.
Brig Sir Mark Henniker, Bt, CBE, DSO, MC, CRE, 43 (W) Inf Div.

Brig G. Taylor, CBE, DSO, OC 5 DCLI, 43 (W) Inf Div.

Major M. A. Edwards, 5 Dorsets, 43 (W) Inf Div.

Major G. R. Hartwell, MC, TD, 5 Dorsets, 43 (W) Inf Div.

Major A. C. Packer, 43 Recce Regt, 43 (W) Inf Div.

J. McMahon, RAF.

Maj Gen R. F. K. Goldsmith, CB, CBE, HQ First Allied Airborne Army.

Maj Gen W. T. Campbell, CBE, HQ First Allied Airborne Army.

Major J. A. Hibbert, Bde Major, 1 Para Bde, 1 Br Airborne Div.

Capt A. P. Wood, MC, DCM, 2 Para Bn, 1 Br Airborne Div.

Rev C. A. Cardale, 2 Para Bn, 1 Br Airborne Div.

Major G. A. Paull, 2 A/L A/Tk Bty, RA, 1 Br Airborne Div.

Capt S. J. D. Moorwood, Glider Pilot Regt, 1 Br Airborne Div.

Lt D. J. Simpson, 1 Para Sqn, RE, 1 Br Airborne Div.

Pte J. Wilson, 21 Indep Para Coy, 1 Br Airborne Div.

General James M. Gavin, Cmdr, 82 US Airborne Div.

Maj Gen R. H. Tucker, OC 504 Para Inf Regt, 82 US Airborne Div.

W. F. Boni, American War Correspondent, 82 US Airborne Div.

Cyril Ray, British War Correspondent, 82 US Airborne Div.

Eric Rafter, Glider Pilot, 91st Air Sqn, 439-Tp Carrier Gp.

Oberst Walter Harzer, 9 SS Panzer Division 'Hohenstauffen'.

Herbert Kessler, Fall Panzer Division 'Hermann Goering'.

Pastor Willi Schiffer, 1 Fallschirmarmee.

K. M. Wietzorek, 1 Fallschirmarmee.

Herr Ing, One-man Submarine Pilot.

Forst Lowery, 656 Tk Destr Bn, 9 US Armoured Div.

John E. Slater, 9 US Infantry Div.

Armand J. Duplantier, Jr, 373 Fd Arty Bn, 99 US Infantry Div.

Roger J. Moore, 3 Bn, 365 Regt, 99 US Infantry Div.

Lt Col William H. Anthony, 809 Fd Arty Bn, First US Army.

William C. Hendrix, 467 AAA (AW) Bn, First US Army.

Bennett H. Fishler, Jr, 8 Tk Bn, 4 US Armoured Div.

Joseph Payne Brennan, 26 US Infantry Div.

Max Gissen, 26 US Infantry Div.

Col Maurice E. Kaiser, Chief Planner, HQ XIII Corps.

Lt W. W. Gemmell, 30 Fd Coy, RCE.

Sgt Sidney F. Smith, 23 Fd Coy, RCE.

W. L. Lugrin, 20 Fd Coy, RCE.

Major Percy J. Maggs, OC, 32 Fd Coy, RCE.

Lt Col E. H. Capstick, 32 Fd Coy, RCE.

E. H. Isley, 34 Fd Coy, RCE.

T. L. Smith, 34 Fd Coy, RCE.

Geo H. Reid, RCE.

Miss M. E. Chettle, MBE, YMCA Canteen No 699.

Leo Gariepy, 6 Cdn Armd Regt (1st Hussars).

Cornelius Jerome Riedel, MM, HLI of Canada, 3 Cdn Inf Div.

Malcolm B. Buchanan, HLI of Canada, 3 Cdn Inf Div.

Sam Dearden, HLI of Canada, 3 Cdn Inf Div.

Bruce F. Leckie, HLI of Canada, 3 Cdn Inf Div.

George Colley, HLI of Canada, 3 Cdn Inf Div.

William H. Smith, HLI of Canada, 3 Cdn Inf Div.

Robert Bennett, HLI of Canada, 3 Cdn Inf Div.

J. A. Collins, 1 Cdn Para Bn, 6 Br Airborne Div.

Ray Newman, 1 Cdn Para Bn, 6 Br Airborne Div.

James Cramer, 1 RUR, 6 Br Airborne Div.

R. S. Trout, RAF, Tug Pilot, 12 Devons, 6 Br Airborne Div.

R. G. Saunders, 108 Regt, RA.

General Sir Evelyn Barker, CBE, DSO, MC, Cmdr 49 (WR) Inf Div.

Lt Col A. H. R. Chalmers, OBE, MC, TD, 2 Glosters, 49 (WR) Inf Div.

D. B. Hollins, 2 SWB, 49 (WR) Inf Div.

J. L. Spencer, 2 Essex, 49 (WR) Inf Div.

G. T. W. Tunbridge, 2 Essex, 49 (WR) Inf Div.

R. Dursley, 2 Essex, 49 (WR) Inf Div.

L. Bould, 2 Essex, 49 (WR) Inf Div.

Major J. O. Flint, DSO, MC, 4 Lincolns, 49 (WR) Inf Div.

Major J. R. Ainger, MC, 4 Lincolns, 49 (WR) Inf Div.

Maj Gen M. G. K. Halford, DSO, OC Hallams Y & L, 49 (WR) Inf Div.

Brig T. Harte-Dyke, DSO, OC Hallams Y & L, 49 (WR) Inf Div.

Chris Somers, Hallams Y & L, 49 (WR) Inf Div.

B. W. Baker-Poole, 1/4 KOYLI, 49 (WR) Inf Div.

R. J. Dunkley, 7 DWR, 49 (WR) Inf Div.

R. H. Day, 1 Leicesters, 49 (WR) Inf Div.

Norman E. Cooper, 294 Fd Coy, RE, 49 (WR) Inf Div.

D. F. Gentle, 756 Fd Coy, RE, 49 (WR) Inf Div.

Capt H. W. Macdonald, MC, 11 Cdn Armd Regt (Ontario).

Lt Col F. S. Wotton, 11 Cdn Armd Regt (Ontario).

The principal books, articles and unpublished works consulted were as follows:

'De Strijd op Nederlands Grondgebeid Tijdens Wereldoorlog II' (The Hague, 1952).

Deel 2: Onderdeel C: *De verdediging van het Maas-Waalkanaal.*

Deel 2: Onderdeel D: *De verdediging van de Over-Betuwe.*

Deel 2: Onderdeel E: *De krijgsverrichtingen ten O. van de IJssel an in de IJssellinie.*

The German Fifth Column in the Second World War by Luis de Jong (Routledge & Kegan Paul, 1956).

Die Geschichte der 22 Infanterie-Division by F. A. v. Metzsch (Verlag Hans-Henning Podzun, Kiel, 1952).

Grenadier Regiment 16: Tagebuch-Erinnerungen by Oberstlt D. Bruns (Wiesbaden, 1959).

Article: 'Holland' by Hptmann Walter Gericke (*Soldaten Fallen von Himmel,* Schutzen-Verlag, Berlin, 1940).

Article: 'Fallschirmjäger Besetzen Waalhaven' by Patra Hptmann (*Sieg Uber Frankreich,* OKW, 1940).

Article: 'Uber den Rhein nach Kolmar' (*Sieg Uber Frankreich* OKW, 1940).

Article: 'Das Adler-Geschwader Greift An' by Oblt W. Baumbach (*Adler Jahrbuch,* Verlag Scherl, 1941).

Article: 'Airborne Assault on Holland' by Lt Cdr F. C. van Oosten (*History of the Second World War,* Purnell).

Article: 'The Capture of Fort Eben-Emael' by Oberstlt Rudolf Witzig (*History of the Second World War,* Purnell).

Hitler's War Directives 1939–1945 ed H. R. Trevor-Roper (Sidgwick & Jackson, 1964).

Panzer Leader by General Heinz Guderian (Michael Joseph, 1952).

The Other Side of the Hill by B. H. Liddell Hart (Cassell, 1951).

Swastika in the Air by Karl Bartz (Kimber, 1956).

The Downfall of the German Secret Service by Karl Bartz (Kimber, 1956).

Hitler's Secret Army by Tim Colvin (Gollancz, 1951).

The Luftwaffe War Diaries by Cajus Bekker (McDonald).

Skorzeny's Special Missions by Otto Skorzeny (Hale, 1957).

Commando Extraordinary by Charles Foley (Longmans, Green, 1954).

The Frogmen by T. J. Waldron & James Gleeson (Evans, 1950).

Normandy to the Baltic by Field Marshal Montgomery (Hutchinson, 1947).

A Short Story of 21 Army Group by Hugh Darby and Marcus Cunliffe (Gale & Polden, 1949).

A Short History of 30 Corps by Major P. B. Randel (BAOR lim ed, 1945).

A Full Life by Lt Gen Sir Brian Horrocks (Fontana, 1962).

Booklet: *Storm Over Nijmegen 1944–1945* by W. Imar Kula (Jensen, Nijmegen).

Booklet: *Fury Over Arnhem* by H. B. van der Horst (Arnhem, 1946).

The Road from Normandy by Margaret E. Chettle, MBE (Titus Wilson, 1946).

The Struggle for Europe by Chester Wilmot (Collins, 1952).

The Guards Armoured Division by Maj Gen G. L. Verney (Hutchinson, 1955).

The Story of the Guards Armoured Division by Capt the Earl of Rosse, MBE and Col E. R. Hill, DSO (Biles, 1956).

History of the Irish Guards in the Second World War by Major D. J. L. Fitzgerald, MC (Gale & Polden, 1949).

A Soldier's Story by Brig J. O. E. Vandeleur, DSO (Gale & Polden, 1967).

The Grenadier Guards in the War of 1939–1945 by Patrick Forbes (Gale & Polden, 1949).

Unpublished History of 2 Grenadier Guards.

Report on the 'Bridge' by Sgt P. T. Robinson, DCM.

Letter from Guardsman Leslie Johnson to his father.

Second Household Cavalry Regiment by Major Roden Orde (Gale & Polden, 1953).

The 43rd Wessex Division at War: 1944–1945 by Maj Gen H. Essame (Clowes, 1952).

The History of the Duke of Cornwall's Light Infantry: 1939–1945 by Major E. G. Godfrey, MC and Maj Gen R. F. K. Goldsmith, CB, CBE (DCLI, 1966).

From Normandy to the Weser (Regimental History, 4 Dorsets).

The Story of the 5th Battalion The Dorsetshire Regiment in North-west Europe by Majors G. R. Hartwell, G. R. Pack, M. A. Edwards (BAOR, 1945).

Articles by Brig Sir Mark Henniker: 'Pegasus & the Wyvern' (*RE Journal*, 1946).

'Strategems that failed' (*The Military Engineer*, 1967).

Unpublished Article: 'Recce Island' by SSM W. Critchley.

Unpublished 'Brief List of Actions and Events' (43 Recce Regt).

Unpublished ' "A" Squadron's Action at Randwijk' (43 Recce Regt).

Arnhem by Maj Gen R. E. Urquhart, CB, DSO (Cassell, 1958).

The Battle of Arnhem by C. Bauer and Lt Col Th. A. Boeree (Hodder & Stoughton).

Aan Theodor Alexander Boeree (De Walburg Pevs, Zutphen, 1967).

Draft booklet on British Airborne Operations: The Parachute Regimental Association.

Diary of Events: 2 Para Bn and other documents: The Parachute Regimental Association.

Misc Articles, Narratives, Documents and Personal Diaries: Major J. A. Hibbert.

Misc Articles & Documents: The Institution of Royal Engineers.

Article: 'The Battle of Arnhem Bridge' by Major E. M. Mackay, MBE (*RE Journal,* Dec 1954).

Article: 'Do You Remember?' by J. A. G. (*Pegasus,* July 1946).

Article: 'The Bridge' by Col Rathvon McC. Tompkins (*Marine Corps Gazette,* April & May, 1951).

Commemorative Edition: *Arnhems Dagblad,* 1946.

Commemorative Booklet: 'Arnhem September 1944' (Gemeentearchief Arnhem, 1969).

Verkauft und Verraten by L. v. Greelen (Verlag Welsermühl, 1963).

Article: 'Arnhem–letzter deutscher Erfolg' by Generaloberst Kurt Student (*Der Frontsoldat,* 1952).

Article: 'The Fight of the Elite' by Erwin Kirchhof (*West-Kurier,* Oct 1944).

Unpublished reports & letters by: Sepp Krafft, General Krebs, Oberst vd Heydte, Major Schliefenbaum.

The Siegfried Line Campaign by Charles B. MacDonald (OCMH, Washington, 1963).

Airborne Warfare by Gen James M. Gavin (Washington Infantry Journal Press, 1947).

The Battle of the Ardennes by Robert E. Merriam (Souvenir Press, 1958).

A Soldier's Story by Gen Omar Bradley (Eyre & Spottiswoode, (1951).

Patton: Ordeal and Triumph by Ladislas Farago (Barker, 1966).

The Bridge at Remagen by Ken Hechler (Panther, 1969).

The Last 100 Days by John Toland (Barker, 1966).

The Maple Leaf Scrapbook (Edition Belgique, No 3 Cdn PR Group, 1945).

Article: 'Across the Rhine' by Martin Blumenson (*History of the Second World War*, Purnell).

The Victory Campaign by Col C. P. Stacey (Ottawa).

1st Battalion the Highland Light Infantry of Canada by Jack Fortune Bartlett (Regtl Assoc 1951).

The Royal Ulster Rifles by Charles Graves (RUR Regtl Com 1950).

The History of the Tenth Foot 1919–1950 ed Maj Gen J. A. A. Griffin, DSO & compiled by Major L. C. Gates, MBE, MC (Gale & Polden, 1953).

La Geste du Régiment de la Chaudière by Major A. Ross, DSO & Major M. Gauvin, DSO (1945).

A Short History of the 49th West Riding & Midland Infantry Division, TA by Lt Col F. K. Hughes (Stellar Press, 1957).

2nd Bn South Wales Borderers: D-Day to VE Day ed H. P. Gillespie (BAOR, 1945).

Normandy to Arnhem by Brig T. Hart Dyke, DSO (privately published, 1966).

The Yorkshire Pud (Polar Bear Press, Iserlohn).

A Short History of 294 Field Company RE by Capt. M. Langley.

The Story of 79th Armoured Division (BAOR, 1945).

A Short Account of the Lothians & Border Yeomanry by W. A. Woolward (1946).

Newsletter: '4 Lincolns Activities for the Month of April, 1945.'

Article: 'The Fighting 49th' by Capt R. D. Marshall (*Soldier Magazine*).

Article: 'Remember Arnhem' by Major W. L. Bell, MBE (*Polar Bear News*, 1946).

Article: 'The 2nd Battalion at Arnhem' by Lt E. F. Burkart (*Back Badge*, 1948).

Article: 'De Laatste Slag om Arnhem April 1945' by Col R. H. Tierney (*De Spindop*, 1962).

The History of the Ontario Regiment.

Article: 'Arnhem Assault' (*Oshawa Times* 'Welcome Home' edition, 1945).

Intelligence Report: 2–24 April 1945 by Lt J. Black, 11 Cdn Armd Regt.

Normandy Campaign Diaries, Vols I & II: A. McKee (HQ First Cdn Army).

Archaeological Report: 'Der Rhein bei Duisburg im Mittelalter' by Hans Scheller (*Duisburger Forschungen Schriffenreihe für Geschichte und Heimatskunde Duisburgs*, Duisburg 1957, Vol 1).

Report: 'Inland Water Transport Operating on the Rhine' (*Niedersachsen News*, 8 Nov 1951).

The Finest Legends of the Rhine by Wilhelm Ruland (Verlag von Hoursch & Bechstedt, Köln).

Nijmegen en omstreken (VVV, Nijmegen).

Finally, I must express my gratitude to Eneke Oakley, Ilse McKee and Gerald Jepson for their labours in translating into English from military narratives and histories written in Dutch, French and German.

Index

*For specific corps, brigades, divisions, etc, see under 'Army'; for names
of bridges, canals and rivers, see under 'Bridges', 'Canals' and 'Rivers'.*